500 FISHING EXPERTS

AND

How They Catch Fish

VLAD EVANOFF

500

FISHING EXPERTS

AND

How They Catch Fish

1978

DOUBLEDAY & COMPANY, INC.

GARDEN CITY, NEW YORK

Library of Congress Cataloging in Publication Data

Evanoff, Vlad.
500 fishing experts and how they catch fish.
1. Fishing.   I. Title.
SH441.E854   799.1
ISBN 0-385-07940-0
Library of Congress Catalog Card Number 77–80884

FOREWORD

When my earlier book *Fishing Secrets of the Experts* was published, quite a while back, by this same publisher, it met with immediate acclaim and turned out to be the best-selling fishing book I had written up to that time. In that book I had eighteen skilled and knowledgeable anglers each write about a single fish or method of fishing he was especially good at. It covered both fresh and salt water, but we had to leave out many important fish and methods of fishing as well as interesting areas or fishing spots.

Then I got the idea for a much bigger and more complete book, covering almost every major game fish in both fresh and salt water. I reasoned that if a book by eighteen experts proved so popular and helpful, then a book covering five hundred experts would be even better and more valuable. So here is the final result—a book that includes advice from some of the most skilled fresh- and salt-water anglers in this country.

If this book reads like the "Fishing Hall of Fame" or a "Who's Who in the Fishing World," it's because many of the anglers in it are well known, and some have national reputations. Many of them are pros who compete in and win fishing tournaments. Others are outdoors writers with columns in newspapers or articles in magazines or authors of fishing books. Still others in the book are boat captains or fishing guides. However, most of the anglers included are best known in certain areas.

While the majority of the anglers in this book are known for a particular species of fish or method of fishing, quite a few are also skilled in catching several kinds of fish or use various kinds of fishing tackle and methods with equal skill. So you'll find these men offering tips, tricks, and ideas on how to catch two or three different kinds of fish.

In recent years there have been many new developments in the fishing field. By reading this book, the wise angler who wants to improve his fishing skills and techniques will keep abreast of these improvements and new ideas and acquire the know-how to catch more and bigger fish no matter where he lives or where he fishes.

VLAD EVANOFF

CONTENTS

1

TROUT IN STREAMS AND RIVERS

We couldn't start this chapter on trout fishing with a more expert angler than Joe Brooks. Although a highly skilled fisherman in both fresh and salt water for many species, Joe preferred to fish for trout in waters all over the world.

Joe Brooks spent many a summer and fall fishing for big brown trout in the streams and rivers of Montana and other parts of this country. He was very careful when approaching a pool or run he was going to fish. He'd stand by the pool and study it. If he saw trout rising he would first cast to the fish that was lowest in the pool or run, so as not to scare the other fish, rising upstream. And if he hooked the fish, he would fight it downstream as much as possible to avoid disturbing the other trout.

Joe also enjoyed fishing for the big rainbow trout found in our western states. Because rainbows lie and feed in fast water, he believed in using big flies, which could be seen in the white water. He liked such flies as the Adams, Light Cahill, Black Gnat, Blue Dun, Brown Hackle, and Royal Coachman, tied on No. 10 to 16 hooks. He used such flies in the rushing rapids at the head of a pool.

When rainbows were slow to rise to the surface, Joe turned to nymphs such as the Stone Fly, May Fly, March Brown, Dark Olive, Ginger Quill, Gray Drake, and Black and Yellow, in sizes No. 10 to 14. In shallow water, up to three feet or so, Joe would use a floating fly line and cast upstream, then pay out plenty of line to make the nymph sink. Or he used a weighted nymph.

One of Joe's favorite flies was the Muddler, and he always carried dozens of these, in sizes from No. 10 up to 1/0. He found them especially effective during the early fall, when big trout were feeding heavily.

Byron W. Dalrymple, one of the nation's most prolific outdoors writers, enjoys fishing for brown trout because he feels that they offer a greater challenge than most fresh-water fish. One of his favorite flies in a shallow section of a stream and for fishing in the evening is a White Miller tied Palmer style. He makes repeated casts until the brown trout suddenly decides to take the fly.

Harold Blaisdell also likes to fish late, between sundown and dark. He feels that this is the best part of the trout fishing day. He believes that too many trout fishermen knock themselves out fishing earlier, during midday, and then quit or are too tired to fish at dusk.

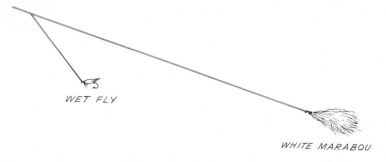

WET FLY

WHITE MARABOU

Slaymaker's rig for after-dark trout fishing

Catching trout during the hot summer months can be tough when the water is low and clear. S. R. Slaymaker II waits for some heavy rains to fall, which will wash terrestrial insects such as ants into the stream. Then he uses an ant tied on a No. 14 hook and catches the trout looking for such land insects. He also likes to fish at night during the summer months, and then he finds that a White Marabou streamer tied on the end of his leader and a wet fly tied on a dropper above is the pay-off combination.

To locate big trout in the Pennsylvania streams he fishes, Don Shiner will flip some live Japanese beetles into the water and then watch as they drift downstream. When he sees a trout come up and take a beetle, he remembers the spot. Then he casts a dry fly tied to imitate the beetle so that it drifts into the spot where the trout is lying, and is usually rewarded with a strike.

Many of the nation's foremost trout anglers go to Montana to fish the streams and rivers of that state. This fly caster is fishing the Madison River. (*Photo by Bill Browning*)

Bill Browning, who lives, fishes, writes, and takes photos in the state of Montana, claims that too many trout fishermen fish the well-known streams and rivers such as the Madison, Gallatin, Big Hole, Missouri, Flathead, and Yellowstone, in his state. Bill advises visiting anglers to try some of the lesser-known rivers, which offer as good or even better trout fishing. He recommends such rivers as the Smith, Big Blackfoot, Beaverhead, the Shields, Dearborn, Bighorn, Jocko, and Jefferson.

Bill recommends such flies as the Grizzly Wulff, Royal Wulff, Muddler, Wooly Worm, Joe's Hopper, and the Cahill. One of the best things about many of these rivers is that the trout are of the wild variety and you have plenty of solitude and elbow room when fishing for them.

Another angler who does a lot of his fishing in Montana is Norman Strung, a guide and outfitter. One of his most successful methods for trout is bottom bouncing with a bait or lure so that it drifts naturally, hugging the rocks, gravel, and sand. Norm uses a long, 8-foot rod he makes himself using the tip of a fly rod and the butt of a spinning rod. He loads his reel with 8- or 10-pound-test mono line. He feels he makes longer and more accurate casts with such a rod and has better control over the bait or lure during the drift.

Norm will use such baits as night crawlers, minnows, nymphs, hellgrammites, and crayfish for this fishing, especially when the water is high and roily. When the water is clear he uses lures such as spoons and spinners. He fishes mostly the slow-moving runs that are about 2 to 4 feet deep. The heads of holes and eddies and the slick water at the tail are also good spots. One of the most productive spots is the water riffles or falls. Norm also concentrates on the smaller streams during the summer months, because the water there is cooler and the trout are more active.

Tom Wendelburg used to pass up the fast, pocket water of streams and rivers until he learned that these are some of the best spots you can fish. So now he concentrates on the pockets, which are usually created by obstructions such as rocks, logs, and depressions. He especially looks for rocks underwater with buffer areas around them. Trout will lie in front, behind, and along the sides of such rocks.

He finds these pockets are especially productive during the summer months, when streams and rivers are clear, low, and warm. Trout then seek the faster water, because it contains more oxygen. And they are easier to fool in the fast water because they have to decide quickly whether they want the fly or not. Tom likes buoyant-hair dry flies such as the Wulffs, the Goofus Bug, and Joe's Hopper, in sizes No. 2 to 14 for this fishing.

When Ernest Schweibert fishes a big western stream or river, he uses a system that covers the water in a pool, flat, or riffle thoroughly. He starts at the head of such waters and casts across the current, using a sinking line and a big, weighted nymph. He lets the fly swing as deep as possible as it drifts downstream, giving it only a slight action with his rod but without taking in any line. He may make a few other casts from the same position. Then he'll move downstream several feet and repeat his casts and drifts with the fly. After working from the new spot awhile, he'll move again, and so on until all the good water is covered. This gives most of the fish there a chance to see the fly.

Dave Harbour fishes early-season trout streams even if they are high and roily, because he has found that trout feed heavily at such times and good catches can be made. But you have to know how to locate the trout, choose the right lures, and present them where the fish can see and hit them.

Dave avoids fishing the fast, churning stretches of the stream or river. Instead he concentrates on the quieter, clearer sections of the stream, where trout are more apt to be holding and feeding. These include pools, eddies, undercut banks, and spots behind boulders, rocks, and logs.

Harbour relies mainly on small spoons, spinners, and small plugs for this early fishing. Big streamers and bucktails will also produce, and so will baits such as minnows and night crawlers. He works these lures or baits downstream, since he can then work them at all levels. And he tries every possible spot and depth, fishing as slowly and as thoroughly as possible.

Joseph D. Bates, Jr., has been creating, tying, and using streamers and bucktails most of his life, and his advice on choosing and using these flies will put more and bigger trout in your creel. To choose the right streamer or bucktail, you must know what kind of minnows, or baitfish, are found in the stream or river you plan to fish. Your streamer should imitate these baitfish in size, looks, and color.

He recommends a dull streamer or bucktail if the day is bright. If the day is dark, a lighter, brighter fly should be used. He also chooses his flies according to the water conditions. When the streams and rivers are high and discolored he uses light, bright flies. In clear water he uses more somber flies.

Although Joe feels that most trout will hit a streamer or bucktail because they are hungry, he also knows that you can make them hit by making them angry. So he often works a streamer in one spot where a big trout is lying, holding it for long periods of time, until the fish decides to hit.

One thing expert trout fishermen have in common is the ability to read a stream and locate spots where trout will be lying and feeding; and of course they all know how to present the fly or lure or bait so that the trout takes it. (*Pennsylvania Fish Commission photo*)

Another skilled angler who likes to use streamers and bucktails for trout is Bob Zwirz. He feels they are highly effective throughout the season, not only in the spring or when the water is high and roily.

Bob likes such patterns as the Miracle Marabous, White Marabou,

Sanborn, Parmachene Belle, Silver Darter, Gray Smelt, Male Dace, Doctor Oatman, Blacknose Dace, and Muddler Minnow. He uses these on a floating line, a floating-sinking line, or a fast-sinking line, depending on the spot he is fishing. When he wants to present the streamer deep he makes upstream casts. And he works the fly so that it makes short darts and spurts like a disabled minnow. He also believes that patience is very important when fishing streamers, and once he knows the location of a big trout he will tease the fish until it strikes.

During the summer months, Bob Zwirz will fish a large Muddler on top, dressing it with a good floatant and letting it drift with the current. Every so often, he twitches the fly by moving the rod tip and taking in a few inches of line. This makes the Muddler sink below the surface, leaving some bubbles; then it pops back on top, which simulates a crippled minnow.

Ken Asper, of Pennsylvania, catches record brown trout in limestone streams like Big Spring Creek and Yellow Breeches Creek. He caught a 17½-pound brown trout and others going 9, 10, and 11 pounds, not to mention many others weighing less. Ken likes to use a 7-foot spinning rod with a medium-sized spinning reel filled with 12-pound-test line. For bait he uses a big night crawler and hooks it through the head and again through the collar with a No. 6 hook.

Ken catches big trout because he specializes in big fish and doesn't waste time fishing for small ones. He will stalk a trout carefully and quietly or he will work his bait under banks, stumps, roots, fallen trees, logs, and in deep holes or pockets where big trout lurk. He tries to make the worm drift as naturally as possible with the current and hug the bottom.

Dick Pobst created the Keel hook, which he designed to fish spots where ordinary flies on regular hooks get hung up and are lost. His fly has an up-riding hook, which enables him to cast into log jams, brush, bushes, weeds, and similar difficult locations.

Keel hook and fly

The Keel hook can be used to tie dry flies, wet flies, nymphs, and streamers. Most of these flies are tied so that the feathers or hair cover the hook point and barb. This helps make the fly weedless. When using these flies Dick deliberately casts into spots that other anglers, using regular flies, avoid. And this is where the big trout like to lie and hide.

Fred McKinley fishes the trout streams in the East, and he found that western steelhead flies such as the Thor and Atomic are killers in the spring of the year. He uses these weighted flies, casts out, lets them sink to the bottom, then retrieves them in short pulls. He casts the fly across and slightly upstream in a run or pool and then twitches it along the bottom. After the fly is swept downstream, he retrieves it by stripping in the line in short, quick jerks. Fred uses a slow-sinking fly line with these flies and finds that they work equally well on brook trout, rainbow trout, and brown trout.

Fred will often use two flies at the same time, such as the Thor and a wet fly or nymph such as the March Brown or Brown Hackle. He ties one of these flies on the end of his leader and the second one on a short, 4-inch dropper at the middle of the leader. This dropper material should test 6 or 8 pounds for best results.

John Reubens used to cast long lines for trout until he found out that he could catch more fish by keeping the line off the water and just letting his fly move with the current naturally, with no drag from the line or leader. It is similar to the technique known as "dapping"; you fish with a fly rod with an equal length of leader extending from the tip.

This technique works in either clear or discolored water, and you can control the movement of your fly better than you could if you had a long line and leader in the water. Of course, John contends that in order to be successful you also have to know the spots where trout lie—in the runs, riffles, eddies, holes, and pockets in a stream. And you have to approach these with extreme care and quiet, because you are fishing so close to the fish.

Well-known outdoors writer Ted Trueblood fishes many of the big trout streams in the West and finds that those fish avoid the large, still, deep pools, because there is little food for them in such waters. He also finds that trout avoid water that is too fast over clean bottoms with no place to take shelter. Instead, these western trout prefer heavy water with a rough bottom of rocks and boulders, where they can rest. Ted also claims that trout in these big rivers tend to avoid the shallow, slow-moving water near shore unless there is a hatch of insects, when they may move in to feed on them for short periods.

David Whitlock catches big trout in the tail waters of southern rivers that have been dammed. He discovered that the fish in the river below the dam change according to the rise and fall of the water level. When the water is being released and the river is rising, Dave finds the fish become very active and move into many areas. During the high-water period, which usually runs from six to twelve hours, the trout move to the edges of the river and hold in the deep, main channels.

During falling water, which may last anywhere from one to six hours, the fish range almost anywhere and then start moving out as the water recedes and the flow slows down. Then, during the low-water period, which lasts from six to eight hours, the trout will be found in the pools, holes, pockets, and deeper rapids and around cover such as boulders, rocks, and logs, and under banks and ledges.

During high water Dave recommends spinning or bait-casting tackle. During low water, ultra-light spinning outfits and fly rods come into their own. Wet flies and big nymphs can be used with the fly rod. With the spinning or casting outfit, you can use spoons, weighted spinners, and small plugs. Natural baits such as worms, crayfish, and minnows also produce well in this tail-water fishing.

Ray Harris has made a specialty of fishing in the Battenkill, in Vermont, which contains some big brown trout. But as anyone who has fished this famous trout stream knows, the trout found there are smart and wary and not easy to catch. Ray gets more than his share of fish, and his methods and techniques deserve close study. First, he approaches with extreme care each spot or any fish he sees rising. He usually waits until flies begin hatching and the fish feeding before he starts fishing. As soon as he sees a good fish rising he stalks it—on his knees! He believes in keeping low even in the water and getting as close as possible so that he can make a short cast and have better control over his line, leader, and fly.

His favorite flies for this fishing—depending on the season—are the Hendrickson, Pheasant Tail, Red Quill, Cream Variant, Olive Quill, and Pale Evening Dun. He uses these in sizes from No. 14 to

18. But when the water gets low and clear he may use flies in sizes No. 20 and 22. Ray also fishes at night, up to midnight, and catches some of his biggest trout then. For after-dark fishing he likes the Wulff flies in sizes 10 to 16.

Ed Kano catches a lot of big brown trout in the streams and rivers of Arizona. One of his secrets is to wait until shadows fall under the trees, alongside logs, banks, and boulders. That's where the big browns like to lurk, and he fishes these shady spots very successfully.

Unlike many trout fishermen, George B. Gordon actually prefers fishing streams and rivers for trout during the hot, summer months. He claims that some of the best fishing of the year takes place at this time. He fishes the pools early in the morning and the riffles and fast water during the day. During the low-water periods, he concentrates on the upstream reaches of the stream. Gordon uses mostly small, No. 14, 16, 18 or 20 flies. The Royal Coachman is one of the most consistent producers. For flat-water fishing he uses spider and variant flies tied on a No. 16 hook.

Gordon often waits for a heavy rain or shower; then, when the water drops to a normal level, he fishes it hard. The cooler water from the shower or rain usually invigorates the trout and starts them feeding. He finds the fishing more enjoyable, too, during the summer months. Most of the opening-day and early-spring crowds are gone and you have miles of water to yourself.

John T. Fowler says that you can catch bigger trout with nymphs than with dry flies or even wet flies. He uses three types of nymphs: May-fly nymphs, stone-fly nymphs, and caddis larvae. He believes in general, rather than exact, imitations and carries both weighted and unweighted nymphs.

John works the water thoroughly and carefully, starting at the lower end of a pool, and then makes short casts first and progressively longer ones until he covers all of the water. He also wades and changes his position often so that he doesn't have to make too long a cast. He claims the short cast is more accurate and he can see a fish hit and can hook him better on a short line. He also finds some of his best nymph fishing takes place during heavy rainstorms. The trout become more active, and "tailing" fish are often seen; these are the trout that are feeding on nymphs drifting along the bottom of a stream.

Chester Chatfield fishes the western rivers, and he claims that a single salmon egg properly fished will catch early-season trout when everything else fails. He likes to use a light, 7-foot fly rod and fly reel loaded with 4-pound-test monofilament line and a 1-pound-test leader. He uses a No. 12 shankless hook, buries this until it is concealed inside the big single salmon egg and then adds two split-shot sinkers a few inches above the hook.

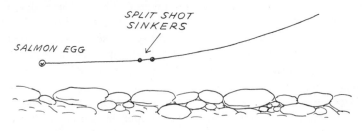

Single-salmon-egg rig for trout

Care must be taken when casting out the egg, because it flies off the hook at the slightest jerk. Actually, the egg is flipped or tossed out, rather than cast. He flips the egg out in fairly shallow running water that has pockets where trout lie. The egg is allowed to drift freely into these pockets and deeper spots; yet the line is kept tight enough to feel a bite. Chatfield finds that soft salmon eggs that dissolve slowly in the water are better than tough, rubbery eggs.

Art Lee seeks rainbow trout in the Delaware River between New York and Pennsylvania, and he feels that it is one of the most productive trout streams in the Northeast. But catching these rainbows in the Delaware is also a challenge. The river is so big that casting blind is usually a waste of time, Art feels. Instead, he waits until he sees a single trout rising or feeding, then presents the fly to the fish before it moves on to a new spot. In other words, he leads the fish and casts well ahead of the spot where it was last seen in order to present the fly in the right spot at the right time. Art finds that both dry flies and wet flies can be used for the Delaware rainbows and brown trout, which are also present in fair numbers. Such patterns as the Adams and the Wulffs are good producers.

Anyone who has read *Field and Stream* magazine through the years knows Al McClane and is familiar with his articles on fishing. A highly skilled all-around angler, Al is particularly fond of fly fishing for trout. He has fished for trout throughout the United States and in many parts of the world. When Al fishes western streams and rivers, he tries to get there when stone flies are hatching. At such times, big trout, which are normally cautious, go on a feeding frenzy and can be caught even during the daytime. Then Al uses dry, wet, and nymph-stone-fly imitations such as the Large Stone Fly, the Dark Stone Fly, and the Golden Stone Fly. These are usually tied on hooks ranging from No. 4 to No. 10. Somewhat heavier leaders are also used in order to hook and hold the bigger trout encountered at this time.

When Al McClane wants big trout during the summer and early fall he starts using the various grasshopper imitations such as the Michigan Hopper or Joe's Hopper and the Muddler. He finds the best fishing with these big terrestrials is found on open-meadow rivers. There the trout will often lie and feed right up against the grassy banks. Sometimes you can see them boil or make little waves as they feed on the hoppers that jump or are blown into the water. Windy days usually produce better fishing than quiet days.

Al also likes to use nymphs early in the season and throughout the year, because he knows that trout feed on underwater insects most of the time. Al usually casts his nymph upstream and lets the current carry it along as naturally as possible. This means avoiding drag, stripping in line by hand. The depth at which you fish the nymph is very important; there are times when the trout are feeding almost on the surface and other times when they are well below the surface, and still other times when you have to make the nymph drift close to the bottom. In the deeper, quieter spots, Al will often let the nymph sink all the way to the bottom and let it lie there for quite a while before retrieving it.

Jim Dean fishes for trout late in the season, when most of the crowd has gone. But because the water is often low and clear then, the fishing can be tough. So he avoids wading if possible and tries to hide behind a tree, a boulder, or some brush. He uses a short line and concentrates on any white water flowing into a pool. He often gets close and daps the fly in this fast water for a drag-free float. Jim uses mostly flies imitating the terrestrials, or land insects, with the black

One look at this fishy spot and you are almost certain it contains trout. Trout anglers spend a lot of time fishing below falls and in white water, since such spots carry food and have cool water and plenty of oxygen. (*Canadian Government Travel Bureau photo*)

ant in size No. 16 or 18 as one of his favorites. But he also uses jassids and beetles in sizes ranging from No. 14 to 22.

Robert H. Reagan enjoys fishing the smaller streams, or "cricks," as he calls them, when seeking trout. The trout there are usually smaller, but because many of these waters are unknown or hard to reach, the fishing is often faster than on the bigger, better-known streams and rivers.

Bob finds dry flies excellent on such small streams, because the water is usually shallow and the fish rise readily for the floaters. One problem he runs into is that the tiny trout will grab your flies and beat the bigger fish to them. So he brings along a few larger flies to use at such times. He also uses nymphs, and finds that casting straight upstream is the best method.

Bob Saile believes in starting the trout-fishing season on western streams earlier than most anglers and is rewarded by some nice catches. In the Colorado streams and rivers, where he fishes, most anglers are not out in March or even April. But there are plenty of big trout to be caught if you use the right lures, methods, and techniques.

One of these is using a nymph such as the Hare's Ear with a floating fly line and adding some lead twisted on the leader about a foot and a half above the fly. This is cast across and upstream and allowed to drift downstream. It should sink fast to the bottom, where the trout lie.

Hart Wixom also fishes the Rocky Mountain states for trout, and he feels that a spinner is the deadliest lure for big trout in these waters. The technique that is most effective in the streams and rivers is to cast the spinner upstream and reel slowly so that it travels close to the bottom. He feels that this downstream reeling is most effective because trout face upstream and can see your lure coming and acting like a crippled minnow.

Of course he has to reel a bit faster than the current to give the spinner action and avoid hanging up on the bottom. To keep the spinner from fouling on the bottom and moving just above the rocks, he raises and lowers his rod tip as needed.

Larry Koller was a great advocate of night fishing for big brown trout, especially during the late-spring, summer, and early-fall months. He fished the famous eastern streams often, and there he found that big brown trout would come out to feed mostly at night during that period. He liked to use big, bushy wet flies with Palmer hackle, tied on No. 4 or 6 hooks. Big streamers, bucktails, and small bass bugs were also successful for him. In dry flies he liked the White Wulff and the Gray Wulff.

Larry retrieved these lures slowly all the way in to the spot where he was standing. Trout at night would often follow the lure right up to where he was fishing. And he found that drag wasn't too important at night. In fact, it often brought more strikes, because the fish could see the ripples or wake that the lure created on top of the water.

Bill Cairns, who teaches at the Orvis fly-fishing schools, knows his trout fishing and his flies. He likes to use such divided-wing patterns as the Adams, Light Cahill, March Brown, and Hendrickson when flies are hatching. He also likes to use spiders, such as the Ginger, the Blue Dun, and the Brown, when the water is low and clear during the summer months. For rough or broken water he prefers the Royal Coachman, Gray Wulff, and the Irresistibles, and casts them around rocks and boulders in fast water. Bill turns to jassids, beetles, and ant flies when trout are looking for such land insects, in the late summer and early fall.

Leonard M. Wright, who wrote *Fishing the Dry Fly as a Living Insect,* claims that many trout fishermen fish at the wrong times of day during the various seasons. He always takes temperature readings of a stream, and after years of fishing can usually predict with fair accuracy when the trout will be feeding.

For example, he contends that if you are using a dry fly it is best to wait until around 11:00 A.M. before fishing in June on the cool mountain streams. Then the fishing will be good for about two hours or so. Another good period is from 7:00 P.M. until dark.

He also spent many hours observing trout underwater to find out where they lie and feed. One of his major discoveries is that trout that are feeding in a pool do not necessarily live or lie in that spot all the time. Usually they move quite a distance from their real hide-out to the feeding position. And he also found out that the big trout do not always choose the deepest water for their hiding place. They often lie in shallow water, only 2 to 3 feet in depth. The trout also avoid strong currents and choose bottoms where they are camouflaged. They shun light, sand bottoms, or flat ledges if there are rocks, gravel, or other dark, broken bottoms nearby. He also learned that pools and long, deep flats hold many more trout than he had formerly thought, so now he spends more time fishing these thoroughly.

Claude Kreider fished western rivers for big trout, and he advocated big flies. One of his favorite lures was a streamer with a silver body and the shoulders of jungle cock. He would cast the streamer across a river and then retrieve it in short jerks as the current swept it down. In the deeper, slower pools he let it sink deep and then would activate it gently.

Claude also used Wooly Worms with black, brown, or gray bodies tied on long-shank No. 6, 4, and 2 hooks. He liked using the big dry flies not only because they caught big trout but also because they rode high and could be used on rough, white water, where smaller flies sank. They were also easier to see and watch when fishing them at a distance or toward dusk.

H. G. Tappley often skates a dry fly on top of the water when trout refuse to rise to a floater fished in the regular manner. He uses bivisibles and spiders, and casts across current with a slack line. Then he lets the fly float naturally until the line straightens. When it begins to drag he skates it across the surface with an up-and-down motion of the rod tip.

Dan Gapen, who designs flies and lures, such as the well-known Muddler, is also a highly skilled fisherman. And when he wants big brook trout he heads for the Winisk River system in Ontario, Canada. He claims that those are the best brook-trout waters he has ever fished. Many of the brook trout there go over 4 pounds and some run up to 7 and 8 pounds.

Like most anglers visiting this wilderness country, Dan uses Indian guides with canoes to take him to the best waters and to control the boat while he fishes. Dan finds that the brook trout there go for various spoons, spinners, jigs, and streamer flies. One of the most effective lures is a hair jig with a short section of plastic worm on the hook and an L-shaped spinner. He casts this with a spinning outfit and allows it to sink to the bottom before retrieving it.

When Dan locates a good concentration of fish with the spinning outfit, he usually changes to a fly rod and uses a weighted Muddler or a Magus Streamer, which he created and tied on one of his fishing trips to the area. This has long, slim black or dark-brown feathers, and he adds a tiny spinner a short distance behind the hook.

The great fisherman and writer Roderick L. Haig-Brown used large dry flies for western trout. He found that the bushy-hair flies on No. 8 or 9 hooks are best when fishing the big, rough rivers for rainbow and cutthroat trout. One trick he used with these floating flies was to drag the fly directly upstream against the broken water, then let it drift back on the slack line that was recovered.

George Heinold fishes for the sea-run brook, rainbow, and brown trout in New England, especially in his native state of Connecticut. For these fish George likes to use a light spinning outfit and cast-weighted streamers and bucktails, spinners, spoons, jigs, and tiny plugs. He has found that when the brown trout first enter a tidal stream or creek, they are fairly easy to catch. Then, in a few days, they become more wary and less inclined to hit a lure in the daytime.

Dan Gapen, well-known lure designer and angler, is shown with two big brook trout caught in Canadian waters. (*Photo by Dan Gapen*)

So he fishes for them at night and finds that they hit much better, especially on a flood tide.

Ted Janes also fishes tidal waters for sea-run trout, on Cape Cod, Massachusetts, and he finds that one of the best baits for them is a live killifish, especially in the spring of the year. He casts it out with a light spinning outfit. Other times of the year, he may use weighted streamers, spoons, and spinners. Ted finds that the trout in the tidal streams and creeks come and go with the tides and that fishing a couple of hours before high tide and a couple of hours after it are most productive.

Wynn Davis used to write a fresh-water fishing column in *Outdoor Life* magazine and has fished many of the country's best trout streams. He prefers to use flies and lures but has discovered that on many rivers nothing beats a soft-shell crayfish drifted through the pools, holes, pockets, runs, and riffles. In quiet pools he fishes the crayfish on a plain line and hook. In somewhat faster currents he adds a few split-shot sinkers above the hook. And in the fast rapids he uses a bottom rig with a sinker to get the crayfish down and hold it there. He hooks the crayfish by placing the hook shank alongside the underpart of the craw's body and holds it in place with rubber bands or dark thread. This way the bait lives longer and acts more lively.

If you want to catch lunker Dolly Varden trout, you couldn't fish a better river than the Flathead in Montana, according to Dale Burk. The trout will average between 6 and 7 pounds and often reach 15 pounds, with some fish going up to 20 pounds! Fish under 18 inches have to be thrown back.

The best time to catch these "bull" trout, says Dale, is in late May, June, and into July, when they run up the river to spawn. But the river shouldn't be too high or muddy or full of debris. Dale Burk uses a boat or rubber raft to float the river to reach the best spots. Then he gets out and wades to fish. The most productive spots are the long gravel bars. From there you cast plugs or spoons with a spinning outfit as far as you can into the river. Then retrieve the lure slowly as it swings in the current. Light-colored lures work best when the water is discolored, while darker ones can be used when the river is clear.

2

TROUT IN PONDS, LAKES, AND RESERVOIRS

Almost all trout fishermen agree that trout in ponds, lakes, and reservoirs are more difficult to catch than in streams or rivers. Since they offer more of a challenge, many trout anglers spend many hours trying to fool these fish. One such angler is Ted Trueblood, who seeks the trout in the clear, cold mountain lakes found in our western states.

Ted has found that lures and streamer flies that imitate minnows do not work on many of the high-country lakes. These waters contain few minnows, so the fish feed mostly on insects. Through the years, he has caught more trout on nymphs in these lakes than on any other lure. He likes nymphs, which are very effective especially when tied with dubbing or fur bodies in such colors as cream, gray, brown, and black on hook sizes from No. 8 to 12. He also uses flies that look like small fresh-water shrimp.

When Ted is casting in waters where he cannot see the trout, he uses a sinking fly line and counts as it sinks. Once he hooks a trout, he then knows how far to let the nymph sink again. Other times, he may troll the nymphs near shore about 60 to 70 feet behind the boat.

But Ted prefers to cast to cruising trout in shallow water near shore, either from a boat or while wading. Then you have to be quiet until you see a trout swimming by. You cast your nymph well ahead of the trout, anywhere from 6 to 20 feet or more, depending on how spooky it acts. Then you let the nymph sink slowly. If the trout refuses to hit it but keeps watching the fly, Ted gives it a slight twitch, and this often results in a hit.

When the trout start rising and feeding on hatching May flies, Ted will switch to a floating fly line and use a dry fly such as the Adams in size No. 10, 12, or 14. He casts to a rising fish and lets the fly float as long as possible; then he may twitch it or retrieve it just below the surface.

When Nelson Bryant wanted to catch wild brook trout in New Hampshire, where he lived for many years, he looked for back-woods beaver ponds. There the trout weren't monsters, but they were usually bigger than those found in small brooks and streams.

It took a lot of hiking and exploring to locate the beaver ponds, but about half of those he found contained some trout. Bryant found that the best fishing in these ponds took place in the spring, early summer, and fall.

John Castle is another angler who likes to fish for brook trout in beaver ponds—in Michigan. He also admits they are hard to find and often require tough hiking to reach, but says that they often provide the type of brook-trout fishing that is not found these days on streams and rivers in more civilized areas.

John usually takes along a fly rod and a light spinning outfit when he is looking for new ponds. On some ponds he has found that small spoons and spinners work better than flies. But, most of the time, he prefers to use dry flies, wet flies, and small streamers. He advises anglers to stay as far back from the edge of the pond as possible when fishing the beaver ponds, to avoid spooking the trout.

Bob Elliot has fished for brook trout in Maine lakes and ponds most of his life and knows most of the lures, methods, and tech-niques that pay off for these fish. Early in the spring, he trolls streamer flies close to shore, especially near the mouths of streams entering a pond or lake. He finds that trolling is usually more pro-ductive when the water is ruffled by a breeze. One trick he uses is to cast toward shore with another fly rod while trolling, and if the trout doesn't hit near the end of the cast it will often follow the fly toward the boat and hit the trolled streamer.

When using streamers or bucktails such as the Black Ghost, he will cast it out with a sinking line and let it go all the way to the bot-tom. Then he lifts the rod smartly with his right hand and jerks it up and down while retrieving the fly line with his left hand. The streamer is brought in sharply, then allowed to quiver and breathe while it is almost stopped. Then the line is jerked again along with

Some of the best fishing is found in beaver ponds situated in remote areas, such as this one in New Hampshire. They usually contain brook trout. (*Photo by Vel Gardner, State of New Hampshire*)

the rod; this procedure is continued until the fly is near the boat or shore.

Stan Berchulski fishes Windsor Pond, in Berkshire County, Massachusetts, when the trout season opens, in April. This lake contains good-sized brook trout, brown trout, and rainbow trout. Stan trolls for these fish with a 9-foot fly rod, single-action fly reel, and a sinking fly line. He ties a 30- to 40-foot, 4-pound-test leader and a streamer fly on the end. He likes the Gray Ghost, Barnes Special, Dark Tiger, Pumpkinseed, Silver Minnow, and the Professor for such trolling.

Stan will troll at various speeds, letting out most of the fly line until he finds what the fish want. If the fish are deep he will use either a fast-sinking fly line or attach a short length of lead-core line between the leader and the fly line. He believes in giving his flies added action by working his rod all the time.

Don Maddocks, of Ellsworth, Maine, catches brown trout in Branch Lake and is more successful than most anglers. He uses live smelt, chubs, and shiners, and trolls them very slowly over bars and shoals, and near inlets. He does most of his fishing early in the morning, at daybreak and for an hour or two after. Then he may go out again in the evening and fish until dark.

Lee Kernan, a biologist who had a lot to do with stocking and managing the brown trout in Lake Michigan off Wisconsin, is also a skilled angler. Now there is good fishing for big brown trout in Moonlight Bay and other waters along Wisconsin's Door Peninsula. These trout run from 3 to 20 pounds.

When the big trout come into shallow water near shore in the fall, Lee likes to wade and cast weighted spinners with silver or brass blades. He also uses spoons and small plugs at times. These are cast toward rocks or reeds seen in the water or toward drop-offs. At times, Lee sees the fish itself in the clear, shallow water, and then he casts and works the spinner so it passes in front of the trout. An erratic retrieve at various levels should be tried with the spinner. Letting it sink and flutter toward the bottom and then jerking it in a "crippled" manner is usually better than a steady retrieve. The best fishing takes place when the water is fairly calm early in the morning and toward dusk.

The big brown trout there can also be taken by trolling, but they are spooky in the clear, shallow water, so Kernan advises trolling the lure 200 to 300 feet behind the boat at low speed.

Ken Botty fishes for big brown trout in Quabbin Reservoir, in Massachusetts, and catches them by trolling with streamers. He uses a 9-foot fly rod, a sinking line, and a 50- to 60-foot, 8-pound-test mono leader. He likes the two-hook, or tandem, streamers such as the Nine-Three, Supervisor, Pink Ghost, Grizzly King, and Spencer Bay. Ken trolls these flies fast and gives them added action by working his line back and forth. If flies fail to produce, he may try Rapala plugs, spoons, and spinners.

Ed Gregory fishes Lake McConaughy, in Nebraska, and catches big rainbow trout, getting most of them near shore by wading. He gets many rainbows running from 3 to 8 pounds and will wait until he sees a fish near shore before casting. One of his secrets is to work a big trout persistently until the fish decides to hit. He will use such lures as small plugs, spoons, and spinners and keep casting and changing them until the big trout gets mad and hits. He worked over one 5-pound trout for thirty minutes and tried eight lures until it finally took one of them.

Peter Barrett, who was outdoors editor of *True* magazine for many years, often fished the western lakes for the big trout found there. In Wade Lake, Montana, he found that the dark, fat nymph called the Fledermaus was a killer on trout, especially when they were feeding on snails.

When the trout were spooky he would cast the fly toward shore, let it sink, then wait until a fish came cruising by. As the trout neared the fly he would give the nymph a twitch or two. Some of the trout would flee, others would ignore the offering, but enough trout would hit it to make the fishing worthwhile. The fastest action often occurred right after sundown. When it got dark he would change to streamers and take some trout on these, too.

Howard Brant fishes twenty-five-mile Pepacton Reservoir, in New York State's Catskill Mountains. There the brown trout have been running from 5 to 12 pounds. This reservoir supplies water to New York City, so you need a reservoir permit, which allows you to fish from shore. To fish from a boat you also need a boat permit. Motors are not permitted on the reservoir, so you have to row to the fishing spots.

Brant uses a light spinning outfit with 6- or 8-pound-test line. He slides a ⅛- or ¼-ounce egg sinker on the line, then ties a small-barrel swivel on the end to act as a stop. To complete the rig he ties a 2-foot leader, with a No. 4 or 6 hook, on the end.

The best bait to use in the Pepacton Reservoir is a live sawbelly, or alewife, hooked through the lips or back. This is lowered to a depth anywhere from 15 to 25 feet in May and June. During July

This 8-pound brown trout was caught by Howard Brant in Pepacton Reservoir, New York. (*Photo by Howard Brant*)

and August when fishing is usually best, you let the bait down from 25 to 35 feet. The best spots to fish, according to Brant, are the old river beds, channels, and drop-offs, with morning and evening hours the best.

Chester Chatfield fishes the ponds and lakes in the mountains of Washington State, and he uses a light spinning outfit and a plastic bubble and fly to take most of his trout. This is a small plastic float you fill with water to provide casting weight. You attach it to your line, add a 3- to 4-foot leader to the bubble, and then tie on the fly.

Chet uses plastic bubbles that weigh from ⅛ to ½ ounce when filled with water. The line on the spinning reel will test 6 to 8 pounds and the leader will test from 2 to 4 pounds depending on the weight of the spinning outfit used. Chet uses dry flies, wet flies, and streamers with the bubble and finds that the float doesn't frighten too many fish. In fact, he feels that it attracts fish to the spot.

Ted Janes fishes the lakes and ponds of New England, trolling with a fly rod using streamer flies. He finds this trolling is best soon after ice-out, when big trout come in to feed on smelt and other small fish. He trolls close to shore and around inlets and finds that the best shore to troll is one against which the wind blows, piling up waves and tossing the small baitfish around. Ted likes to troll against the wind, rather than with it, feeling that his fly has better action. He also finds that fast trolling is more productive than slow trolling.

John Hewston fishes for rainbow trout in the Flaming Gorge Reservoir, where the dam backed up the Green River from Utah across the border into Wyoming. He finds that trolling in the open water is best in May and June, using spoons, spinners, and small underwater plugs. Later on, in July and August, slow trolling in depths from 15 to 30 feet pays off.

He also casts from shore in the spring of the year, using a fly rod or spinning rod, and concentrates on any partly submerged sagebrush, clumps of grass, or rocks. He finds fly fishing is best from about midsummer to the fall, when rainbow trout move into the shallow water in the evening.

Mike Hayden has fished the "high lakes" in California's High Sierras with his wife for many years, and usually comes back with some trout. But he has found that the trout in such high altitudes can be hard to please and you have to vary your lures, baits, techniques, and methods.

Some of the best trout lakes, such as Todd Lake, in Oregon, shown here, are in scenic surroundings and mountain areas. Most of them are fished from shore, because they are reached by hiking and backpacking. (*Oregon State Highway Dept. photo*)

Mike finds that it is better to fish an area with several good lakes, rather than take your chances with only one lake no matter how good its reputation. He looks for streams or brooks entering a lake and fishes there. Or he looks for spots where he can reach a drop-off with his cast.

If the trout are rising he uses dry flies. But if there is no surface action he uses spinning tackle and casts spoons, spinners, and small plugs. Or he may try worms, salmon eggs, grasshoppers, or other insects. He casts the live baits with a plastic bobber or float to fish them near the surface. Or he adds some split-shot sinkers to fish them deeper. He finds that the trout will hit the baits better if you give them some movement by reeling them in slowly.

When Rod Cochran wants to catch early brook trout he uses a rig that is more effective and takes bigger trout than any other lure or bait. He takes a spoon weighing anywhere from ¼ to 1 ounce (red-and-white or bronze or copper spoons are preferred) and removes the treble hook on the lure. Then he ties a short, 5- to 8-inch leader with a tandem, or double, hook on the end. After which, he impales a worm on the hooks. Rod trolls this rig in water anywhere from 10 to 20 feet deep and pretty close to the bottom. He also casts the rig from a boat or shore into likely spots and reels it down deep.

Spoon and worm used for brook trout

Don LaDuke catches big brown trout in Wickiup Reservoir, in Oregon; he once caught one going 24 pounds 14 ounces! He catches most of them by trolling with a fly rod and a white bucktail fly he ties himself with long, white bucktail hair, jungle cock, and a woven silver tinsel piping for a body. Don trolls this fly around points over submerged reefs where the big brown trout feed. The fly travels a few inches below the surface, and to obtain strikes Don jerks the rod so that the fly darts to one side, and that is when the trout usually hit it.

When Ernest Schweibert fishes western lakes and reservoirs, he looks for trout cruising and searching for food. Such trout often leave a string of ripples from successive rises. But instead of casting to the last rise seen, he casts ahead of it, to the spot where the moving trout is mostly likely to rise the next time.

When trout are not showing in the lakes and reservoirs, Schweibert fishes for them in the shallows near shore, especially around the mouths of brooks or streams entering the lake. He finds that one of the best ways to fish there is to cast in a semicircle starting from the left and making successive casts about a yard apart until the last one is made on the right, near shore.

David Whitlock enjoys fishing with nymphs for big trout in such hard-to-fish waters as slow-moving streams, spring-fed ponds, reservoirs, and mountain lakes. There the water is clear, and with little or no current the trout have plenty of time to look over the fly. They are also difficult to approach without being seen. So Dave dresses in dark clothing and wades carefully without splashing, then stops and waits until he sees a fish come cruising by.

Dave uses a slow-action 7½- or 8-foot rod with a shooting-head line in a No. 4 or 5 weight. He likes knotless tapered leaders from 9 to 12 feet long and finds that nymphs tied to resemble May flies or damsel flies are most effective in sizes No. 10, 14, and 16. The tan, gray, and olive shades seem to work best for him.

In slow-moving water Dave will cast upstream a few feet and then let the nymph drift as long as possible, mending the belly in the line several times during the drift. In ponds, lakes, and reservoirs, he casts the nymph out and lets it sink to the bottom. If he sees a fish approaching he starts retrieving the nymph so that it passes in front of the fish.

Norman Strung finds fast fishing for rainbow trout in Montana's high country lakes soon after there is some open water in the spring. The rainbows go on a feeding spree then for about two weeks. He finds most of the fish grouped close to shore off long, rocky points on the side toward which the wind is blowing. And they are down fairly deep. He either trolls for them with a boat or casts from shore. He has his best luck with spoons, weighted spinners, and small plugs such as the Flatfish.

Don Waggoner is an expert nymph fisherman who has fished many western lakes. When the trout were feeding on fresh-water shrimp, he would use a shrimp fly with a yellow chenille body tied on a No. 8 hook. Wooly Worms tied with yellow or gray bodies also worked well for him. These were allowed to sink to the underwater weeds or grass beds and then were retrieved in slow, hesitating jerks to imitate the swimming motion of a live shrimp.

When Gene Hackney wants to catch some husky rainbow trout in one of the lakes near Spokane, Washington, where he lives, he turns to marshmallows for bait. The rig he uses with this bait is simple. He slips a sliding egg sinker on his line, then ties a small split ring on the end of the line. Next he ties a foot-long 3-pound-test leader and a No. 8 hook to the ring. Gene then takes a piece of the marshmallow and buries most of the hook in it, kneading some of it around the hook shank, eye, point, and barb in a tiny pear shape.

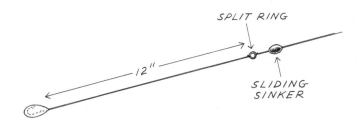

Rig for fishing marshmallow bait

To fish the marshmallow on this rig he casts it out about 50 to 60 feet and lets it sink to the bottom. Then he pulls about 10 feet of line off the reel and lets it settle in a big belly. This lets the trout take the bait and move off with it without feeling any pull.

Rex Gerlach fishes for cutthroat trout in the Pacific Northwest, especially in the state of Washington, where he lives. He heads for Badger Lake in early May to catch the fly hatches, which provide fast surface fishing for the cutthroats and also rainbow trout. When this happens he ties on a March Brown dry fly and gets plenty of action. He also fishes other lakes for cutthroats with flies and finds fishing good from April to October. But dry-fly fishing is best early in May and during September.

Charles Farmer finds excellent fishing for golden trout in the high-altitude lakes of Wyoming's Bridger Wilderness. One such lake is Wall Lake, which is reached by a tough backpacking hike of fourteen miles. But you can also take a pack trip with a guide on horseback to this lake.

Farmer uses ultra-light spinning tackle and casts such streamer flies as the Platte River Special. He adds some split shot on the leader for casting weight and to take the fly deep. He lets the streamer sink to the bottom, then retrieves it at a steady pace. Other times, he has good luck with spinners, also worked in a slow, steady retrieve near the bottom. The best time to fish for the golden trout in Wall Lake is from July through September.

3

STEELHEAD

Claude Kreider spent a lifetime fishing for steelhead, often following the fall and winter steelhead trail in California, Oregon, Washington, and British Columbia. He fished such famous steelhead rivers as the Eel, Klamath, Trinity, Deschutes, Rogue, Quinault, Umpqua, Skeena, and Kispiox.

Claude felt that steelhead in a river follow a definite course, defined by gouged-out troughs, submerged boulders, or a certain action of the water they like and they follow this devious route every year. He took a steelhead or two in a gouged-out channel below a wood snag breaking the current, for eight years straight; Claude knew of similar spots that produced steelhead year after year.

Claude passed up the slow pools, shallow eddies, and small riffles, which trout like. Instead he looked for long stretches of moderately fast water, not too deep. He knew steelhead rested in the depressions on the bottom below a boulder or beneath an underwater ledge in a strong current.

Another angler who specialized in steelhead fishing was Clark C. Van Fleet, who spent more than forty years fishing for them on most of the Pacific Northwest rivers. He found that when fishing the low, clear streams in the late-summer and early-fall months, overcast or cloudy days were better than light, clear days. And a breeze was also needed on quiet waters. So the best fishing usually took place from about nine until noon and in the later afternoon and evening, when such conditions usually prevailed.

Van Fleet did most of his fishing for steelhead with a fly. He particularly enjoyed fishing the fly an inch or two below the surface and seeing a big steelhead come up and take it. So he looked for boils, or rises, which indicate feeding fish, and cast toward the circles left by the fish, often getting an immediate strike.

Herb Duerksen, who fishes for steelhead in Oregon streams and rivers, keeps a close watch on those he plans to fish. He finds that drift fishing is best after the water level has reached a peak and starts dropping. When the color of the river changes from dirty green to a clear green, the steelhead often start hitting. This will usually occur first along the upper reaches of a river. These stretches can be fished early, and then, later on, the angler can move down to the lower sections of the river as they begin to clear.

When fishing for summer steelhead, he finds that the fish will often gather in the deeper holes in large numbers when the water is low and clear. They will be difficult to catch then, but he waits until a rain or a shower comes along and raises the level of the water or discolors it, at which time the steelhead often start to hit. For this fishing he likes to use large hair or streamer flies with bright, tinsel-wrapped bodies.

Wes Blair fishes for steelhead in the state of Washington, and he feels that it is highly important to learn the migration paths and resting areas in each river in order to plan a successful fishing trip. The best months for winter steelhead fishing, according to Wes, are November to March.

Wes looks for steelhead in water from 4 to 8 feet deep with a strong current. There the fish lie right on the bottom, usually in front of or behind a boulder. They also lie alongside riverbanks and drop-offs. These winter steelhead won't move very far to the left or right and will not rise off the bottom more than a foot or two, so you have to present your bait or lure at that level.

Wes uses an 8-foot drift rod with a level-wind bait-casting reel for his fishing, or a similar-length spinning rod with a medium-weight spinning reel. He likes to use fresh eggs for this drifting and adds some green yarn above the hook. He also uses spinners, spinner-bobber lures, and spoons.

He does his drift fishing from both shore and boats but considers boat fishing more productive than shore fishing, because you reach more of the best spots in a river. The main thing in drift fishing, he claims, is always to try to feel bottom with your sinker and keep changing weights until you do this.

Russell Chatham fishes for steelhead with a fly rod, and one of his most productive flies is the Comet fly. These are slim flies with long tails and sparse hackle, usually tied on a No. 4 or 6 hook for low-water or normal-water fishing. For high-water fishing they can be tied on No. 2 or larger hooks. Russell likes orange or fluorescent colors for clear water and black for murky water. He wraps a few turns of lead around the hook of the smaller flies to add weight for sinking and make them cast better. He uses the Comet fly with a sinking line and finds it is particularly suited for the deeper, slower waters found in the Pacific Northwest rivers near the coast.

Comet fly used for steelhead

James Freeman wrote a book called *Practical Steelhead Fishing* and has fished for seagoing rainbows for many years and in many waters. He advises visiting or beginning anglers to look for local anglers fishing. These people usually know when and where the steelhead are in a river. So follow the crowds and you'll be fishing in productive water.

When drifting a lure or bait for steelhead down deep, Freeman usually watches the tip of his rod and tries to feel the weight bouncing along the bottom. He tries to feel the weight tapping or hopping or gliding over the rocks. If this bouncing stops, it often indicates that the lure or bait is moving into a hole or deeper spot. This is where steelhead like to lie in a river. When this happens he lowers his rod tip to permit the lure or bait to sink deeper in the hole. You can also release some slack line to do the same thing.

Like most steelheaders, he changes the weight on his rig often to match the speed of the current, the depth of the water, and the distance he must cast to reach a good spot. To locate fish, Freeman works a stretch as fast as possible, making casts into likely spots and making a few drifts, then moving on to the next spot. However, if he knows that steelhead are present in a certain spot or sees them leaping, he stops and fishes that location long and hard.

Jim Freeman also catches steelhead with a fly rod during the win-

Some of the biggest steelhead are caught in the waters of British Columbia, Canada—like this beauty taken in the Kispiox River. (*Garcia Corporation photo*)

ter months. Then he uses the larger, brighter-colored flies, which are weighted to sink fast. He fishes these as slowly and as close to the bottom as he can get them.

P. J. Tronquet concentrates on the smaller, lightly fished steelhead streams and finds better fishing than on the heavily fished, well-known, bigger rivers. He finds that in addition to more elbow room and less competition on the smaller streams, he also has a better chance to catch more fish.

He finds that heavy winter rains often raise and muddy the bigger rivers. They usually stay that way for days or much of the season. But the smaller streams clear quickly even after heavy rains and can be fished. The steelhead are hard to fool there, so he uses light rods with bait-casting reels and lines testing only 8 to 10 pounds. The leader may be as light as 4 to 6 pounds if the stream is low and clear. He uses fresh steelhead roe cut into small clusters for bait, to which he adds a couple of strands of pink yarn as an added attractor.

Since many of the small steelhead streams have banks overgrown with trees and brush, Tronquet finds that pin-point casting is usually necessary to place the bait in the right spots between the openings and the growth. Since these waters are fairly shallow, you have to wade from one side to another to position yourself in the right spot to fish each drift effectively.

Francis H. Ames has fished most of the top steelhead rivers in the Pacific Northwest, and he says that to catch winter steelhead you have to keep a close check on the weather, water level, water condition, and the movements of the fish, to locate them constantly.

He finds that when the steelhead are moving upstream fast you have to follow them as they run up the river. The spot that was good yesterday may not produce today. According to Ames, steelhead like fast-flowing, heavy water, and you should avoid fishing in still water. When the water is high and discolored he uses natural baits, but when it is clear and warm he uses lures and flies. He also likes to fish toward dusk when the rivers are clear and low, especially just below riffles and rapids.

Emil Dean is a fishing guide who fishes for the steelhead on the Manistee River, in Michigan. His system is to anchor the boat upstream from a hole where steelhead lie and then let the current carry the lure down to that location. He lets the lure drift down to the head of the hole and lets it work there for a while, then lets it drift down 3 to 4 feet and keeps it in that spot for twenty seconds or so. He keeps doing this until the entire length of the hole is covered. The lure— usually a small plug such as the Flatfish—should bump bottom often. Emil finds that a casting rod and casting reel filled with 20-pound-test mono is best for this fishing.

Dave Borgeson had a lot to do with introducing steelhead and salmon into Michigan streams, and he also likes to fish for them for sport. He has found that the Michigan steelhead can be caught on flies from February to April, when they enter the rivers to spawn.

Dave uses a special rig to get the flies down to the right depth. He attaches a small three-way swivel to the end of his line, then a 2-foot leader, which holds the fly, and to the remaining eye he ties on a short, 6-inch dropper that will hold split-shot sinkers. The number of sinkers he uses depends on the depth and speed of the current. For flies, he uses weighted nymphs that imitate stone flies, May flies, or dragonflies. One of these is called Spring's Wiggler and is tied on a No. 4, 6, or 8 hook.

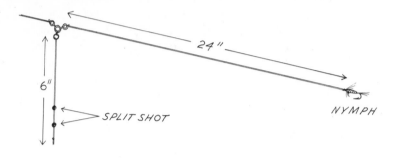

Steelhead rig used by Dave Borgeson

Dave finds that steelhead will lie in the deeper water and holes during the middle of the day but will move out into the riffles where they make their spawning beds just before dark. So, early morning is one of the best times to fish for them. You cast the fly to the fish that are seen or to the spawning beds, which show up lighter than the rest of the bottom. The trick is to let the fly drift, as close to the bottom as possible, toward the fish as you feel the split-shot sinkers bouncing along the bottom.

Bill McMillan continues fishing for steelhead with a fly rod and fly even during the fall months and finds that the fish in a river's upper reaches in shallow riffles and pockets can be caught this way. He usually sees the individual fish and casts to them using the Muddler in sizes from No. 6 to 1/0 for fall steelhead. He fishes this fly on the surface or just below it and twitches and jerks it for added action. He also uses a No. 4 Brad's Brat; in the shallow riffles, he works it across the current, and the strike is readily seen. If these patterns fail he tries the Steelhead Bee on or near the surface. If a steelhead "shows" but doesn't take the fly, he will often rest the water for five to ten minutes and then try again, with the same fly or a different one. Finally, if the steelhead aren't rising, he will use a Stone Fly nymph and fish it deep.

Dory Lavier is a biologist who works for the Washington State Game Department; he helped manage the steelhead fisheries there for twenty-five years. He is also an expert rod-and-reel fisherman for steelhead, so his advice about these fish is valuable. He knows his rivers and waters—which ones to fish and which ones produce best under varying conditions; after a heavy rain, he knows which rivers clear quickly and which ones take longer. He claims one of the best times to fish for steelhead is when the river starts to drop after a heavy rain.

For winter steelheading, when big fish are around, Dory uses an 8½-foot glass rod with fairly stiff action. He attaches a Heddon Winona side-winding reel to his rod and fills it with 10-pound-test mono line. He uses salmon and steelhead eggs on a sliding-sinker rig, though he finds that steelhead eggs are better than salmon eggs, and he often adds some fluorescent or bright-orange yarn just above the big, No. 1/0 or 2/0 hook. When the water is low and clear he may try small spoons with a single hook. Once Dory catches a fish, he makes a mental note of the spot and fishes it again at a later date, often catching more steelies from the same spot.

David Richey fishes the Little Manistee River, in Michigan, for the steelhead that spawn there in April. He casts a lure toward their spawning beds and finds that extreme care is needed when approaching the fish, which usually lie in water from 1½ to 4 feet deep. He starts fishing at the crack of dawn and takes a position downstream from the fish and casts a spinner upstream so that it drifts toward the fish. It may take many casts before the steelie gets angry enough to hit the lure.

In the fall of the year, Richey uses a different method to catch the steelhead. Then he looks for spots where steelhead like to lie in the current. He knows that they like the edge where the water is not too slow or too fast. They also lie in front of or alongside a rock. The tail end of a deep hole is also a prime location. Then he anchors a boat upstream from such a spot and drops back a Tadpolly or a Flatfish. He lets these lures back about 3 feet at a time, holding the plug in the current in each spot before letting it drop back again. Every so often, he may give the lure additional action with the rod tip.

Tom Jeeson uses weighted spinners for steelhead, but he makes his own spinners to suit the conditions and fishing found during the vari-

David Richey is shown here with a 14-pound steelhead taken in Michigan's Platte River. The fishing is best during the spring, when the big fish are getting ready to spawn. (*David Richey photo*)

ous seasons. He cuts slip-on pencil sinkers into varied lengths and adds these to the wire below the bead and spinner blade. Then he adds a single hook behind that. The blades are usually gold, in size No. 4 or 2, for summer fishing. He may also paint the lead body a fluorescent color. In high, roily water he may use spinners with the blade also painted in a fluorescent color.

Tom will cast the spinner upstream and reel a bit faster than the current when fishing holes or fast riffles. When he casts to a rock or a log, he drops the lure a few feet above the obstruction and lets the spinner swing close to it.

Robert Curtis has fished for steelhead on the West Coast for many years. He knows which rivers can be ruined by prolonged storms or rains and which ones clear rapidly. So he concentrates most of his efforts on such rivers in California as the Ten Mile River, the Noyo River, the Big River, and the Navarro River, in the Mendocino area. He knows from past experience that these rivers will clear quickly in a few days.

Like most winter steelheaders, he finds that fresh-roe baits are best. He ties the eggs in small squares of red netting and fishes this on an 18-inch leader with the hook and a 6- or 8-inch dropper, which holds the sinker. The sinker will weigh from ⅜ to ¾ of an ounce. He ties the dropper holding the sinker with a weaker line so it breaks off if snagged, saving the rest of the rig.

Frank Metcalf is a fisheries biologist who also fishes for steelhead for sport. He has examined the stomach contents of hundreds of steelhead and has found that, on their spawning runs upstream, they do feed. He has observed that the steelhead usually refuse to hit on both sides of a barrier blocking the mouth of a river. So he digs a channel to the surf. As soon as the water starts flowing through this channel, the steelhead start moving through it to the river, and they also start hitting baits and lures.

Bill Luch fishes for summer steelhead the same way he does for resident trout, which means he fishes each spot thoroughly, casting behind rocks and in riffles, chutes, and pockets where trout are usually found. He also approaches the water he will be fishing with extreme care and avoids wading if possible. This is especially important on the smaller streams that are low and clear.

John B. Gleason does his steelhead fishing on the Pere Marquette River, in Michigan, and he finds that a long, 8-foot rod with a spinning reel makes a good outfit for using spawn sacks in the spring and fall. He likes to use fresh eggs and toughens them with boric-acid powder. Then he gets some nylon stockings and cuts these into 2- to 3-inch squares. He usually ties about three to five eggs in each nylon sack, because he feels small sacks work better than big ones.

John fishes the eggs on a drifting rig with a sinker and makes it move along the bottom at all times. This means using a weight that permits the bait to drift at the right speed and depth in the water you are fishing. So he prefers a dropper with split-shot sinkers, which can be added or removed as needed. And like most expert steelheaders, he assumes he has a bite when the sack stops, hesitates, or acts differently, so he sets the hook time and again in order not to miss a real strike. Sure, he loses many rigs and gets hung up often, but that is the price you have to pay if you want to catch steelhead.

Don Ingle also fishes for the steelhead that run in the Pere Marquette River, from January to early May, and he catches them on a fly rod. He uses weighted streamers on a fairly heavy fly rod and likes such patterns as the Skunk, Parmachene Belle, Silver Doctor, Royal Coachman, Jock Scott, and the black-and-white types.

When fishing the river, he looks for steelhead on their spawning beds and works his way carefully toward the fish from upstream. He quarters his cast and lets the current swing the fly toward the steelhead. Then he works the fly, making it move forward, after which he drops it back, in a teasing action.

4

ATLANTIC SALMON AND LANDLOCKED SALMON

Lee Wulff is well known as an author, photographer, TV sportsman, and skilled all-around angler in both fresh and salt water. But most fresh-water anglers associate him with the Atlantic salmon. Lee Wulff has spent a lifetime fishing for salmon in Canada and many rivers of the world. His book *The Atlantic Salmon* is a classic, and he has made many contributions to the sport of fishing.

Lee finds that salmon fishing varies in all rivers, depending on changes in water level, temperature, and the seasons of the year. He knows that salmon are unpredictable fish, so he is always experimenting—trying new techniques and novel twists that will make a salmon rise and take the fly.

According to Lee, when salmon are scattered over the length of the river, wet flies are the most productive. And wet flies are also best when the rivers are high and the water cold and rough. Lee also feels that wet flies cover more water, are seen by more fish and can be presented for a longer period of time than dry flies. And he also believes that salmon are not conditioned to rise to a tiny insect on the surface when they first enter a river from the ocean. So, early in the season he uses mostly wet flies.

Lee Wulff fishes the wet fly in the conventional manner by casting across and downstream at an angle of about 45 degrees and then allows it to swing with the current in an arc until the line is directly downstream. Then he picks it up and makes another cast. He will make a cast or two from one spot, then move downstream a few feet and fish new water. Of course, if he knows a salmon is lying in a cer-

Lee Wulff, well-known angler and sportsman, with a big salmon caught in Canada. Lee often flies in with a plane to wilderness streams and rivers for this type of fishing (*Lee Wulff photo*)

tain spot or a fish shows by rising or leaping, he'll spend more time fishing that spot.

When the water is low, and the salmon gather in groups in pools, and he sees fish rolling on the surface, Lee turns to dry flies. He uses the White Wulff, Gray Wulff, Royal Wulff, Adams, Rat-faced Mac-Dougall, and the bivisibles for this fishing, in sizes from No. 6 to 16. Usually, the clearer the water the better the fishing is with the dry flies. He fishes a dry fly in much the same way as for brown trout, avoiding drag as much as possible. But if that fails after repeated casts, Lee will deliberately pull the fly across the surface or even pull it underwater in front of a fish. This sometimes triggers a response and the fish takes the fly.

When using dry flies Lee is constantly alert and watches for flashes of a fish below the surface. This indicates restless fish, which are more inclined than others to rise and take the fly later. He finds that salmon may make false rises: just coming up and looking at a fly. They do not always take a fly on the first pass but may make two, three, or more passes before taking it for good.

John Atherton was a talented artist and skilled fly fisherman who fished for trout and Atlantic salmon. When he used small wet flies for salmon during average or low water conditions, he used a floating line and kept it well greased. This way, he felt, he could control the fly better and mending the line to give the fly the right action was easier. He could also follow the drift of the fly, notice any drag, correct it, and always know where the fly was in the water. In addition, he could see the salmon rise and thus locate the fish. John would then keep working the same spot with different flies, try varied techniques and hook the fish later on.

When fishing a wet fly in very slow water, John Atherton would strip in line with his left hand in a slow, steady retrieve while waggling his rod tip up and down about 3 to 4 inches. This gave the fly a lifelike action in the water.

Joseph D. Bates has written many fishing books, and one of these, *Atlantic Salmon Flies and Fishing,* covers almost all of the important flies used for this great fish. He also gives excellent information on how to locate salmon and how to use the flies.

One important observation Joe makes about salmon rivers is that the lies of the fish change according to the changes in the volume and depth of the water. When the water drops, salmon will leave certain lies that are too shallow and take up new ones. When the water rises, some shallow spots that formerly didn't appeal to the fish now attract and hold them. If the water gets really high, the shallower bars usually provide better fishing than the big, deep pools.

During warm-weather periods, when a river's water temperature reaches or passes 70 degrees, Joe finds that the salmon will seek and move into cold-water pools, where the best fishing will usually take place in the faster water rather than in the slower portions of the pool.

Joe Bates will use streamers or bucktails for salmon in the fall when the water temperature is 50 degrees or lower. And he finds that they can be used in all kinds of water from shallow to deep and in rough or smooth water. He feels that the splash of a streamer will often attract salmon rather than frighten them. To work the streamers or bucktails, he casts straight across and lets the current create a belly in the line, which speeds up the fly. Joe also uses streamers and bucktails during the summer months after a rain, which raises the water level and discolors the water. He likes the Herb Johnson Special, the Gray Ghost, and the Mickey Finn, but finds many other streamer patterns work well too.

Atlantic salmon alongside rock

Bill MacDonald has fished the famed Miramichi River, in New Brunswick, Canada, for many years. He likes to fish from shore by wading, if possible, but many stretches of this river are best approached from mid-river in a canoe. Bill has found that in the runs between deep pools, Atlantic salmon tend to hug the bottom alongside a rock rather than behind it. So he tries to cast his fly so that it is carried past this spot.

Al McClane has fished for Atlantic salmon in the major rivers of the world. He claims that even though you have fished for trout with flies, salmon fishing is a brand-new ball game. You look for salmon in spots different from those where you look for trout, according to Al. Salmon usually choose a spot where the flow is strong enough to bring them the necessary oxygen yet weak enough for them to lie in without using too much energy fighting the current. You can waste a lot of time fishing and casting in unproductive water between such lies. So blind casting is not as productive as casting to spots where fish are known to lie or where you can actually see the salmon lying or showing.

Al usually casts his wet fly across and slightly downstream with a straight line so that the fly drifts naturally right from the beginning. In fast currents he lowers his rod to give some line to slow down the speed of the fly. In slow water he lifts his rod and strips in line to speed up the fly. At the end of the drift, Al retrieves the fly gently after a short pause. He increases the speed of the retrieve after other casts and has found that at times a fly that is retrieved so fast that it skims over the surface sometimes brings a smashing strike.

When fishing a river with plenty of salmon, Al McClane spends about twenty minutes working over a single fish, trying various flies. Then he moves on to the next fish. But where salmon are scarce and when fishing public salmon waters, it pays to work on a single fish for longer periods of time. Then you try various fly patterns and sizes, and switch from wet to dry flies and try different techniques; sooner or later the fish may show interest and hit.

Don Leyden also fishes for salmon on the Miramichi River, and while salmon can be caught in the river from the middle of June and during the summer months, he prefers September, when the peak fishing usually takes place.

Instead of using the time-honored English and Scottish salmon flies, Don prefers the more simply tied hair-winged flies. He likes the Squirrel Tail, Black Bear Hair, Green Hornet, Oriole, Silver Turkey, and Gold Turkey, in hook sizes from No. 2 to 12.

Don fishes the flies slow in fast water and fast in slow water. He is always mending his line to give the fly the speed that will appeal to the fish. In slow currents he mends his line downstream to give the fly more speed. He likes to use a floating line and keeps it clean and well dressed. When a salmon hits short or just nudges the fly, he casts out again, and when the fly reaches the spot, he pulls on the line to increase its speed. At times, this makes the salmon take the fly.

Edward R. Hewitt was America's master trout-and-salmon angler early in this century and was using dry flies for Atlantic salmon when other anglers still used wet flies only. He wrote *Secrets of the Salmon,* which was published in 1922. Hewitt was a scientific angler, who was always experimenting and developing theories and techniques, many of which are valid to this day.

He claimed that wet-fly fishing early in the season for salmon was too easy and preferred to wait until later on, when the water was warmer and the salmon would rise to dry flies. He found that they

The happy angler shown here caught this salmon in the Miramichi River, near Blackville, New Brunswick. This is a favorite river with many avid salmon fishermen. (*Canadian Government Travel Bureau photo*)

strike best when the water temperature is between 60 and 66 degrees. He used a 14-foot leader and bushy, high-floating, all-hackle dry flies in sizes No. 6 to 10.

Hewitt would try to cast his fly so that it floated directly over the fish, where it could see it with both eyes but not notice the leader. He had his best luck with flies that floated high on the tips of their hackles. But he also pulled the fly under the surface at times and once hooked fifteen salmon in one afternoon fishing in this manner.

Norman Hathaway is the Atlantic-salmon champ of Maine and has caught as many as thirty-three salmon in one season (from three different rivers in that state). Most anglers are lucky if they get one or two fish during Maine's salmon season.

One of his tricks is to tease a salmon with a bright orange fly that he created and calls the Orange Crate. This fly rides high and is not actually taken by the salmon. But Norm will cast it three or four times to the same spot where a salmon is lying or jumping, and if the fish shows interest he switches to a more conventional fly pattern and casts that to the same spot. He gets many hits and fish this way.

Edgar Eastman, who guided for salmon anglers in a canoe on the Humber River, in Newfoundland, for many years, said that salmon fishing is usually better when the day is overcast rather than bright. He also said that when he could hear the rocks tumbling under a falls, the big salmon usually hit best.

When it comes to landlocked salmon, we find many more anglers who are skilled in taking these close relatives of the Atlantic salmon. One of these is Harold Blaisdell, who catches the landlocks in various ways. But his favorite way is to catch them on dry flies in fast water such as the Moose River, near Jackman, Maine. There the landlocks can be caught in May, June, and September. Fishing can also be good in July at times if the weather and water are cool and the river is high from recent rains.

Harold fishes the spots just above the rapids or falls, where the water is slick and fast. Some of the river has to be fished from a canoe, but there are also spots where you can wade and fish. He uses a light, 2- to 3-ounce fly rod, a floating fly line, and a dark dry fly tied on a No. 12 hook for most of this fishing. He finds that one trick that often makes landlocks rise and take a dry fly is to swing the fly in an arc on a tight line so that it actually skims the water. Often, a salmon will swirl or make several passes at the fly before taking it for good. So it pays to continue casting and fishing if a fish shows some interest in the fly.

When dry flies aren't producing, Blaisdell will try streamers and wet flies in a river. He likes heavily dressed wet flies on No. 8 hooks. These usually have dark wool bodies ribbed with narrow gold tinsel or yellow silk floss. He finds that they not only work on salmon but also catch good-sized brook trout. He will sometimes let the current carry out all of his fly line and even some of the backing, then will reel in the fly at a rapid, steady pace. He often gets strikes from salmon before his line is wound back on the reel.

Bill Geagan trolls for landlocks in Maine soon after ice-out. He uses either a smelt sewn on a treble hook or tandem-hook streamers. Bill is very careful about handling the bait or lure with clean hands.

To eliminate any odor from gasoline or oil, or other strong smells, he washes his hands before handling the baits or lures.

Bill likes to troll a smelt or a streamer about 60 to 70 feet behind the boat. He trolls such streamers as the Supervisor, Nine-Three, Green King, Pink Lady, Black Ghost, and Gray Ghost at high speed. He trolls the smelt at a lower speed. If straight trolling doesn't produce, he'll try a serpentine course. He does most of his trolling off bars, points, and islands, and in inlets. He finds that early-morning and evening hours are best for landlock fishing, especially during the warmer months.

Ken Botty fishes deep for landlocks during the summer months, but he feels you lose a lot of the action and sport if you use the regular trolling outfits. So he puts his wire line on a big single-action fly reel and then on a fly rod, and really enjoys fishing and fighting the high leapers on such gear.

Ken puts about a hundred yards of .010- or .022-inch wire line on his reel, and to it he attaches a 35-foot, 10-pound-test monofilament leader and then another 10-foot section of lighter leader material to the end. For lures he uses spoons or small plugs and lets these out anywhere from 75 to 200 feet, depending on the depth he is trying to reach. He marks the wire line every 50 feet or so, so he knows how much line is out at all times.

Ken also varies his trolling speed depending on whether he is trolling with the wind or current or against it. The trolling speed will also vary according to the lure he is using and the depth he wants to reach.

Although most anglers fish for landlocked salmon in the lakes in the spring, Jerome B. Robinson prefers to catch them in the rivers. He feels that this is the closest thing to Atlantic salmon fishing. So he seeks landlocks in Maine and New Hampshire waters soon after ice-out. The fish aren't easy to locate, because they move quickly and often up the river, not lingering too long in one spot. But Robinson has observed that the salmon will often reveal their presence by leaping or swirling, especially when the sun breaks through the clouds. He uses streamers and wet flies but enjoys catching the salmon on dry flies best of all. He relies mainly on a Gray Wulff tied on a No. 10 hook.

When trolling deep for landlocked salmon, Carrol Cutting recom-

Maine offers the best landlocked-salmon fishing in the country. Many are caught by trolling with fly rods from canoes and other small boats on such scenic lakes as this. (*Maine Development Commission photo*)

mends trolling in circles or figure eights. This creates a varied speed and depth at which the lure or bait travels.

Gene Letourneau, who writes an outdoors column in the Portland (Maine) *Press-Herald,* recommends the following waters in his state for landlocked salmon: Sebago Lake, Mooselookmeguntic Lake, Chesuncook Lake, Moosehead Lake, Square Lake in the Fish River chain, East Grand Lake, and West Grand Lake. He says you should hit these lakes soon after ice-out and that the best fishing is on cloudy days with a chop, or small waves. He suggests trolling with such flies as the Nine-Three, Liggett Special, and Sportsman.

Ted Janes looks for landlocks in the early spring close to shore, especially around river mouths where smelt have gathered for their spawning run. Then he trolls streamers fast right in the wake of the boat. He feels that a zigzag course while trolling is more effective than a straight course, since it covers more water and varies the speed and depth of the lures. He also gives his fly added action by sawing the line up and down ,through the guides or lifts and lowers his rod tip to do the same thing. Later on in the season he looks for landlocks in deeper water but watches for them coming up to feed on the surface on insects. Then he fishes for them with a fly rod and dry flies.

Charles V. Kihlmire fished for landlocks in such Maine rivers as the upper Kennebec. He found that most of the salmon like to lie in the shelter of rocks at the edge of the white water. Fishing in such rapids, he would cast to the white water below the rocks. He would also wade in the river and cast across stream and allow the fly to swing downstream with the current until it was directly below him. Then he would bring the streamer fly back in short, rapid jerks against the current. When he was doing this, a salmon would often leave its shelter and slash at the fly. He found that such a salmon would often make several attempts to catch the fly until it finally did so for good.

Harry Drew, of Waterville, Maine, spent more than sixty years fishing in the waters of that state. One of his favorite tricks when trolling for landlocks was to slow down and let the lures or bait sink deep. Then he would speed up so that the lure or bait would rise. He claimed that most of his strikes came during such a speed-up of the lure or bait.

Philip S. Andrews is a biologist in Maine who enjoys fishing for landlocked salmon, especially when they are in rivers and hitting flies. He recommends for this fishing such waters as the Eagle Lake outlet, Mattagamon Lake outlet, St. Croix River at East Grand Lake, the Kennebago River, and the Crooked River. Fishing in these waters is usually best in the spring and fall, with September a top month on many of these rivers.

Phil recommends streamers on No. 4 or 6 long-shank hooks, and he fishes these by casting across and a bit downstream and retrieving at various speeds as the fly swings with the current. Wet flies can also be fished the same way with a somewhat slower retrieve. Or they can be fished on a slack line or "dead drift" manner.

With dry flies, Andrews feels that specific patterns are not too important, but you should use flies ranging from light to dark shades of brown on size No. 12 or 14 hooks. At times, he finds large dry flies such as the Wulffs or bivisibles up to 2 inches in diameter effective.

5

COHO SALMON AND
LAKE TROUT

At one time not too long ago, coho salmon were fished for mostly along the Pacific coast in salt water. That was before Michigan decided to plant fingerling salmon in the creeks and rivers feeding into Lake Michigan. Results were quick and amazing: only ninety days after stocking the 5-inch salmon had grown to 15 inches and a weight of 1¼ pounds. The coho found the deep, cold water of Lake Michigan to their liking, and the abundance of alewives and smelt provided plenty of food for them. A year later, fishing for the cohos began in earnest and has been fast and furious to this day. Since then, coho and Chinook salmon have been stocked throughout the Great Lakes, and today thousands of fishermen descend on these waters for a piece of the action—hooking a wild, silvery coho salmon.

Anglers trying to catch cohos for the first time would learn how to do it more quickly if they first went out with an expert angler or chartered a boat from one of the ports along the Great Lakes. One such charter-boat captain is Ogden Hamachek, who operates out of Kewaunee, Wisconsin, and fishes Lake Michigan. He has been catching plenty of coho salmon, Chinook salmon, and lake trout for his customers.

Captain Hamachek likes to use 6½-foot salt-water trolling rods with level-wind reels. The reels are filled with 20- or 25-pound-test monofilament line. When the fish are down deep, however, he will use outfits with wire line on the reels. One of the rigs he uses consists of a three-way swivel with a dropper of 3 to 6 feet, holding the sinker or other weight tied to one eye of the swivel. Then he attaches a 6-foot leader and the lure to the other eye of the swivel.

Coho salmon are usually caught by trolling at various depths with weights or wire lines. This one was caught in Lake Michigan. (*Michigan Tourist Council photo*)

Captain Hamachek uses spoons and plugs for coho and prefers lures with single hooks rather than treble hooks. He finds treble hooks too weak: they get crushed or twisted by the tough jaws of the salmon. He trolls at varying speeds depending on the lure he is using at the time. He tests each lure alongside the boat to see if the speed is the right one to bring out the best action. The lures are trolled at varying distances behind the boat, anywhere from 150 to 300 feet. He changes the trolling weights also, depending on the depth to be fished, and these usually range between 2 and 8 ounces.

Captain Hamachek may troll up to six or eight lines from his boat, and if he gets two or three fish on at the same time he usually throws over a floating buoy to mark the spot. Then he runs clockwise around and through the school of fish.

Tom Opre also fishes for coho in Lake Michigan, and he finds that they will usually be found where the water temperature is between 50 and 55 degrees. This could be anywhere from 20 to 100 feet or more during the summer months. So a depth-sounder, or fish-finder, and an underwater thermometer are musts in locating this thermocline. Once the fish are located you troll your lures at the right depth all the time. Various lures can be used for the coho, but the one that Tom

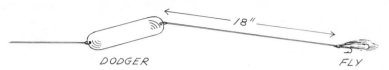

Dodger and fly used for coho salmon

Opre prefers is a shiny metal "dodger" with a silver or gold finish and a streamer fly trailing about 18 inches behind it.

Jerry Chiappetta also fishes for cohos in Lake Michigan during the entire season that they run and hit, but he prefers to fish for the smaller cohos that run early in the season, during April and May. Then the salmon are close to the surface and in shallow water, where you can use light tackle when trolling or casting for them. They even swim in close enough to land so that shore anglers can get a crack at them. These early salmon run mostly from 2 to 4 pounds, but they are fast, lively fighters and also make excellent eating.

Jerry finds that lures that imitate the alewives and smelt that these salmon are feeding on are the most effective fish catchers. Among the more popular lures are the Flatfish, the Rapalas, the Rebels, and spoons, spinners, and streamer flies.

Henry Zeman likes to fish for the cohos when they come into the surf in the spring of the year. Then he can cast from shore with light surf-fishing tackle and catch these great game fish. The best fishing usually takes place at the mouths of streams and rivers entering Lake Michigan. One such river is the Platte. Points of land that jut out into the lake and can be waded a bit are also good spots to try. Zeman finds that the best lures for this fishing are long, narrow spoons heavy enough to cast a good distance. He also uses underwater plugs that can be cast far enough to reach the fish.

Jim Bashline also likes to catch cohos when they come close to shore in the spring and fall. He prefers to use a fly rod and either casts or trolls close to shore for the salmon. He also finds his best fishing around the mouths of streams or creeks emptying into the lake.

Jim recommends a No. 8 or No. 9 weight fly rod and a good-sized fly reel with a sinking fly line. For lures, bright, flashy streamers with some Mylar on them work best. Those with blue or green feathers or hair on their backs and white or yellow below and silver bodies are most effective, since they imitate the alewives and smelt and emerald shiners that cohos feed on.

These anglers are fishing for and catching coho salmon from shore in the surf. This fishing is best near the mouths of streams and rivers during the spring. (*Henry Zeman photo*)

David Richey catches hundreds of coho salmon in Michigan streams and rivers during the spawning season. And he catches most of them on streamer flies or spinners. It is not unusual for him to hook ten, twenty, thirty, or more fish in one day. He releases most of these fish and keeps only an occasional salmon for the table. What he enjoys about this fishing is that he has the stream or river mostly to himself during October, November, and December, when the cohos are in the river.

Richey finds that the salmon are easy to locate on their spawning beds in the shallow water. First he spots the fish, then he casts the fly so that it passes in front of the fish's snout, close to the bottom. He uses such streamers as the Royal Coachman, Golden Girl, Mickey Finn, Orange P. M. Special, Red P. M. Special, Little Manistee, and Skykomish Sunrise.

He tries to approach the salmon from upstream and gets as close as he can to make his cast. Then he casts across and downstream so that the fly drops about 6 feet above and to the far side of the salmon. Often the fish will take the fly on the first cast, but if it doesn't he keeps casting until the fish decides to hit. Other times, when the fish are spooky, he may approach them from downstream. In this case, he usually casts from about 30 feet below the fish and places his fly about 6 feet in front of the salmon. Then he strips in line slowly or raises his rod tip so that the fly moves where the fish can see it.

Dick Seamans, chief of the New Hampshire Fisheries Division, says the coho salmon fishing can be good in the bays and rivers of his state during the summer and fall months, but few anglers take advantage of this fishing. He and other biologists in New Hampshire have been stocking coho-salmon smolts since 1967, and fishing has been improving each year. They can be caught either by trolling or casting spoons, plugs, and jigs, in the bays and rivers. So far, the most productive rivers have been the Piscataqua, Lamprey, and Exeter. The best time to catch the cohos moving upstream is from September to mid-December.

Lyle Budnick, boat captain and guide, takes out sportsmen on Lake Michigan for coho salmon and lake trout. And his customers often catch lake trout on top even during the summer months. Lyle has found that the key to this fishing is the water temperature. He discovered that on the Wisconsin shore of Lake Michigan, prevailing westerly winds during the summer may push the warm surface water out toward the middle of the lake. The cold water from the depths wells up to replace it. This creates a temperature close to 50 degrees which the lakers like. They can then be caught in depths of 15 to 20 feet.

Budnick trolls spoons on outriggers at these depths using Dacron line. He uses a depth-sounder or fish-finder and picks up the schools of lake trout on it. If the fish are present but do not hit, he tries various speeds while trolling to find the right one. Or he experiments with different lures or different colors until he finds what the fish want.

Harry Holubes fishes Priest Lake, in Idaho, and he has acquired a reputation for catching big lake trout. He's called "Mackinaw Harry" by other anglers, who respect his ability to catch the lakers. Harry's favorite method is to troll with a light salt-water rod and a star-drag salt-water reel filled with Monel wire line. He lets out about 600 feet of line and needs no additional weight to get the lure down to the right depth. On the end of the wire line he adds 100 feet of monofilament line and then attaches an underwater plug. He believes in using light leaders, testing no more than 12 to 15 pounds. While being trolled at low speed the wire line occasionally bumps bottom, but the plug stays high enough off the bottom to keep from snagging.

Jerry Tricomi, who runs Camp Manitou, in Ontario, Canada,

found out that lake trout can be taken by jigging even during the hot summer months. He likes to use a very light spinning outfit and such lures as the Eelet or spoons or jigs. He lets the lure down to the bottom in water from 60 to 100 feet deep. Then he starts to reel it back toward the surface, at the same time raising and lowering his rod tip. Most of the strikes he gets come after the lure is about half-way up. He jigs in the spots which he knows contain lake trout and which he discovered years earlier while trolling for the fish. He finds that the same holes and spots produce year after year.

John Gleason does a lot of trolling for lake trout, using braided wire line in depths up to 60 feet and solid Monel wire line at greater depths. He attaches a small barrel swivel to the end of the wire and then ties on a short, 3- or 4-foot monofilament leader to the end and attaches a snap to hold the lure. He uses a salt-water-type reel to hold at least two hundred yards of line and a stiff trolling rod made of solid glass. For lures he uses mostly spoons and plugs.

John claims that it is very important when trolling for lake trout to feel bottom at all times, so he is always letting out line or taking it in. He also pumps the rod regularly up and down, since he feels that is the key to taking lake trout at these depths. To do this properly, you let out enough line so that the lure is almost on the bottom. Then you lower your rod so that the lure hits bottom. Now raise your rod so that the lure jumps off the bottom. Then lower again so that it flutters back toward the bottom. John claims that most of your strikes will come when you lift up the rod.

Jim Axtell, who is a conservation officer in New York State, fishes for lake trout in the Adirondacks State Forest. One of these lakes is the Seventh Lake of the Fulton Chain Lakes. In the spring of the year, when lake trout come into shallow water, Jim looks for swallows diving. This means that flies are hatching, an event that attracts the sawbellies, or alewives, and they in turn bring the lake trout to the spot. Jim casts a silver spoon with a hookless nymph fly attached in front of the spoon on a short leader. He casts the spoon in the spot where the swallows are swooping and lets it sink to the bottom; then he starts retrieving it by lifting his rod tip sharply and then lowering it, at the same time reeling in the slack line. He raises the rod again, then lowers it, and so on, making the spoon rise and flutter on the way in.

If you want big lake trout like this lunker, head for one of the far northern lakes such as Great Slave Lake, where this one was caught. There are many other lakes in Canada where big lake trout abound. (*Canadian Government Travel Bureau photo*)

This inshore fishing is best early in the morning; later in the day and during the summer months Jim trolls for the lakers with wire line. He lets out enough line so that the spoon digs into the bottom mud every so often. He also gives it the same up-and-down action as he does with his casting outfit.

Bob Mushrush, who owns the Evergreen Lodge on Clearwater Lake, in Manitoba, Canada, knows this lake like his back yard and can find the best spots for lake trout without using a depth-sounder. He knows all the ledges and drop-offs and holes, and fishes them successfully. One of his most effective methods for the lakers is to use a jig weighing about 2 ounces on a light spinning outfit. He sweetens the jig with a strip of fish, usually from a tullibee, or cisco. Then he sends it down to the bottom and jigs it a couple of times as he starts to reel it back toward the surface.

Wally Niemuth trolls for lake trout in Lake Superior soon after ice-out, when they are close to shore. He uses a medium-action spinning or bait-casting rod with 10- to 15-pound-test lines. He finds that lightweight, minnow-type plugs are best for this trolling, but will also try spoons and spinners. He trolls with two rods and tries various depths. Wally has the best action early in the morning and late in the afternoon and finds that cloudy days are more productive than bright days.

John T. Fowler also likes to fish for lake trout early in the spring when they are near shore in shallow water. Then he trolls with a fly rod using streamers. If he runs into a school of fish, he will often drift and cast into them. He also keeps a spinning or casting outfit handy while trolling, and if he sees a lake trout boiling to the surface he will cast a lure toward the fish.

John carries a map of the lake and an underwater thermometer with him when looking for lake trout. He searches for steep, rocky shorelines or points of land, or streams entering the lake. Then he starts sounding with the thermometer until he finds a temperature between 40 and 45 degrees, and starts fishing there.

He also fishes for lake trout with a laced or sewn minnow or smelt on the hook. This is sewn on the hook so that it has a bend and revolves in a wide, lazy arc when trolled. He trolls the baitfish on a wire line with a chain swivel on the end and a 25-foot nylon leader, which holds the baitfish. This is trolled so that it moves just above the bottom.

When Oren Bates wants to catch big lake trout, he heads for Great Bear Lake, in Canada's Northwest Territories. There lunker lake trout are eager to do battle even during July and August. In fact, Oren claims, these are the two best months for this fishing. The big lakers can be taken by either trolling or casting in fairly shallow water near rocky shores. Spoons are the most productive lures.

Although many kinds of outfits are used at Great Bear Lake, Oren Bates likes to use a light spinning rod to cast for the big brutes. He once caught a 40-pound lake trout on 8-pound-test line! And they have been caught in the 50- and 60-pound classes in this fabulous lake.

David O'Connor fishes for lake trout in the lakes of Maine, with big Moosehead Lake one of his favorites. He trolls for them with 40-pound-test lead-core line and a big spinner ahead of a smelt, minnow, or small fish sewn on a treble hook. He finds that slow trolling over the gravel bars, rocks, boulders, and submerged stumps in water from 60 to 100 feet is most productive.

Jack Sevigney, of Sanford, Maine, also fishes Moosehead Lake, but he does it through the ice. He looks for underwater ridges, and bores several holes through the ice in a line about 150 feet apart over varying depths. He finds that lake trout will cruise along a ridge and feed at various depths. When he catches a fish at a certain depth, he adjusts all the lines to the same level.

Jack uses live smelt for bait. When one of the flags on his tip-up pops up, indicating a bite, he takes his time going over to the hole. He knows that lake trout will usually toy with the bait for two minutes or more before really taking it. If he gets a bite, but the fish doesn't take it for good, he will often raise the smelt and then drop it back several times, trying to tease the fish into grabbing it again.

Jack insists on fresh, live bait on his line, and if a smelt is killed by a fish biting it or acts dead, he will quickly replace it with a lively one.

Fishing guide Bud Norton also fishes for lake trout through the ice, in Wisconsin's Green Lake. He has found that putting several small minnows on one hook makes a good bait for these fish. He lowers this bait to the bottom in 100 feet of water.

When Henry Zeman fishes for lake trout through the ice in Lake Michigan he does it by jigging. Grand Traverse Bay is one of his fa-

vorite spots for such fishing when the ice is thick. He uses a short rod
made from a wooden handle and the mid section of a fly rod. To this
handle he attaches a closed-faced spinning reel that holds 15-pound-
test monofilament line.

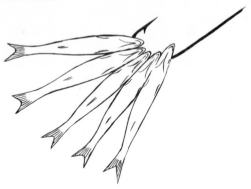

Several minnows on hook for lake trout

Zeman's favorite lure for this jigging is a 3-inch gold-and-silver
spoon. This lure is lowered into the deep water, at times up to 150
feet, and when it hits bottom he reels in a few turns and starts to
raise and lower it in a snappy jigging motion.

Another lake-trout ice fisherman is Earl Leitz, who fishes in
Whitefish Bay, on Lake Superior. He fishes from a shanty out on the
ice and uses a short ice rod and a rig consisting of two spoons. One
spoon is attached to the end of the line, and the second one is tied on
a dropper about 18 inches above the other spoon. He often adds
strips of smelt, which are folded on the hooks of the spoons.

Earl lowers the spoons through the hole in the ice until they reach
bottom; then he starts jigging up and down. He varies his jigging
speed and motion according to what the lake trout want on a given
day. Usually he jigs so that the motion isn't too fast or too slow. He
finds you have to be alert to feel a fish hit the spoon and bait, then
set the hooks fast, or the laker will be gone. Earl Leitz seems to an-
ticipate the strike and sets the hook at the right moment.

6

LARGEMOUTH BASS

The largemouth bass is sought by skilled and expert anglers in this country more than any other fresh-water species. And more fresh-water lures have been designed and created to catch the largemouth than for any other fish. In recent years more and more systems, techniques, and different ways of using the lures have been developed and perfected to catch largemouth bass.

One of the men who helped revolutionize bass fishing in recent years is Buck Perry, of Hickory, North Carolina. He has been called the father of "structure" fishing and has amazed many other anglers by his catches of bass in lakes that were labeled "dead" or "fished-out" because few fish were taken from them.

Perry created the lure called the Spoonplug—a metal lure bent and curved like a shoehorn, which he trolled to locate the best fishing spots in a lake. These Spoonplugs come in various sizes and weights from ⅛ ounce to 1 ounce for trolling in water from 2 to 20 feet in depth. They can also be cast out and reeled in at various depths.

Perry feels that depth and speed are more important in a lure than size or action. Color, he feels, can be a factor at times, so his lures do come in various colors. He recommends a light lure on bright, sunny days and clear water and dark lures on cloudy days and murky waters for deep fishing.

Perry trolls his Spoonplug fast with a stiff rod and a reel filled with a marked monofilament line with most of the stretch removed. Once he finds the depth he wants to fish, he chooses a Spoonplug that will travel at the correct level when trolled at a fast speed. The lure should bump bottom often for best results. He starts trolling in shallow water, then moves out into deeper water until he locates the structure that has fish. After he catches a fish or two from a spot, he anchors there and starts casting. Here, again, he lets the Spoonplug sink to the bottom and then retrieves it so that it digs into the bottom on the way in.

One thing Perry learned early in the game is that bass have regular migration routes, which they follow on their way to their feeding areas. They follow such routes every day, year after year. Most of these movements are along structure and once you locate such structure you can be pretty sure that the fish will pass that way or stop to rest or feed there sometime during the day.

Of course, there is a lot more to it than this, so Buck Perry has written a book called *Spoonplugging—Your Guide to Lunker Catches,* in which he deals with catching more and bigger bass in all kinds of waters. It is available by mail from the Northwoods Publishing Co., Inc., P. O. Box 4169, Milwaukee, Wisconsin 53210. It comes in hard-cover and paperback, and you can write them for the prices.

Bob Underwood fishes for bass in Florida, and he trolls a plastic worm with a curve in it, because he feels the spinning action that results brings more strikes and gets him more bass. He rigs a soft 6-inch plastic worm that has a flat side with a No. 1 Eagle Claw hook. He threads the worm on the hook well past the eye and on the leader and brings the hook out of the side of the worm up to the bend of the hook. This gives the worm a curve at the head, which gives it the spinning action. Then he adds a small barrel swivel about a foot above the worm to help prevent twisting of the line. To get the

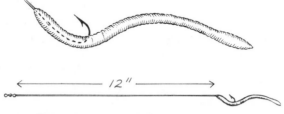

Plastic worm with curve for trolling

worm down to the right depth, he adds anywhere from one to three split-shot sinkers to the leader between the worm and the swivel.

Bob trolls the worm slowly about 50 feet out and close to the bottom. Then he takes in some line and slips it under a hairpin that he has taped on the cork grip of the rod just above the reel. The reel is left in free spool with the bail off, and the line is slipped under the hairpin, where it is held until a fish hits and pulls it free. Then Bob puts his boat into neutral, grabs the rod, takes in the slack line, and sets the hook hard.

Roger Arnett also fishes a plastic worm in Minnesota lakes, but he likes to cast his worm along a shoreline and finds this is highly effective when the water is murky. He casts as close to shore as possible, lets the worm sink about a foot, then lifts the rod so that the worm moves a short distance. Next he lowers the rod and reels in the slack. After lifting the rod again, he repeats the same process for a few more feet. Then he reels in fast all the way and makes a new cast. He likes purple and black worms and adds a No. 3 split-shot sinker just above the eye of the hook.

An even more novel way of using a plastic worm is practiced by Reggie Hathorn. He uses a stiff 8- to 9-foot bass-action fly rod, fills the reel with 20- or 25-pound-test nylon, and attaches a floating plastic worm to the end. This worm has most of the hook buried to make it weedless, and he adds a light slip sinker on the line. Then he looks for spots with heavy cover, such as lily pads, sunken trees, brush, and logs, and eases up to these quietly in his boat. He lowers the worm into an opening and lets it sink to the bottom. This is done with his hand by letting out or taking in line. He can then feel the worm as it sinks or rises and also feel a fish grabbing it. Reg doesn't wait too long after a bass grabs the worm. Maybe a second or two, then he sets the hook hard.

A. D. Livingston fishes for big bass in Florida, and he favors live baits such as shiners. He uses the shiner on a big, 4/0 or 5/0 hook and runs it through the back of the bait. He uses the shiner with a green sliding float, which slips down for the cast but moves up the line after it hits the water. He ties a knot in his line and adds a bead below it to create a stop for the float. Then he casts his shiner out to the spot he wants to fish and makes it land with a big splash. He feels this attracts bass to the scene. When a bass takes the float down, he lets the fish swim off with the shiner for a few seconds; then he sets the hook.

Art Reid heard that experiments at Southern Illinois University revealed that bass need and take food about every forty-eight hours and that they do most of their feeding in the morning hours from just before daybreak to noon. So he experimented by fishing Lake Jack-

son, in Florida, and other nearby lakes, and after fishing for an entire month he found that more than 75 per cent of all the bass he
caught were taken during the morning hours. So now he starts fishing
at daybreak and doesn't quit until noon.

Jack Lovett wasn't satisfied with the regular plastic worms he used.
So he started to experiment by cutting them into sections and creating his own worms with novel shapes. He found that he could take
sections of the worm he cut, hold the two ends over a flame, then
when they start to melt, press them together until they fuse and
harden. Now he makes worms with two or three different colors, or
he adds legs or tails to the body. One of his most successful worms
was created by cutting a worm into three or four sections and then
fusing them together to make a zigzag worm.

Zigzag plastic worm

Homer Circle, who designed and manufactured fishing tackle and
lures for many years, is now fresh-water fishing editor of *Sports
Afield* magazine. He is also a highly skilled black-bass fisherman and
has wet his line in some of the best bass waters in this country.
Homer's advice on catching this popular fish is followed by thousands of anglers who read his column and articles.

Like most bass anglers, Homer enjoys catching bass on top if they
are co-operative. He uses poppers, swimmers, crippled minnows,
noisemakers, and the slim, torpedo-type plugs. Homer is a strong
believer in using sound to attract bass. He feels the noise gets the attention of the fish and lures them to see what is causing the commotion.

When using poppers he will often cast out the lure and when it hits
the water, jerk it hard to make a loud pop. Then he'll wait a few seconds, after which he will retrieve it slowly in the beginning and then
increase the speed during the final retrieve.

When using crippled minnows with spinners or propellers, Homer
will cast them out and then wait until things quiet down. After

Homer Circle is shown here with a hefty string of big bass. Fresh-water fishing editor of *Sports Afield* magazine, Homer fishes in many parts of the country for bass. (*Homer Circle photo*)

which, he reels the plug in with a series of long and short swishes. Or he may make a series of swishes and then let the plug rest in one spot for ten seconds.

When he uses the quiet, torpedo type of plug he casts out, reels in the slack line and then barely moves the rod tip so that the plug just nods in one spot. After fishing this way for a while, he may work the plug back in a zigzag fashion by reeling and with rod action so that the lure swings crazily from side to side on top of the water.

When using surface lures after dark, Homer Circle recommends casting at least twice in each spot. He claims that the first cast may attract the fish but he gets to the spot too late to see your lure. So, on the next cast, he'll be right there waiting and more apt to see and hit it.

When he's using plastic worms, Homer holds the rod tip high; then, when he feels a bass mouth his worm, he quickly lowers the rod and leans forward so that the fish doesn't feel any pull on the line. Then he leans back and sets the hook hard.

Charles Waterman, of Deland, Florida, catches many bass in the lakes around his home, and he fishes for the big ones in January, February, March, and April, because that is when the big "hawgs" are most likely to be on spawning beds or in shallow water and cover. He makes it a point to fish the "heavy stuff," as he calls it. His favorite surface lure for this is a weedless rubber-skirted wiggler. He uses this with a bait-casting outfit and 12- or 15-pound-test line. He casts right into the lily pads, hyacinths, sawgrass, and weeds, where the bass like to lie, hide, and feed. Then he works the lure back on top fairly fast. But when it gets to an opening or clear spot, he lets it sink for a short time, then reels in to the next patch of vegetation.

Leonard M. Wright, Jr., catches big bass using 4- to 5-inch sunfish. He uses a heavy fly rod, floating level line, and 10- or 12-pound-test monofilament leader. He hooks the sunfish with a small, No. 6 treble hook through the back, and strips about 50 feet of line off the reel, coiling it on the bottom of the boat. Then he slip-casts the sunfish toward shore and lets it swim around. When the bait reaches shore, he retrieves it slowly, making it flash and act in a crippled manner. When the sunfish acts nervous or spurts, he feeds slack line and lets the bass grab it and swim away with it to swallow it. Then he sets the hook hard two or three times.

Larry Green likes to catch both largemouth and smallmouth bass with a fly rod and bass bugs. One of the deadliest bugs he uses is called a Fluff Bug, which was created by his friend Irwin M. Thompson, of Sebastopol, California. These Fluff Bugs are tied with deer hair with a bulky body up front and a slimmer tail. Larry ties various color combinations such as a red body with white tail or a white body with red tail or a yellow body with black tail or a blue body with red tail.

This bug does not make a loud pop or noise or commotion on top but skims quietly along the surface. Larry casts it close to shore or some cover, then retrieves it with a slow, steady pull varied with fast, snappy jerks. For this surface fishing he uses a floating line and coats his bug with a floating solution or spray. But this bug can also be used below the surface, and then he uses a sinking line and adds no coating to the bug.

Fluff Bug used by Larry Green

Dick Kotis is president of the Fred Arbogast Company, which makes some of the top lures for bass. He is also a skilled bass fisherman who knows how to use his lures. When the bass are on top or in shallow water, he uses such plugs as the Jitterbug and the Hula Popper. When using the popper, he casts it out so that it lands softly and quietly. He lets the lure rest until the ripples disappear. Then he twitches it a bit to give it a slight movement. He repeats these light twitches two or three times. Then he makes louder and quicker pops, which attract fish from greater distances. He retrieves surface lures more slowly on calm water and at night than when the water is rippled or choppy.

When using his underwater lures, such as the Hawaiian Wiggler, Dick likes to cast into shady spots or right over logs, sunken trees, brush, and weed beds. Then he eases his lure over or around these obstructions. When fishing southern waters in the late winter or early spring, he uses deep-running lures in 10- to 25-foot depths.

Jim Dean starts off the bass season as early as January or February in North Carolina, where he lives and fishes. And surprisingly he finds most of the bass in shallow water near shore around submerged brush, trees, weeds, logs, stumps, and treetops. Even more surprising is that he uses a floating-diving plug or spinner and reels it in at fairly high speed. Jim feels that the bass find warmer water near shore and also some minnows and small fish to feed on. Anyway, by choosing the warmer, sunny days, he is reasonably comfortable and has good early fishing for bass.

Another bass angler who starts early is Ron De Nardo, who catches big bass in March, when most anglers are still dreaming about fishing. He fishes in Indiana, where the weather and water are much colder than in our southern states, where most winter fishing is done for bass.

Ron waits until the ice breaks up on the lakes he plans to fish and then goes to work. He looks for weed beds in water from 6 to 10 feet deep and finds that bass often gather in such spots and he can catch several fish without moving the boat. He uses a black jig and adds either black pork rind, a black plastic worm or a mud-puppy imitation to the hook.

Ron finds that to be effective the lure should move along the bottom. He makes sure of this by casting the jig out and letting it sink until he sees the line go slack. Then he reels in three or four turns of the handle and lets the lure settle again. When the line goes slack, he reels in again three or four turns and lets the lure settle once more. He keeps doing this until the lure is finally retrieved.

Robert E. Price is convinced that bass go on a feeding spree when a storm approaches and during the period when it first hits. So when he hears that a storm front is coming he heads for his favorite bass lake. He can't explain why this happens and why bass start feeding and hitting then, but records kept through the years prove that the fishing is excellent during such approaching storm fronts.

Call him a master bass fisherman or a pro, but Roland Martin has been winning many of the major bass tournaments in recent years and winning the big money. When you realize that he is competing with some of the best bass anglers in the country, you can't help but respect his fishing know-how.

Martin believes that bass will be found at various depths depending on water temperature and how much light there is. He tends to fish in shallow water when it is muddy and in deeper water when it is clear. He'll also fish the shallow water in the spring if the fish are there and the deeper water during the summer months, when the water is warm.

Martin looks for bass in various places according to the type of lake he is fishing. In shallow lakes he has his best fishing close to creek channels. In deep lakes he concentrates on the points and drop-offs. He tries to fish as many spots as he can in a day and doesn't waste much time in any one spot if he gets no hits. After a half dozen casts he's off to a new spot. In shallow water he may make only one or two casts, then move on.

Martin fishes with many lures and has the know-how to use most of them, but his favorite is the plastic worm, which accounts for around half of his fish. He often fishes in heavy cover and brush, so he uses 14-pound-test line and prefers the Stren Fluorescent because he likes to watch his line closely for indications of a strike.

On cloudy or rainy days he may use surface plugs or spinner baits. In recent years he has been using the plastic grub with good results. He may cast out a grub and let it sink. Or he may hold the boat over the spot he wants to fish and let the grub straight down to the bottom. He gets many hits while it is sinking. In deep water, from 20 to 45 feet over brush piles, he likes a hammered metal spoon for vertical jigging. He uses this with a stiff rod and 25- or 30-pound-test line. There the bass like to lie among the branches and he works the spoon right in the stuff.

Many bass fishermen will tell you that fishing in shallow water near shore during the middle of the day in hot weather is a waste of time or slim pickings. But not John O. Cartier, who often makes some good catches under such conditions. His only secret, if you can call it that, is to look for spots that have shade and plenty of cover. He looks for bass around stumps, logs, sunken trees, boat docks, and piers, and finds that such choice locations will produce again and again. Once you catch a bass from one of these spots, you can return in the future and get more. New bass are always moving into spots vacated by the former residents.

James Brang likes to fish farm ponds and makes good catches from shore early in the morning and in the late afternoon and evening. He walks slowly around the pond always facing the sun so that no shadow is cast in front of him on the water. Then he casts so that his lure travels parallel to the shoreline and close to it. He finds small surface plugs that resemble frogs or minnows best for this fishing. But when the weather warms he fishes the deepest parts of the pond with deep-running or sinking lures.

Lloyd Eiserman fishes the lakes of California for bass, and he uses a fly rod—a few rods in fact, since he takes along several, each one rigged with a different bass bug so he doesn't have to waste time tying on new bugs. And unlike most bass fishermen he doesn't let his bug rest at any time. Instead he casts out and retrieves it fast with short, popping jerks. He feels that this way a bass doesn't get a chance to examine the bug closely and has to make up his mind fast. He finds this fast retrieve especially effective when the water is clear.

Carl Malz is managing editor of *Fishing Facts* magazine and also a skilled bass fisherman. Like most modern anglers, he looks for and fishes over "structure" and "breaks" in a lake or reservoir. But once he finds a good spot and starts fishing, he also concentrates on "feeling the bottom" for variations in depth and hardness, and logs, stumps, brush, weeds, and other objects.

Carl feels that the type of lure you use and its weight and shape are important in establishing this feel with the bottom. In other words, too heavy a lure isn't good and too light a lure won't work too well either. He also tries to feel for clean spots and paths, especially next to or right in a large section of structure. Such clean spots often produce good fishing, because bass are either present there or will move through there sometime during the day.

Paul Kalman fishes for brackish-water bass in Louisiana and Mississippi. He finds that some of the best fishing takes place on the outgoing tide, when the water pours out of the marshes into tidal streams or creeks. He anchors a boat in a cut through which the tide is pouring and often finds fast and continuous action. He casts toward the shoreline and finds that brackish-water bass usually hit a faster-moving lure than those found in strictly fresh water.

Warren Shepard enjoys fishing for bass with light fly rods and what he calls "mini-bugs." These are smaller versions of the standard bass bugs. He ties his own on No. 6 and 8 hooks and small pan-fish corks. He adds long, splay hackles, which make the bug about 3 inches in total length. Warren finds that such small bugs frighten fewer bass, and he makes good catches with them even on hard-fished ponds and lakes. And surprisingly he finds he catches bigger bass on these tiny bugs than on the larger-sized ones.

Tom Mann, of Eufaula, Alabama, manufactures fishing lures but still manages to fish thirty hours a week and has achieved a reputation as a top bass fisherman. He believes that lures should not only look attractive but should also give off sound vibrations, so he designed a tail-spinner lure called the Little George as well as a plastic grub-tail lure. These two lures are the ones he uses most of the time.

The grub-tail is useful when the water is very clear; Mann casts it over sunken islands or high spots or over moss beds. He also finds the white grub good for schooling bass. He'll cast it into the fish, let it sink a couple of seconds, then start it back in a fast swimming and jigging motion.

Mann finds his tail-spinner lure very versatile and uses it in shallow water and in water as deep as 35 feet. Or he may jig it vertically up and down during the summer months when the bass are deep. But, most of the time, he casts the lure out and lets it sink to the bottom, taking in the slack, then he points his rod tip toward the lure and lifts the rod up. This makes the lure "rip" off the bottom; then he lets it drop back again to the bottom on a tight line.

Despite all the new lures on the market, Kenneth Hassler still relies on the good, old-time pork-chunk and pork-rind lures for most of his bass fishing. He catches fish out of hard-fished lakes in Pennsylvania, where other anglers usually draw blanks or few fish.

One of his favorite lures is a bait-casting-size pork frog on a weedless hook. He uses this on a bait-casting rod and casts it into weeds, dead tree limbs, logs, snags, and other hard-to-fish spots. He will cast right into this heavy cover and works his pork frog slowly in among the pockets and openings. He finds that most of the other anglers avoid such spots, so he usually has them all to himself.

Ken may also add a few red beads ahead of the pork-chunk frog, and then in front of this he adds a spinner. This sputters along on top and draws bass from a distance.

Bob Gallagher catches a lot of bass in ponds and lakes by fishing from shore. But he doesn't wade in the water or rush up to the edge of the pond or lake. Instead he stands well back from the shoreline and casts his lure. He may even sit in a chair or crouch on the ground to avoid being seen. He uses mostly underwater lures, because he feels loud poppers or surface lures tend to frighten the fish in the daytime. At night he does use the surface poppers and finds that bass are less wary then.

Bill Dance is a top bass-fishing pro who wins a lot of tournaments and the big money. His approach is highly scientific; he uses a fathometer to indicate the depth and type of bottom, an electric thermometer to give him the water temperature at various depths, and a topographic or hydrographic map of the bottom and the contours of a lake or reservoir. He also uses a barometer, and studies lunar and solar influences on the fishing.

Bill knows that largemouth bass feed and are most active at a temperature that ranges between 68 and 72 degrees, so he fishes the depths where these temperatures are found. He looks especially for spots where this temperature range is present along the bottom. He fishes deep water most of the time, but may fish for bass in shallow water in the spring, when they are spawning.

Dance likes a 5½-foot medium- to heavy-action bait-casting rod and bait-casting reel filled with 12- to 14-pound-test line. He may occasionally go to 17- to 20-pound-test line when fishing heavy cover. Although he uses jigs and eels, spoons, and surface and underwater plugs, most of his fish are caught on a plastic worm. He rigs this worm with a sliding sinker and a single No. 4/0 hook. He runs the point of the hook into the head of the worm and out the side and then buries the point and barb in the body to make it weedless. He prefers blue, purple, or black worms of the floating type that clear the bottom and weeds and can be seen more easily by the fish.

Dance casts out the worm and lets it sink to the bottom, then he raises the worm with his rod and lets it settle back again to the bottom, at the same time dropping his rod tip and taking up the slack line. He keeps repeating this all the way in. When a bass takes the worm, he waits a second or two to make sure the fish has it and is moving off, and then sets the hook.

Claude Cantwell consistently catches big bass even during the winter months in the southern impoundments in Kentucky and Arkansas. He uses a Sonar lure with a silver finish, which gives off sound waves during a fast retrieve. He anchors in shallow water, casts into depths from 30 to 40 feet and lets the lure sink to the bottom, after which he reels it in as fast as possible for three or four turns, then lets it sink to the bottom again and repeats.

Leon (Buddy) Kelly fishes Orange Lake, in central Florida, and has caught many bass over 10 pounds in that lake. He often releases bass under 5 pounds unless he wants to keep a few for eating. He uses a bait-casting outfit with a reel filled with 20- or 25-pound-test line. He likes surface plugs, underwater balsa and plastic minnows, plastic worms, and weedless spoons with pork rind. He likes these in the larger sizes for big bass. But his real secret is to fish between the hours of 10 P.M. and 2 A.M. in the dark.

Stan Fagerstrom, who wrote the book *Catch More Bass,* does most of his bass fishing in the lakes of the Pacific Northwest. He believes in carrying three or four rods already rigged and each equipped with a different lure. When fishing in heavy lily pads and using weedless pork chunk or spoon and pork strip, he often raises bass but they miss the lure. When this happens he quickly grabs one of the rods rigged with a surface lure and casts into the opening or pocket left in the pads by the fish. Accuracy is required to place the lure in the small opening. Then he lets the lure rest awhile and twitches it gently. This often results in an explosive strike.

Bill Phillips, of Alabama, swears by plastic strips added to such lures as spoons, spinners, and plugs. He uses plastic garbage bags and similar plastic bags, which come in white, yellow, black, red, blue, or green. He cuts most of these strips 4 to 8 inches long depending on the size of the lure. But he also adds strips as long as 10 to 12 inches, because he feels they imitate small snakes, on which big bass feed.

Bill Plummer catches big bass in New England waters, where big fish and big catches are not too common. One of the reasons he does so is because he looks for tough spots such as fallen trees, brush, overhanging trees, logs, water lilies, duckweed, and eelgrass, which other anglers avoid. He uses a bait-casting outfit with a 15-pound-test line and casts right into these hazards. Bill believes in short casts and brings his boat as close to the spot being fished as possible. He uses a long, 7-foot rod to keep most of the line off the water and to give him better control over the lure in the heavy cover. He uses mostly the sponge-rubber frog, pork chunk and spinner, jig with pork strip, and a black eel or plastic worm, all with weedless hooks.

Bob Whaley claims that 90 per cent of a lake is barren of fish. The secret in bass fishing is to locate the 10 per cent that produces, and fish that only. So he looks for old riverbeds, creek channels, edges and drop-offs, stumps, sunken trees, brush, and other cover. He also

Stan Fagerstrom does most of his fishing in the Pacific Northwest and catches lunkers like this largemouth bass. (*Stan Fagerstrom photo*)

Grits Gresham, outdoors writer and bass fisherman, is shown with a nice string of bass. Like most bass-fishing pros and regulars, he uses a modern bass boat, depth-sounder or fish-finder, and other aids, when fishing for bass. (*Ray Jefferson photo*)

finds that the shallow areas and shorelines adjacent to deep water or drop-offs are also good spots to fish. Bass like the security the deep water offers and do not venture too far from it to feed.

Grits Gresham, who wrote *The Complete Book of Bass Fishing*, fishes the backwater areas of Louisiana, where he lives. These waters are usually created by the overflowing rivers that flood the low-lying fields and woodlands. When these waters begin to recede, in the late spring, he finds the fishing fast and furious. Grits likes to use top-water plugs for fishing these backwaters. He casts these around stumps and cypress-tree trunks and lets the plug lie for quite a while before starting to activate or retrieve it.

Brick Owens is shown with two of the many "hawg" bass he has caught in Florida waters. Brick likes to wade in the water for his big fish among and along the edges of lily pads. (*Garcia Corporation photo*)

One angler who has caught real "hawgs" in Florida waters is Brick Owens, of St. Cloud. He has caught 12-pound, 13-pound, and 16-pound bass. And he estimates he has caught over five thousand bass in thirty years of fishing! Brick likes to fish the lakes by wading in water often above his waist and even swimming out into deeper water to fight a big bass.

He doesn't believe in fishing a spot too long but casts into a spot about three times, then moves on to the next one. He feels that the first two casts catch a bass's attention and annoy him. Then, the third cast makes him angry enough to hit the lure. Or else Brick casts once or twice in a spot, then leaves and comes back later to try there again.

He uses surface plugs such as plunkers and poppers or torpedo types and works these in among the lily pads and hyacinths. Or he tries deep-running plugs with big lips in deeper water. Brick does most of his fishing near shore in shallow water from daybreak until about two hours later. Then he may return a couple of hours before dark and fish again.

One of the most exciting ways to catch bass is by "jump" fishing on the big impoundments in our southern states. Frank Phipps does this fishing on Cumberland Lake, Kentucky Lake, and Dale Hollow. The bass come to the surface to chase and feed on young gizzard shad, and the fishing is often fast. He finds June is a top month for this, and it may last into the summer months. Early morning and evening are the best time to find the bass feeding on top. They usually show when the water is calm and clear.

Frank finds that long casts are required to reach the fish and obtain strikes. And he finds that surface plugs produce best, especially the type that have spinners in the front and rear. He casts the plug toward the disturbance and then lets it rest a second or two before he twitches the lure. Most of the bass caught in this jump fishing will be on the small side, but the action is often out of this world.

Bruce Brady fishes in Louisiana and Mississippi, and he prefers night fishing for bass over daytime fishing. He finds it much better and has caught as many as twenty-three bass in one night. Despite the prevalent belief that dark nights are better than moonlit nights, he has found that the bright nights with a moon are best. Especially just before the full moon. One reason for this is that on such nights he can cast closer to cover, where most of the bass hang out.

Bruce uses a bait-casting rod for his fishing and mostly underwater lures. He likes spinners with plastic skirts or strips of pork rind, and he prefers black lures. He fishes the deeper water, from 5 to 12 feet, early in the year and shallower water near shore later on, during the warmer months. He works the lures as slowly as possible. Brady has found that the bass lie in the shady parts of the lake, rather than in the moonlit sections. So he casts to the shadowed side of trees, logs, or other cover.

Milton "Red" Packer fishes Lake Beulah, in Mississippi, and consistently catches big bass. He likes a black spinner with skirts or floating deep-diving plugs, which he works very slowly from the cast to the final retrieve. He doesn't even speed up when his lure is crawling over a log or tree branch or other obstruction. After the lure clears the obstruction, he stops reeling for a second or two. That is when a bass usually hits.

Sam Welch does what most bass fishermen dream of doing: fishes day after day for big bass in his favorite waters, such as Lake Norfolk and Bull Shoals Lake, in Arkansas and Missouri. He has fished bass for more than forty years and has caught thousands. In one seven-year period he caught 360 bass weighing 4 pounds or more. Two of these were 10 pounds apiece.

Sam also kept score for many other resort owners, float-trip operators, and fishing camps on Bull Shoals Lake. He kept a record of most of the big bass caught in these waters. For a long time, he fished in shallow water near shore, but later shifted operations to deeper water, studying temperatures, depths, and bottom structure; he then began catching the big ones.

For day-in-and-day-out fishing, Sam Welch prefers a jig or lead head with pork eel or plastic worm. He likes these eels or worms in white, yellow, red, and black and about 6 inches long. When he's after a really big bass, he may go to a 9-inch eel or worm. He lets the jig and eel or worm sink all the way to the bottom and then reels it in very slowly. He doesn't give it any rod action but just winds in very slowly. And he keeps it on the bottom all the way in. He concentrates his fishing on the points, bars, ridges, bluffs, rocky ledges, submerged islands, and weed beds. He works the area methodically, at fishing depths from 15 to 60 feet.

Charlie Richie is a professional fishing guide in Livingston, Texas, who favors light spinning tackle for his fishing. He uses the lighter, smaller lures on 8-pound-test line. And he doesn't believe in giving his lures too much action, rather he works them slow and easy, with no violent jerks, twitches, or jumps. To locate bass in a lake, Richie looks for steep-sided or quick-breaking creek beds. He especially looks for the sharp bends in such creeks, because they tend to hold large concentrations of bass.

Charlie Richie feels that it is very important to position a boat in exactly the right spot so you can present your lure naturally and from the right direction. He feels that since bass will lie facing in a certain direction and intercept any baitfish coming their way, that is the same path your lure should follow. Thus, when fishing a point, he

Many expert bass anglers like to use an electric motor for approaching fish quietly and maneuvering the boat in close quarters. It can also be used for slow trolling. (*Tempo Products Co. photo*)

holds the boat in a spot where he can reel in the lure from deep water to shallow water.

Anthony A. Ciuffa fishes the small ponds and lakes near his home, in St. Louis, Missouri, and catches over one hundred big bass a year from them. He finds the quiet approach important, because bass are wary in these confined, shallow waters. He also fishes mostly early in the morning, in the evening or at night. Most of these fish are caught on spinner lures with lead heads. He likes white and yellow in the spring, and red, blue, and black in the summer. He lets the lure sink to the bottom and then retrieves it very slowly.

Jack Wingate fishes Lake Seminole, on the Florida-Georgia border, for bass, and claims that the biggest ones are caught during the winter months. He likes the Spring Creek area of the lake, where

there are many deep channels, stumps and brush. He uses a surface plug or plastic worm and casts it right next to the stump or
brush and works it very slowly. He finds that most of his strikes
occur near the stump. As soon as his lure is two to three feet from it,
he reels in fast and casts to another stump.

Rufus Eubank is a guide, and he feels that the spinner-bait is one
of the best lures you can use for bass. He fishes it at various depths
from top to bottom and during all seasons of the year. His preferred
spinner-baits are solid white, yellow, blue, or black and he uses
mostly the ¼- and ½-ounce sizes with No. 4 or 5 blades.

When working the spinner-bait along the surface, he casts into a
bass hideout and starts reeling it back as soon as it hits the water,
raising the rod high. As the spinner gets closer, he lowers his rod. He
also fishes the lure during the cold-weather months, because he feels
the spinner blade vibrations attract bass and make them hit. He will
at that time fish the lure along the bottom, slowly lifting it off the
bottom every so often to make the blade revolve.

Charley Mooney fishes the lakes of central Florida, which contain
big bass, and he catches them consistently. His biggest was a
16-pound lunker, and he has caught two others, each going 15
pounds! Many other bass went between 8 and 14 pounds. Charley
catches all his big bass on live shiners up to 10 inches in length. He
usually catches these baitfish by chumming an area with oats and then
using small doughballs on a No. 14 or 16 hook.

Charley believes in using heavy tackle for these bass, and his reel
is filled with 30-pound-test line. He's after a world-record bass, and
he doesn't want to lose him when he hooks him.

Charley fishes the live shiners on a big, 3/0 or 4/0 hook under a
fluorescent float or bobber. He hooks the shiner through the lips and
casts it out in spots where he knows big bass like to lie. When a big
"hawg" grabs his shiner, he lets it run for only a couple of seconds or
so, then sets the hook hard.

7

SMALLMOUTH BASS

There are many more outstanding largemouth-bass fishermen than smallmouth-bass anglers. For one thing, the smallmouth bass has a more limited range and is confined to the cleaner, colder waters of our northern states, a few southeastern states, and Canada. So, fewer fresh-water anglers get the opportunity to fish for them. But those anglers who live in areas where the smallmouth bass are plentiful, or those who can travel to such areas, find that the scrappy smallmouth offers even more of a challenge than the largemouth bass.

One angler who has acquired a reputation for catching smallmouth bass in the bigger sizes is Billy Westmoreland of Celina, Tennessee. He does a lot of his fishing in Dale Hollow Lake, on the border of Tennessee and Kentucky. His biggest smallmouth is a 10-pound 2-ounce fish, but he has taken many others, running from 3 to 9 pounds.

Billy catches these big bass on light spinning tackle with 4- to 8-pound-test line on his reel. His favorite lure is the Hoss Fly, which is a lead-head jig with hair. He usually adds pork rind or a plastic worm or lizard to the hook of the lure. He also uses a plastic grub and a tail-spin lure. He likes these in the smaller sizes and weights from ⅛ to ¼ ounce.

Billy fishes water from 15 to 40 feet deep for the smallmouths, depending on the time of year. He looks for the bass off deep points, rocky shores or shelves, and flats or bars leading to deep water or drop-offs. He also fishes over underwater reefs, sunken islands and ridges. Most of the bass are found over a clean bottom near such spots.

Westmoreland is very careful when approaching a fishing spot, and he eases up to it with his electric motor. He prefers to move inshore into shallow water and make long casts toward deeper water. After casting he keeps a taut line and watches it carefully. If it stops or hesitates or he feels a light tap, he sets the hook. Many of his bass are hooked while the lure is sinking. If the lure reaches bottom without being hit, he lifts his rod a short distance, then holds it still while the lure settles on the bottom again. Then he will lift the rod again, hold it still, let the lure bump bottom again, and keep repeating this during the entire retrieve.

Dave Marston finds live crayfish deadly for smallmouth bass in the Juniata River, in Pennsylvania, where he fishes. He catches his crayfish by turning over rocks carefully without making too much silt. Then he places one hand behind the crayfish and the other in front of the bait, which then backs up into the hand behind it. Dave hooks the crayfish through the back with a No. 4 or 6 hook and casts it into deep pools and lets it sink toward the bottom. But once it reaches the bottom, he doesn't let it stay there too long. He lifts it off the bottom to prevent the crayfish from hiding under a stone or in the weeds.

Michele Caraher also uses live crayfish for smallmouth bass in the lakes and reservoirs near Baltimore, Maryland, where she lives and fishes. She likes soft-shelled crayfish and uses big ones for big bass. To keep the crayfish on a hook, she wraps some plastic tie or pipe cleaner around the bait's mid section and inserts the hook under it. Michele fishes the crayfish from a drifting boat, adding and removing split-shot sinkers on the leader above the hook so that the bait moves along the bottom. She leaves the bail on her spinning reel open, and when a bass picks up the crayfish she lets it take plenty of line to swallow it. She has had her best success with crayfish when fishing in the late afternoon and evening right up until dark.

Ken Smith claims that there are a lot more smallmouth bass present in many rivers and lakes than most anglers believe. You just have to locate the spots where they hang out. He looks for them along rocky shores, piles of rock and coarse gravel, and close to bridge dikes or pilings, wing dams, and ledges. And because smallmouth bass do a lot of their living and feeding in clean, clear rivers he approaches each spot with extreme care so as not to frighten the fish.

Ken likes to use a fly rod for the fish and casts wet flies early in the season and streamers later on. During the summer months he finds surface poppers very effective. He believes the time of day is not too important in smallmouth-bass fishing and has caught as many in the middle of the day as in the early morning or evening.

Byron Dalrymple wrote *Modern Book of the Black Bass* and has spent a lifetime fishing for and writing about both the largemouth and the smallmouth bass. When he fishes a lake or a river, he looks for rocks, as that is where the smallmouth bass usually are. Crayfish, hellgrammites, and minnows are most abundant there, and the bass move into such spots to feed on them. He also looks for big boulders and casts his lure or bait so that it drops off the boulder and sinks along its edge. In lakes that have no rocks, he looks for the slender reeds where the minnows and small fish, on which bass feed, take shelter.

Dalrymple finds underwater lures most effective, because smallmouth bass tend to do most of their feeding below the surface. So he uses underwater plugs, spoons, spinners, jigs, streamers, and bucktails for most of his fishing. When artificial lures fail, he turns to natural bait such as a big night crawler. But he has a special way of hooking the worm. He uses a thin wire hook and threads the worm all the way up on the shank of the hook and leader so that the point emerges near its tail. He also ties a small hook near the worm's head to keep the bait from slipping down. This way, he doesn't miss as many bass as with one hook.

Night crawler hooked for smallmouth bass

Walter Tingle makes sure that sometime during the last week in May or early June he's out fishing on one of the New Hampshire lakes for smallmouth bass. That's when the bronzebacks go on a feeding frenzy and gorge on the hatching May flies. The action is so fast at times that on some days he may catch and release over one hundred bass! Catches of thirty, forty, or fifty bass are common on so-called "poor" days.

Like most bass fishermen, Tingle believes in the quiet approach and uses an electric motor when actually fishing. He finds the bass at this time of year in water from 2 to 12 feet deep near shore over stony bottoms, where they are on their spawning beds. He uses surface and underwater plugs, spoons, bass bugs, and dry flies. He likes lures with a lot of yellow in them.

When using surface plugs or bugs, he believes in the light touch and soft approach. No loud pops or fast reeling. Instead he lets the lure lie still and then just twitches it to make it quiver. He says that if the bass doesn't hit the lure in the first few seconds of this twitching he probably won't hit it at all. So he lifts the lure off the water or reels in quickly and casts to another spot.

Billy Burns, of Lexington, Kentucky, catches bass in record sizes. Some of his strings of fish have smallmouths running from 5 to 8 pounds! Naturally, it takes plenty of skill and know-how to catch such big smallmouth bass fairly consistently, and Billy has both. One of the reasons why he catches such lunkers is because he concentrates only on the big bass and fishes the spots where they are found.

Billy looks for points that slope gradually under the water and then drop off sharply into a ravine, which is where he does his fishing. Such spots are even better if there are sunken trees or bushes in the ravine. Billy has been known to sink and anchor such trees and bushes in the ravines when the water is low.

Burns favors stiff-action rods and star-drag casting reels. He works his underwater plugs fast right through the brush and trees, and even makes them bump bottom. Naturally he hangs up often, but one of his tricks is to use two rods. If one plug gets hung up, he lets it stay there a while. Then he fishes with the second outfit. If that gets hung up too, he rows over and tries to free his lures. This way he doesn't disturb the spot as much and frightens fewer fish.

Jerry Robinson fishes for smallmouth bass in Vermont and New Hampshire, where he has most of the rivers all to himself except for a few summer visitors and kids. He finds the natives of these New England states prefer to fish for trout and landlocked salmon. But Jerry feels they are missing out on some fine sport and fun. He claims that the smallmouth bass run bigger than most of the trout caught in the same waters and they put up a better fight.

Jerry fishes for smallmouth bass just as he would for trout. He sneaks up on the fish and walks softly on the bank or wades quietly in the river without letting his shadow fall on the water he is fishing.

He casts accurately and avoids making too big a splash. Since, according to Jerry, smallmouth bass do not like too much noise or commotion, he uses lures that are light and do not create too big a splash or make too much of a commotion in the water.

He finds that the best time to fish for smallmouth bass in ponds and lakes is in late May to early June, while late June to early July is best when fishing streams and rivers. When the water warms up and its level drops, in July and August, Jerry resorts to hellgrammites and fishes these in the deep channels and holes.

Bob Nauheim fishes California's Russian River from April to October and usually gets his limit of smallmouth bass. He floats the river in a boat and fishes from it or gets out to wade and cast. He prefers a light 7½-foot fly rod and uses streamers such as the Black Ghost, Gray Ghost, and King's Winter King, the latter being tied locally. He gets best results by working the flies just below the surface. Bob looks for smallmouth bass in fast water, and he finds they usually lie close to shore under the banks, brush, and sunken logs. He also casts into eddies, where the slow and fast waters meet.

Woodie Wheaton owns and runs a fishing camp at Forest City, Maine, and fishes in nearby Spednik Lake. He also acts as a guide and knows the waters intimately; the "sports" who go out with him catch plenty of smallmouth bass most of the time. Woodie also likes to fish himself, and his favorite outfit is a fly rod with a small popping bug, which he casts almost on shore. He lets it lie there for a minute or so and then pulls on the fly line so that the bug quivers and sends out tiny concentric rings. Like most smallmouth-bass fishermen, he avoids making loud pops or other loud noises with his lures.

Woodie also trolls for the bass with streamer flies and spoons early in the spring. Then, when they ccme into shallow water to spawn, he may use top-water plugs and poppers. He has found that the bass will hit the top-water lures even in the summer when the water is calm early and late in the day.

But, most of the time when fishing during the summer months, Woodie turns to frogs, night crawlers, and minnows. At this time, the bass are down deep in the holes and near the bottom along rocky reefs and drop-offs. So he lets such baits sink all the way to the bottom and reels them back slowly, stopping every few feet or so to let them stay in one spot a short time.

Lefty Kreh admires a smallmouth bass he caught. He finds the Potomac River between Maryland and Virginia a good place for catching them. (*Lefty Kreh photo*)

Lefty Kreh fishes the Potomac River for smallmouth bass, and he finds that trolling a nylon or bucktail jig is a highly effective way to catch them. He looks for them in shallow water near piers, bridge supports, and rock ledges, and in the riffles. He also looks for May-fly hatches; when the bass dimple the surface to feed on them he casts a lure just upstream of the ring.

Keith C. Schuyler uses an 8- to 9-foot fly rod with a forward-taper floating line for smallmouth bass. He likes the small popping bass bugs in yellow, brown, or black and he fishes them by wading or from a canoe. He looks for bass in the smooth, glassy water of a deep riffle at the tail of a big pool, especially early in the morning and in the evening. Then he casts quartering upstream and starts working the bug back in short jerks with pauses in between. The bug should have plenty of action but move fairly slow.

Keith also casts around big rocks, logs, debris, and in small eddies along the shore. He finds that some of the fastest action with the bugs takes place toward evening, when shadows fall on the water and insects begin to hatch and rise.

Charles W. Edgehill also finds that fishing with a fly rod for smallmouth bass offers the ultimate in sport and is often deadlier than other tackle. Especially when the bass are actually feeding on hatches of insects, small flies, or nymphs. Then he uses dry flies tied on No. 12, 14, and 16 hooks and nymphs on similar-sized hooks. He employs trout tactics when fishing these flies and nymphs by making natural drifts with them.

George B. Gordon catches many smallmouth bass in muddy rivers when others fail to get a bite and throw up their hands in disgust. He uses a live minnow on a hook and adds a couple of split-shot sinkers on the leader above it. Or he uses a live crayfish. And on some days he may resort to a small, shiny spinner with a worm on the hook behind it.

Gordon found out that in order to take smallmouth bass in muddy water you have to study each spot carefully and then cast so that the bait travels close to the bottom and drifts right into a waiting fish. He finds that bass, especially the big ones, won't move far to hit a bait or lure. And in muddy water they can't see the bait at a distance. So you have to cast it often and work a small spot thoroughly, covering almost every foot of the bottom. Of course, it also helps to know the river well from past fishing and cast into the same spots where you have been catching bass in clear water.

Wynn Davis wrote a fresh-water fishing column in *Outdoor Life* magazine for many years and has caught almost every fresh-water fish that swims. But one of his favorites is the smallmouth bass, especially in fast-moving rivers such as the Delaware. There he finds that the best way to cover most of the water and locate the best spots is by floating down the river in a boat, especially in September, when the bass fishing is likely to be hot. He casts from the boat or beaches it and gets out to wade in the water to fish.

His favorite lure for this fishing is a small surface plug, especially early in the morning and in the evening. During the day, he uses

spoons, spinners, and jigs, which can be worked deep. He also likes
to use a fly rod with streamers and bass bugs.

When smallmouth bass are tough to catch during the hot summer
months in Pennsylvania rivers and creeks, Don Shiner uses a
streamer or bucktail on a fly rod or a weighted streamer on a spinning rod. He concentrates on such spots as the white water under
falls or the riffles entering a deep, cool pool. He also casts close to
logs, rocks, ledges, and undercut banks. Most of his fishing is done
right at daybreak and again toward dusk.

Phil Yost fishes for smallmouth bass in the Potomac River, and he
has caught as many as one hundred bass in one day! And all this
during the summer months, when other anglers are complaining that
the fishing is poor for these fish. His only secret is to use a light,
6-foot spinning rod and a reel filled with 4-pound-test line. He uses a
white jig that weighs $\frac{1}{16}$ ounce. It has a white chenille body and a
short white marabou tail.

Phil casts the jig out and lets it swing with the current with very
little added rod action. But his long, limber rod, which bends in an
arc from the tip to the butt, is held high and he can feel every strike
and the movement of the jig as it bounces along the rocky bottom.

John Hueston fishes for smallmouth bass during float trips on such
rivers as the Buffalo and White rivers, in the Ozarks. He uses a
weighted spinner and casts it toward undercut banks or in eddies
behind boulders. On warm nights he may use a surface plug. But
when lures fail to produce, he hooks a live minnow through the lips
and casts it into shoal water without any weight or float.

Earl F. Dodds fishes the Tennessee River and Pickwick Lake, in
the Florence-Muscle Shoals area of the northwestern corner of Alabama. These waters are noted for the big smallmouth bass, running
from 5 to 8 pounds, usually caught there. Many anglers feel that the
world record for smallmouth bass will be broken in those waters.

Earl uses both spinning and bait-casting tackle for these fish. Since
the fish tend to be line-shy in the clean water there, he uses 10-
pound-test monofilament on his spinning reel and may go down to 6-
or 8-pound at times. He finds that the smallmouth bass can be
caught on surface and underwater plugs, spoons, spinners, and jigs in
the river. But Earl has his best fishing with a plug-spoon combination
rig: You take a surface plug such as the chugger, remove the hooks,
and add a 2-foot, 8-pound-test leader to the tail eye of the plug.

Then, on the end of this leader, you attach a Reflecto spoon with feathers.

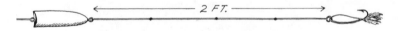

Chugger and spoon for smallmouth bass

Frank Armstrong also fishes the Tennessee River, and most of his fishing takes place below the Wilson Dam. The rig he uses to catch big smallmouth bass with is simple, consisting of a No. 6 hook tied on the end of his line and a split-shot sinker about a foot above the hook. Then he hooks a live minnow through the lips and lets it out from an anchored boat so that it drifts out in the current 70 to 80 feet. He leaves the bail on his reel open and holds his finger on the line. If a bass picks up the minnow, he lets line peel off the reel under his finger for a few seconds. Then he sets the hook hard.

Frank finds that the best fishing usually takes place in the main channels, especially when the turbines are operating and the current is strong. He catches most of his big bass in the spring and again in the fall.

Fenton Roskelly catches hefty smallmouth bass, and he does it in his own state, Washington. Almost every year, he catches two or three bass over 5 pounds and his biggest is a 7-pound 2-ounce bronzeback. He gets almost all of these bass on a jig-and-bob rig, which outfishes any other lure or bait. It consists of a Jig-Fly, with a black head and black marabou feathers, and a short, 3- to 3½-inch plastic worm on the hook. A nail knot is tied so that it can slide up and down on the main line. Then he threads a bead on the line below the knot and adds a bobber, which slides up and down on the line. The distance from the bobber to the jig will depend on the depth he wants to fish. He adjusts the knot so that the lure will be just off the bottom and touching it occasionally.

Roskelly has best results with this rig in the late winter and spring in the sloughs and backwaters where smallmouth bass gather. When there is some wind or waves, very little action is needed by the angler with this rig except reeling in a turn or two of the reel handle every few seconds. When the water is calm, you can lift the rod tip a few inches every few seconds and reel in slowly. You have to watch the bobber all the time, and when it moves you set the hook.

Some of the biggest smallmouth bass are now being caught in the large impoundments found in our southern states. (*North Carolina Department of Development photo*)

Charlie Brewer fishes for smallmouth bass in the spring, when they are spawning. He finds that in the southern states such as Tennessee and Alabama, where he fishes, this action usually begins sometime in April. He looks for the bass in coves or shallow water along the shoreline. These spots should have rock or gravel bottoms and be right off the main channel. Charlie also locates the fish offshore in the main channels or on underwater ridges and gravel bars. Most of these spots should be in water from 4 to 8 feet deep, with still deeper water nearby.

Charlie is a great believer in light tackle for smallmouth bass, and he uses light spinning rods and reels and lines testing from 2 to 8 pounds. Most of the time, he fishes with 6-pound-test line. His favorite lure is a lead-head jig with a plastic worm or plastic lizard or pork rind added to the hook. But he doesn't use the jig heads as they come. Instead he will take a jig head and file it on the bottom side, removing about one third of its weight. This results in a lighter, flatter head, which sinks more slowly. He feels that this makes the lure stay over a bass's spawning bed longer and irritates the fish into hitting.

Charlie also fishes the lure extremely slowly and smoothly, with no extra action. He casts the lure out and when it hits the water he quickly reels in a few turns to take up the slack line. Then he holds the rod fairly high and retrieves the lure slowly. He doesn't bump bottom but keeps the lure traveling just above it. However, he will vary this at times by letting the lure settle to the bottom, then just reel or raise the lure so it slides slowly and smoothly, settling on the bottom at regular intervals. But he avoids any jerking, bumping, or other violent action.

Nick Sisley catches smallmouth bass in the Susquehanna River even during the hot summer months. He uses an ultra-light spinning rod and reel with 4-pound-test line. One of his favorite lures for this fishing is a silver Colorado spinner with a live minnow on the hook behind it. He also uses white marabou and bucktail jigs. Nick fishes many eddies, pools, and riffles in the river but finds some of the best fishing in the tumbling water below dams.

Jerry Gibbs, who is fresh-water fishing editor of *Outdoor Life* magazine, finds that a highly effective lure for smallmouth bass is a double Indiana spinner with No. 2 blades and a fly behind it. He uses such flies as the Muddler, Coachman, Professor, McGinty, and Black Gnat behind the spinners. When using this lure, he varies his retrieve with short jerks, drop-backs, dead drifts, and rod action to obtain strikes. Jerry also uses dry flies in sizes No. 6, 8, 10, and 12 for smallmouth bass. He finds that skating a spider-type fly along the edge of a slick next to fast water often raises these fish.

8

MUSKELLUNGE, PIKE, AND PICKEREL

There are many anglers who would like to catch a big muskellunge, but not too many are willing to pay the price. These fish are moody and unpredictable, and they do not hit too often. You may have to spend many hours, days, weeks, months, and even years before you catch a few of these fish or learn how to do it. So most anglers prefer to fish for trout, bass, walleyes, or panfish. But there are a few anglers who are musky specialists and have acquired reputations for catching these fish year after year. They usually spend most of their time fishing for muskies and waste little time on other species.

One such angler, Percy Haver, made a career of musky fishing and spent more than thirty years seeking these big fish in Michigan in such waters as the Detroit River's Belle Isle and Lake St. Claire sectors. During this period, he caught over three thousand muskies, some of them weighing 56, 58 and 62½ pounds! He has caught eleven big muskies in one day!

Percy Haver caught most of his big muskies in June, September, and October. He believed in using heavy tackle and depended on big spoons and underwater plugs for lures. He made many of his spoons, which were often 8 or 9 inches long. Most of his muskies were caught by trolling and many came from Lake St. Clair, not far from Detroit, Michigan. When he first saw these waters, he was convinced they contained plenty of fish. So he made a survey of the lake, took soundings, checked the bottom, and located the weed beds. Then he began fishing and started catching big muskies, especially along the edges of the heavy weed beds and around the mouths of streams and rivers running into the lake. Like most musky fishermen, he found that fishing as often as possible and spending many hours trolling is the secret in catching big muskies.

Another old-timer who caught plenty of muskellunge was Robert Page Lincoln, one of our earlier outdoors writers, who fished for them in many waters in this country and Canada. He was one of the first anglers to start taking them on top with surface plugs. He felt that this was one of the best lures you can use in the evening, right up until dark and even later. He liked to use noisy surface plugs over reefs, in coves, and the shallow water along shore at dusk. One of his favorite techniques was to cast the lure out and then jerk it hard several times to make a big splash to attract the fish. Then he would let it lie still up to a minute or so before reeling it in.

He also believed in approaching a spot he was going to fish quietly and with little disturbance of the water. He stayed a good distance away and made long casts. He felt that a canoe was best for muskie fishing, since it is silent and easily maneuvered and handled while fishing and when fighting a big muskie.

Ed Johnson, outdoors editor of the Charleston *Daily Mail,* fishes for muskies in the rivers of West Virginia. Although some of the rivers in that state have provided musky fishing for years, they never received the publicity of the more popular musky lakes and rivers farther north. In West Virginia, muskies are found in such rivers as the Elk, Little Kanawha and Big Coal, and in Mill Creek.

Ed Johnson looks for muskies in the long eddies, pools, and deeper holes. If these are filled with logs, trees, snags, and brush, chances are good that muskies are present. Once he locates a musky, Johnson keeps after him, casting to the spot several times during the day or coming back and trying again in the future. Although muskies are caught in these rivers in the spring, summer, and early fall, Johnson likes November best of all, especially the first two weeks of the month.

Tony Burmek has spent a lifetime fishing and guiding sportsmen around Hayward, Wisconsin, for muskellunge. He has never really cared for any other kind of fishing and has concentrated only on muskies. Before fishing a lake he studies it carefully, pin-pointing the best spots. He looks for reefs, bars, and points, using contour maps, and even makes airplane flights over the lakes to study and locate the most productive spots. That's one of the big secrets of his success: he knows many good spots in many lakes, so he can try as many as possible and find some that haven't been fished hard by other anglers.

Once Tony locates a good spot he drifts over it and casts big underwater plugs. He experiments with his retrieve, working the plug at various depths and speeds, and gives it some rod action. He makes short casts and long casts and fishes extra hard when the barometer is rising. He feels the fish feed best during the fall months; in fact, he proved it one season by going out with his brother for twelve days in late October and catching seventeen muskies! Bad weather never stops Burmek from fishing. He fishes in the rain, snow, and cold, and in high winds. It may be uncomfortable for him at times, but he knows you have to be there when the muskies decide to hit.

4-TO-6-OZ.
KEEL WEIGHT

4-FT. WIRE LEADER

Musky trolling rig

Homer LeBlanc is a fishing guide who has helped his customers catch thousands of muskies. He plies his trade mostly on Lake St. Clair, between Lake Huron and Lake Erie. This is a big body of water with few lily pads, rocks, logs, or other typical musky hangouts you can cast to. So Homer has resorted to trolling from his 26-foot boat. He'll troll as many as six lines at a time on medium-action salt-water trolling rods with 50-pound-test lines. Rather heavy tackle, but many of his customers are inexperienced or first-time fishermen. At the end of his lines he has 4-foot stainless-steel leaders with 4- to 6-ounce trolling weights. On the end of the leader he attaches such lures as spinners, spoons, and plugs.

In the spring and fall, Homer trolls in shallow water from 8 to 12 feet deep. In the summer, he trolls the deepest parts of the lake in 20 to 25 feet of water. He finds that many of his muskies hit close to the boat, in the wash of the prop. He often runs into schools of muskies and will take several fish from one spot. He finds that they bite best when the barometer is falling and a storm is coming up. He also likes a wind from the west or northwest in the fall of the year.

One trick Homer LeBlanc uses when letting out his lines is to raise the rod slowly and then drop it back quickly. He'll do the same thing

Homer LeBlanc and Joe Le Page hold a day's catch of muskies caught by trolling in Lake St. Clair, Michigan. (*Homer LeBlanc photo*)

while he is trolling, at regular intervals. This makes the lure sink and flutter in an attractive manner and often excites a musky into hitting it.

Spike Kelderhous, of Maple Springs, New York, is also a guide who knows how to catch muskies—in the deep waters of Chautauqua Lake. In the spring, after the muskies spawn and move into shallow water, he uses jointed wooden plugs and trolls them at depths of 15 to 18 feet. Then he uses lead-core lines and lets the lure out 120 to 180 feet behind the boat. But when he wants to get down 20 to 25 feet he uses Dacron line and adds a 6-ounce weight ahead of the lure. When the muskies move back into shallow water, in the fall, he trolls for them in 8 to 10 feet of water.

Ted Capra used to be a muskie guide in Minnesota and still fishes for big muskies every chance he gets. He feels that the reason more anglers don't catch muskies is that they fish during the poorest season—in the summer—and they don't spend enough time fishing. Ted says that in his section of the country early June, September, and October are the best months to fish.

Capra finds that muskies spend more time in deep water than in shallow water. But he fishes for them in shallow water in June for a while and looks for them in bays or coves with creeks or streams emptying into them. But there should be deep water nearby. He likes to cast into this shallow water and retrieve his lure over the drop-off. He finds that for this early fishing the smaller spinners are good.

Later on, during the summer and early fall, Ted looks for muskies along the drop-offs and over sunken islands and weed beds. Then he uses the larger surface plugs, underwater plugs, and bucktail spinners. For such big, heavy lures he likes a stiff musky rod and bait-casting reel filled with 25- or 30-pound-test mono line. He ties the lure directly to the line, with no wire leader. During the spring he often fishes during the middle of the day, but in the summer Ted likes to be out early in the morning or late in the evening.

Art Mercier feels that a day with a breeze or some wind is better than a calm day and flat water when fishing for muskies. And if it is also cloudy or overcast, conditions are even more favorable for taking these fish.

Len Hartman has specialized in catching big muskies for many years and has taken them on spinning tackle. He once caught a 67-pound 15-ounce muskie on 12-pound-test line! And that's about the heaviest line he'll use on these fish. Len fishes with his wife, Bets, and in one of their best years they caught 152 muskies during the season.

They use 7- or 7½-foot spinning rods, heavy-duty fresh-water spinning reels, and a 30-pound-test wire leader. With such an outfit they can make long casts from their boat and cover a lot of water. They prefer to drift quietly with the wind or current and make the casts so that they fan the water all around the boat. When he finishes his first drift, Len will run the boat up to the starting point and make another drift over new water. He uses spinners, spoons, and plugs and works them deep and slow.

Len Hartman holds a 55-pound 2-ounce muskellunge he caught on 10-pound-test line. He has caught many others, even bigger, on lines testing no more than 12 pounds. (*Garcia Corporation photo*)

Len keeps records of his fishing days, noting where the musky was caught, how big it was, the lure used, time of day it was caught, the weather, wind velocity and direction, and water conditions. This helps establish a pattern, and he can often predict where muskies will be found during a given day, week, or month.

The Hartmans do a lot of their musky fishing in the St. Lawrence River near Ogdensburg, New York. They fish the entire season but find that June, September, and October are the top months. During July and August they will often fish at night, especially after midnight, and cast toward the shallow water near shore.

Al Russell is another musky angler who fishes the St. Lawrence River for these fish, and he catches many of them at night. He trolls for the fish with big, jointed plugs in light colors. And he feels that because the muskies are lying or feeding on the bottom, the plug

should travel deep and hit bottom every so often. He also believes
that a plug hitting a rock makes a sound or vibration that attracts
muskies from a great distance. This trolling is usually done in water
from 15 to 25 feet deep. So he uses light salt-water outfits with a
lead-core line on the reel to get the plugs down to these depths.

Clarence Gall catches muskies in the Niagara River more consistently than anyone else fishing those waters. And the main reasons
for his success are that he knows the bottom like his back yard and
he fishes often. He trolls for most of his fish using jointed underwater
plugs and multicolored line and constantly reels in line or lets it out
according to the depth of the water he is fishing.

He claims that it is very important to make the lure travel just
above the submerged weeds and to let it drop down deeper into
the pockets and holes. So when he is acting as a guide he is always
yelling "two colors" or "three colors" or "four colors," depending on
the depth he is trying to reach. Clarence is always checking his lures
to make sure they haven't picked up any weeds, which will kill the
action of the plug.

Johnny Brantland is a fishing guide who fishes the many lakes and
waters surrounding Vermilion Bay, in Ontario, Canada. This is the
heart of some of the best muskie country in North America and
Johnny can prove it by showing anywhere from ten to twenty
muskies in one day to any of his hard-fishing customers. If you stay
with him for a week and fish every day, he can almost guarantee you
a fish over 30 pounds.

Like most musky fishermen, Johnny doesn't know exactly what the
fish will want at a given time, so he is prepared to use various lures
and baits as the situation demands. Big surface plugs, underwater
plugs, and spinners, however, will raise most of the fish for him.

Art Lawton and his wife, Ruth, spent many years seeking big
muskies and caught some whoppers. Some of the muskies ran as high
as 58, 60, and 69 pounds. And during one fabulous week they
caught thirty muskies! They liked to fish the St. Lawrence River,
using stiff, sturdy rods filled with 30-pound-test line. They used big
plugs, at least 6 inches long and some as big as 8 or 10 inches. Solid,
one-piece underwater plugs were most effective, with the favored
colors being yellow, orange, and red, with green or blue shades
added. They trolled these lures about 125 feet behind the boat as
close to the bottom as they could. They fished over channels, weed

beds, and shoals or bars and off points of an island where the water was from 15 to 25 feet deep. The Lawtons fished the St. Lawrence from late summer and into September and October, especially around the full moon, when the fishing was best.

Bert Claflin spent a lifetime fishing for muskies and wrote a book called *Muskie Fishing,* telling about his experiences and frustrations with these big fish in many waters. He looked for muskies in fairly shallow water off a point or sand bar where small fish such as rock bass, sunfish, yellow perch, and crappies were plentiful. When fishing in deep water, he used a spinner and bucktail and worked slowly near the bottom. He felt that surface lures should be retrieved rapidly, while underwater plugs and lures should be reeled in slowly. He spent many hours casting or trolling and trying various lures and spots. When fishing for muskies in rivers, he avoided casting around snags, logs, sunken trees, and brush, because he felt that such spots harbored mostly the smaller fish. Instead he looked for the bigger muskies in deeper water, close to the bottom.

Kel Krotzer spent many years fishing for muskies in the state of Wisconsin. At first he encountered slow going; then, as he acquired more know-how, his catches increased. He offers some good advice on catching these fish.

First, he believes you should fish a lake that produced good muskie fishing the year before. He also feels that you should know several good muskie lakes or rivers and try as many of them as you can. According to Kel, too many big muskies are lost because anglers do not fish with adequate tackle. He recommends a medium-action spinning rod and reel filled with 10-pound-test line. He also uses a bait-casting outfit if he feels the need for it.

Kel uses small lures from early spring to July, because he finds they will take more fish than big lures. He likes spinner-bucktail combinations, with silver spinners on dark days and gold spinners on bright days. After July he uses bigger lures such as the spinner-bucktail and underwater plugs.

Kel looks for muskies over weed beds, and if these cover a big area he may spend hours casting to every section of this underwater growth. On sunny days he fishes the lakes with deep water and the tops of the weed beds there. When the day is overcast, cloudy, or stormy he heads for the shallow lakes. He finds that some of his best muskie fishing takes place on windy, stormy days.

Another muskie angler who fishes for them on raw, cold, rainy, or stormy days is Charles Nausen. He'll be out there when other anglers are sticking close to the stove. He has found that muskies hit better at such times than on calm, clear, warm days. Of course, like most muskie anglers, he feels it is important to know the waters you are fishing. Once you have fished a lake or river and taken muskies from certain spots, you can go back to them and catch more fish. New muskies are always moving in to take over a good spot, so it doesn't remain empty for long.

Louis Spray held world records for muskies weighing 59 pounds, 61 pounds, and 69 pounds. He used a large sucker on a harness both for casting and trolling, and fished in the spring and fall. He would camp near his favorite waters and fish hard. Once he located the hangout of a big "lunge," he would keep fishing for him day after day, changing lures and baits until the fish hit.

Frank J. Knourek has worked out a system that enables him to catch a legal-sized muskie on an average of every three days of fishing. He uses a spinning outfit with 10- or 12-pound-test line or a bait-casting outfit with 20- or 25-pound-test line. He likes long rods that are fairly stiff for making long casts and also for setting the hooks in the fish's tough jaws.

Part of his system is to choose lakes that are known to contain plenty of muskies and to pick two lakes in the same area so that he can alternate fishing them as conditions demand. Then he gets a hydrographic map of those lakes and tries to locate the best spots for muskies. He tries to find the weed beds, because that is where he does most of his fishing. These should lie in water less than 12 feet deep, where the muskies usually feed. Frank uses spinners and bucktail and surface lures. As the boat drifts they should be cast in an arc in the direction of the drift and should be retrieved fairly fast. Frank fishes mostly from 9 A.M. to 3 P.M. During the summer months, however, he may fish early in the morning, in the late afternoon, and in the evening. If the fishing is poor in the lake he is fishing, he'll try another lake nearby.

John Keats gets most of his muskies by trolling in deep, still water during the daytime. He likes to troll at a good speed. But he also finds muskies in shallow water from dusk to dark and again at daybreak. At such times he uses a big, black popping plug. He fishes in the fall, not only because it's a prime time but also because the summer crowds are gone and he has the water to himself.

Some of the biggest pike are caught in Canada's lakes and rivers. This one came from North Caribou Lake, Ontario. (*Ontario Ministry of Industry and Tourism photo*)

When it comes to pike, we start off with Al Lindner, tackle manufacturer and master angler, who enjoys catching these fish in many of our northern states with deep-water lakes. Here he starts fishing in the bays with weed beds soon after the pike have finished spawning. He finds that a live minnow fished on his "Lindy Rig" (a bottom rig with special slip sinker) works best for him at this time. Later on, in May and June, he looks for the pike along the deeper edges of the weeds, over the weeds, and also over bars or humps along the weed edges. The water usually ranges from 6 to 18 feet in depth. He likes to use a ½- or ¾-ounce jig baited with a 3-inch sucker minnow. He works this lure and fish bait fast by making long sweeps with the rod but letting it drop back to the bottom between lifts.

When July arrives, Al Lindner starts fishing from the deep edges of the weeds toward still deeper water. He may fish in water from 25 to 40 feet at times. Then he uses a shiner minnow with the slip-sinker rig or a spinner-and-minnow combination. He likes big, 3- to 6-inch minnows with the bottom rig and 2- to 4-inch minnows with the spinner rig. He may also try trolling fast with the Spoonplug or the Bomber.

During September, Al finds that the pike start moving into shallow water again. He looks for them on long, flat areas with heavy patches of cabbage weed; the pike will often be scattered all over such flats. Now he uses spinner baits, especially those with a black skirt and an orange blade. He also trolls with big spinners and Rapala plugs.

Then, after this shallow-water stay, the pike move into deeper water again and Al fishes once more in water from 25 to 45 feet deep, using live minnows, or jigs with live minnows, or he may try jigging a spoon up and down. In all this deep-water fishing, Lindner fishes over some kind of structure, such as a hump, a drop-off, or a long point.

Ed Senecal fished for pike in the St. Lawrence River, using only one lure and one method to take these fish plus an occasional musky. All he did was cast a spoon from a drifting boat over weed beds around such spots as Grenadier Island. He'd cast only about 20 to 30 feet, letting the spoon sink toward the bottom. Then, without reeling in, he would work his rod up and down so that the spoon tumbled and fluttered in the depths. Just by using this simple method, he caught as many as one thousand pike in one season!

Peter Dubec, who has held the world record for northern pike for many years with a 46-pound 2-ounce fish taken in Sacandaga Reservoir, in New York, specialized in pike fishing. He spent over thirty years fishing the reservoir and knew the waters and bottom and depths. He caught other pike going 32, 33, and 36 pounds, in the same reservoir.

Peter preferred to cast for his pike but caught most of his fish by trolling. He liked to use underwater plugs. Most of his pike were found around marshy or weedy shores and bottoms rather than in the rocky areas. He also fished around the mouths of creeks emptying into the reservoir. He fished shallow water in the spring and deeper water during the summer months, but he found that pike still came into shallow water during mornings and evenings in the summer, and again in the fall.

When he was casting, he looked for stumps, logs, weeds, sunken trees, submerged brush, lily pads, and similar cover, and cast his lure close to these. He claimed that a pike, especially a big one, is lazy, and you have to drop the lure near him to get a hit.

John B. Gleason has found that the big, slim-line plugs such as the Rebel in a silver finish are killers for big pike. He likes one that runs 15 feet down, and catches many pike on it. But he also uses plugs of this type that travel just below the surface and float. Then he reels them in and jerks them. After a jerk he will often stop and let the plug float to the surface. Usually a pike will hit it as it is rising. Or once the plug reaches the surface, he may make it quiver and look crippled.

When Mel Ellis fishes for big pike in Manitoba, Canada, he finds they will hit surface lures, so he uses big, noisy poppers, wounded minnows, and underwater plugs with lips bent so that they swim on top. Even when he uses a spoon, he reels it fast so it skitters and skips along on top. These surface lures, worked on top, produced the most spectacular and thrilling strikes for Mel.

Dave Harbour has found that the same plastic worm that is so deadly for black bass can also be highly effective for pike. He works the worm in a snake-like wiggle, jerking it steadily to produce the action that obtains the most strikes. For big pike he uses the largest plastic worms he can get and rigs them with weedless hooks. For smaller pike he finds that 6- to 7-inch worms are best.

Harold Blaisdell likes to fish for pike with a fly rod and big popping bugs. He finds that big bass bugs tied on long-shank hooks up to 6/0 or 7/0 are needed. He uses an 8-foot rod with a No. 9 weight-forward fly line to cast the bulky bugs, and finds it adequate. A 4-foot leader of 25- or 30-pound-test monofilament on the end holds the bass bug. He fishes from a boat floating down a creek or river and casts toward shore around snags, sunken trees, logs, rocks, and shady spots, where pike like to lie. He finds that the pike fishing is best in Vermont, where he fishes, during the low-water periods. When casting to a good spot, he works it repeatedly, since pike often have to be teased into striking. He also finds that an erratic retrieval

Hair bug for pike

of the bug with varied speeds, stops, pops, and twitches is better than a single set routine.

Robert Dornquast fishes for big pike in Lake Superior near Marquette, at the top of Michigan's Upper Peninsula. He finds that the best fishing usually takes place during the late-winter months, when the pike gather at the mouths of rivers. He gets best results with small spoons and a whole frozen 8-inch smelt, which he casts out and works to give it a lifelike action. He has caught many big pike, up to 20 and 25 pounds, fishing in cold weather.

Andy Welsch fishes for pike during the winter months in even colder weather, when the lakes are frozen. He fishes through the ice in January and February in Lake Poygan, in Wisconsin. He uses big 8- to 12-inch smelt or chubs on a special Scandinavian V-shaped hook that holds the baitfish in a lifelike, horizontal position. The big hook is inserted into the smelt's vent, and half of it, with the point and barb, is buried inside the bait, with the point of the hook just breaking the skin on top of the head.

Then he lowers the baitfish so that it is just off the bottom. He uses a non-stretch line, such as linen or Dacron, testing 50 pounds, rather than monofilament, which stretches. When a pike grabs the bait and moves off, he sets the hook during the fish's first run, rather than waiting until it stops.

Pickerel, a small member of the pike family, tends to be neglected and underfished in many of our lakes and rivers. But some anglers really appreciate this fish and spend days, hours, weeks, and months fishing for it. One such angler is Bob Gooch, who wrote the book *The Weedy World of the Pickerels* and who has fished for them in many waters. He uses most of the standard lures for pickerel, such as spoons, spinners, surface and underwater plugs, and streamer flies. He likes these in fairly large sizes, in red, yellow, green, and silver.

When using these lures Bob reels them at a brisk pace but varies the speed and occasionally stops reeling spoons or spinners and lets them sink and flutter, then starts reeling again. He casts the lures along the shoreline in weed beds, along lily pads, around logs and fallen trees, and in shallow coves.

In the winter, he uses live minnows, and finds that hooking a killifish with a shad dart through the lips and fishing it below a bobber is

This husky pickerel was caught through the ice on a New Jersey lake.
(*Harry Grosch photo*)

Killifish on shad dart for pickerel

highly effective. It adds color and keeps the baitfish down at the right depth.

Ted Janes fishes for pickerel in New England, especially in the ponds on Cape Cod. He enjoys using a fly rod and a bucktail and casts this toward the edge of the lily pads and retrieves in a stop-and-go fashion, letting the fly sink a few inches between successive forward movements. He finds the red-and-white bucktail best for such fishing, but other colors can also be used.

Alain Wood-Prince fishes for all kinds of fish, but he goes pickerel fishing every chance he gets and has a lot of fun and sport. He likes the way they charge a lure, hit it with abandon, and then, when hooked, put on an aerial display. They often save the day when trout, bass, and salmon do not co-operate.

Alain looks for lily pads or weeds in a lake, where pickerel are likely to be found. He knows that they will come into shallow water only 8 to 10 inches deep if there are lily pads. He likes to use surface lures, and one trick he pulls is to cast a weedless spoon into the pads and let a pickerel follow the lure out to the edge of the open water. Then he casts a surface plug on another rod to the spot where the pickerel is usually waiting.

Alain may also resort to trolling to catch pickerel and to locate the best underwater spots. For this he uses a brass or silver spinner in front of a streamer fly or a plastic minnow. Once he locates the fish by trolling, he stops and casts in the area.

9

WALLEYES

Joe Fellegy, Jr., is a fishing guide who wrote the book *Walleyes and Walleye Fishing;* he has spent more than twenty years fishing an average of one thousand to fifteen hundred hours a year for these fish. So his advice on catching walleyes is valuable and pertinent. He firmly believes that the versatile angler, who uses all kinds of tackle, lures, baits, and rigs, will catch more walleyes than the angler who sticks to one type of tackle and one kind of lure or bait.

Joe has found through the years that you can catch as many walleyes in the daytime as at night. He looks for them in lakes, along slopes and drop-offs near shore, rocks, sand and gravel bars, ledges, reefs, and mud flats. In rivers, he looks for sand or gravel deposits, drop-offs, points, falls, and dams. When trolling for walleyes in shallow water, he lets out a lot of line to avoid spooking the fish.

When casting jigs for walleyes that are schooled up for feeding in a particular spot, he anchors by that spot. This will usually be in water from 8 to 20 feet deep. He casts his jig out as far as possible, letting it sink to the bottom, then he brings his rod forward, keeping a tight line; this lifts his jig off the bottom. Then he lets the jig drop back to the bottom, at the same time reeling in the slack. He lifts again and drops back and keeps repeating this all the way in. If the walleyes are scattered over a wide area, he prefers to drift in the boat with the wind, and does his jig fishing in the moving craft.

When fishing from the shore of a river, Joe casts down current, and with the water pulling on the jig he keeps working it up and down without reeling in much line. He likes white jigs on cloudy days, yellow ones on sunny days, and blue or black jigs at night.

Although he uses a plain jig a lot, there are times when a jig-and-live-bait combination is more effective. Then he adds a worm or a minnow to the jig hook and works it in much the same fashion as a plain jig, but less violently, in order to avoid losing the bait. He finds that when using a big minnow on the hook jig it pays to drop your rod down and even give some slack line so that the walleye has a chance to swallow the bait.

In recent years Joe Fellegy has also started to use leeches as bait for walleyes, but this fishing is covered in detail in the section about Al Lindner.

Doug Swindell and fishing guide Elias Rob tested sixty-seven different walleye lures and found that three lures stood out above the others as the most consistent fish catchers. The best lure was a jig head with a short plastic body or tail. This they found worked best in clear water when cast out and retrieved very slowly right on the bottom. In fact, walleyes would often grab this lure when it was lying on the bottom.

Jig with plastic body for walleyes

The next-most-favored lure was a Doll Fly jig with feathers, to which they added a small strip of white pork rind. This is retrieved in a series of slow jerks to make the feathers "breathe" and the pork rind flutter. This lure also worked best when the water was clear.

The third-best lure, which was most effective when the water was muddy or dirty, was a No. 3 silver spinner with a strip of fish on the hook behind it. This is retrieved near the bottom at a slow, steady pace.

Bud Raskey owns a bait shop in Stronach, near Manistee, Michigan, an area that is very popular with coho-salmon and steelhead fishermen. But Bud also likes to fish for walleyes in Manistee Lake, especially when the moon is full in August. He casts a black-and-white sinking plug and does most of his fishing at night. He casts toward shore in likely spots, and if the fish aren't there he works deeper water. But he finds his best fishing over sand or rock bars, off points, and along drop-offs.

Roger Betz has been a walleye fishing guide and outfitter for many

Walleyes are becoming increasingly popular with many fresh-water anglers; they provide not only fun and sport but fine eating. (*Pennsylvania Fish Commission photo*)

years. He finds that when fishing with lures or bait for these fish you should always present them no more than 10 inches off the bottom. And you have to develop a sense of "touch," or "feel," which will tell you when you are deep enough and also convey the type of bottom you are fishing over.

He recommends a spinning or spin-casting outfit with a matching reel filled with 10- or 12-pound-test monofilament line. He feels you'll save more lures with this heavy line. And he doesn't carry a tackle box loaded with dozens of lures. All he takes along are a No. 3 French spinner, a sinking blue balsa plug, jigs, and plain fishhooks. He uses the hooks when he fishes with minnows.

When trolling for walleyes, Betz recommends the lowest speed possible, even if it means trolling backward with the boat. Once he has a strike or hooks a fish, he stops the boat, and this often results in hooking another fish or two. Where you troll is very important, and he navigates the boat so that the lure or bait passes close to or right over sunken treetops, old snags, edges of weed beds, rock shoals, gravel beds, and drop-offs.

Betz will also use live minnows about 3 inches long with a bottom rig and sinker. He hooks the minnow through the tail and casts it out from the boat, letting line flow off the reel until it goes slack, indicating it has reached bottom. Then he lets the bait stay there awhile, after which he lifts the rod slowly until it points straight up into the air; then he drops it back toward the water again. He keeps doing this until the bait is under the boat, at which point he lifts the sinker off the bottom and lets the minnow lie there for a few minutes. Then he reels in, makes another cast, and repeats the procedure.

Bob McGarry likes to fish for walleyes in the St. Croix River between Stillwater and Taylors Falls, in Minnesota. He uses a boat and fishes around the islands and points found there, usually at daybreak, having found that is the best time. He anchors off the points or the islands and casts out a jig weighing about ¼ ounce. This is the best weight for fishing in the 10- to 12-foot depths found there. If he can get a fathead minnow, he adds this to the jig. Then he casts the jig out, and when it is carried downstream he gives it a fast jigging action at first, then slows down, giving it a slower jigging movement. He finds that the fishing is best when the water is slightly above normal in the river. The spring and fall months are the prime fishing periods.

Al Lindner has made a thorough study of walleye fishing and has perfected rigs, methods, and techniques that catch these fish consistently. In the spring, after the spawning season, Lindner looks for walleyes in water from 4 to 12 feet deep, with a hard bottom, not too far from the spawning areas. At that time he uses minnows such as the redtail chub. He fishes the minnow on his "Lindy Rig," which is a slip-sinker, live-bait rig.

A bit later on, when the walleyes go into deeper water, he looks for them over sunken islands in water from 20 to 35 feet deep. These "humps" are usually productive then and most of the year. Al also looks for points breaking into deep water, especially along rocky bottoms. In the summer in the shallower water he looks for weed beds or weedlines.

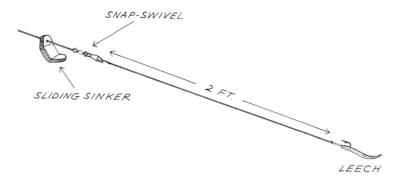

"Lindy Rig" for walleyes

Lindner carries both night crawlers and leeches and uses these during the summer months on his "Lindy Rig." He fishes with these baits over the sunken islands or humps straight up and down, raising and lowering his rod to feel the sinker hit bottom. He likes a ½-ounce sinker for moderate depths but may change to a lighter or heavier weight if needed. Al will also throw markers over an island or hump and make drifts in varied paths so he covers all the good spots. Slow trolling with the rig and baits can also be done with an electric motor or a small outboard motor.

Lindner finds that there are times when walleyes grab the bait and swallow it quickly; then he sets the hook fast. Other times, they are slower and may just play with the bait; then he may wait ten, twenty, or even thirty seconds to set the hook.

Don Walsh, Jr., who has fished for walleyes since boyhood, in Minnesota and Canada, feels that the jig with a minnow hooked through the lips is one of the deadliest combinations you can use for these fish. He casts this into the fast water of a river and lets the jig and minnow sink to the bottom and move close to the rocks. He often gets hung up in the rocks and loses a lot of jigs but also catches plenty of fish. He has found that the fastest fishing usually takes place in the spring, right after the spawning season.

Dave Otto also fishes for walleyes when they run, in the spring, up various rivers in Wisconsin. He finds that a minnow fished with two treble hooks is most effective. This rig has a treble hook on the end of the leader and another one on a sliding sleeve just above the first hook. The upper treble hook goes through the minnow's mouth, while the lower one impales near the tail. In this way you get the walleyes which tend to bite at the tail. This rig is fished with a sinker near the bottom.

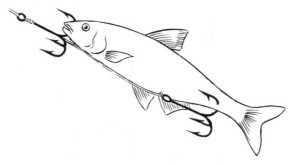

Hooking minnow with two trebles for walleyes

Carlos Vinson fishes for walleyes in Tennessee and catches big ones in Center Hill Lake, in that state. He uses a spinner/night-crawler rig to make most of his catches. This consists of a single No. 4 spinner with a No. 1/0 long-shank hook. He attaches the spinner and hook to a 30-inch leader of 10- or 12-pound-test monofilament attached to a three-way swivel. Next he ties an 8-inch dropper of 8-pound-test monofilament and a bell- or pear-shaped sinker to the end of this weaker dropper. Then he ties a snap-swivel on the end of his line and attaches this to his rig. The hook is baited with two big night crawlers.

Carlos trolls this rig on the bottom very slowly so that he can feel the sinker bouncing on the rocks every so often. In the summer, he trolls deeper waters than in the spring and fall months. In the spring,

Some of the biggest walleyes are now being caught in such southern states as Tennessee, where this 14½-pounder was taken in Center Hill Lake. (*Tennessee Conservation Dept. photo*)

he trolls around gravel and sand points. During the summer, he trolls along the high rock cliffs, where the water is deeper.

Vinson will also fish for big walleyes with a sliding-sinker rig and a live stone-roller minnow. He casts this out from shore and sets the rod in a forked stick or rod holder on the bank, then puts the reel in free spool and sits and waits for a bite. When the walleye takes the minnow, he waits until it starts moving away with it, then stops again, after which he sets the hook.

Jim Thrun is a field editor for *Fishing Facts* magazine; he fishes for walleyes in the fall, during October and November, catching big ones in shallow water at night. He looks for shorelines where there is deep water near by and weeds on the bottom. Creeks or rivers flowing into a lake are also good spots. He finds such conditions in several lakes in Wisconsin, where he fishes.

Jim relies mainly on two lures for this fishing. One is a floating-type Rapala plug, and the other is a ¼-ounce jig. He uses the plug in shallow water and the jig in deep water. He likes white, yellow, and black jigs.

Ray Slogar fishes for walleyes in the rivers of Minnesota, and he finds that a big night crawler hooked through the head about a half inch below the mouth and then inside the body is a potent bait when walleyes are down deep in a river. Then the worm is allowed to sink to the bottom, where it can roll along over the rocks and sink into holes and depressions where the walleyes lie. You hang up a lot and lose a lot of hooks and worms this way, but you also catch some big walleyes. The worm should be fresh, lively, and not mutilated in any way. If the worm is dead or bitten off, put on a fresh one.

If the current is strong or the water is deep, Ray will add a couple of split-shot sinkers or a clincher sinker on the leader above the worm. He has found that river walleyes like to lie at the foot of a pool below fast water, where the current eddies and spills to bring them food.

Gearheart Block, of Ortonville, Minnesota, has fished Big Stone Lake nearby for a lifetime and has a reputation for catching big walleyes. He fishes by the Ottertail Outlet, where the Minnesota River begins. And he keeps only big walleyes—many of his fish run over 10 pounds in weight. He fishes mostly at night, casting the big Hell Cat plug with a long, sturdy spinning rod. He makes the plug move along the bottom close to shore during the fall months, when walleyes come in there to feed. He finds quiet very important when casting into this shallow water. He reels his plug slowly, at a steady pace, with no added rod action.

Carl Malz uses minnows on a bottom rig when fishing for walleyes early in the year. He makes this rig by adding some split-shot sinkers to the end of his line. Then he ties a short, 6-inch dropper with the hook about 30 inches above the sinkers and baits it with a minnow. Split-shot sinkers are added or removed as needed. This rig gets hung up less often than one with a fixed-type sinker, because the split-shot sinkers slide off the line when they get caught in the rocks or other obstructions. And because the minnow is ahead of the sinkers, you can feel the walleye taking the minnow more readily.

Don Beland owns a lodge and canoe-outfitting business on Moose Lake, in northern Minnesota, from where he guides and fishes many of the lakes in the area. One of his tricks is to use two minnows on a single hook. He hooks one in the mouth and the other one under the dorsal fin. Then he adds a couple of split-shot sinkers about 18 inches above the hook so that the minnows will sink deep yet stay off the bottom. He casts them out and reels slowly along the bottom, covering a lot of area.

10

CATFISH

Fishing for catfish is popular with many anglers in our southern and midwestern states. They fish from shore and boats and often go out after work and during the night. Some of them are real catfish specialists and experts, who would rather fish for these than any other fresh-water fish.

One such specialist is Jake Milliron, who lives in Nashville, Tennessee, and has achieved a reputation for catching more catfish than anyone else. He fishes below the Pickwick Dam, in the Tennessee River, and has often caught several hundred pounds of catfish in two or three days' fishing. He claims that catfish won't move very far for a bait, so he tries to anchor his boat where he can drift out, or lower his bait into a spot where catfish are lying. The catfish usually stay in holes among rocks or in junk piles, so this is where he tries to drop his bait. He uses whole small hickory shad or the guts from a big one on his hook. He will squeeze or pinch a shad into two sections, leaving a bloody, ragged bait that attracts the catfish.

When Jake wants a big catfish, he hauls out his salt-water rod and star-drag reel with 60- or 70-pound-test line. He uses a bottom rig with a 9/0 hook and a 12-ounce sinker. Then he baits up and heads for the "boils," or turbulent water rushing out below the powerhouse. He'll drift with his anchor out until it catches on the bottom. But it must catch in the right spot, where he thinks fish are present. Then he lowers the bait and tries to make it drift into a hole he wants to fish. When he hooks a catfish, he frees the anchor, which is marked by a buoy, and fights the catfish while the boat is drifting down the river.

Harry M. Harrison is a biologist for the Iowa State Conservation Commission, and he offers some good advice on catching channel

He's holding a 41-pound catfish caught at Pickwick Dam, in Tennessee. It takes skill and know-how to catch such big cats, and strong tackle too. (*Tennessee Conservation Dept. photo*)

catfish. He says that during periods of clear water the catfish will feed largely at night. And they will often come into the shallows to do this. But when the stream or river rises and gets discolored, they will come out to feed even in the daytime.

He recommends chicken blood as a good bait for the catfish. This is allowed to congeal and is then put on a small treble hook. Another good bait is the guts from a fish or chicken. They can be cut to any length you want and can be still-fished on the bottom or drifted toward likely spots. Usually the best way to fish the baits is to drift them naturally in the current, using just enough lead to keep them down near the bottom. And when you have worked a certain spot for a while, you move downstream a few feet and fish in new water.

Harrison emphasizes that channel catfish in a stream can be very reluctant to take a bait if you create too much noise or disturbance in the water. He recommends wading quietly and walking softly along the banks.

Frank Davis catches a lot of good-sized catfish in Ohio lakes and reservoirs. He fishes mostly at night from a boat and uses a husky salt-water rod and reel filled with 30- or 40-pound-test line. He uses gizzard shad for bait, either dead or alive, and puts it on a No. 4/0 or 5/0 hook. Then he drifts slowly in a boat and lets the bait out, with no weight, to the bottom, usually in 15 to 20 feet of water.

Sam Goodwin is known as "Catfish Sam" around Moncks Corner, South Carolina, because he catches so many of these fish in the Santee-Cooper region. He operates a bait shop but spends most of his time fishing for catfish. He uses a long surf-type rod and a salt-water reel, which he fills with 15- or 20-pound-test line. He uses a bottom rig consisting of a three-way swivel and a 10-inch snell, which holds the hook, while a 12-inch dropper holds the 3-ounce sinker. He puts a needlefish or a gizzard shad, cut up into chunks, on the hook. Sam likes to fish from a boat and casts his rig and bait a good distance to-

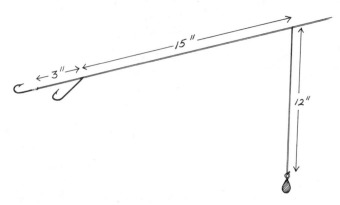

Two-hook rig used for catfish

ward shore from the middle of the river, where he anchors. He finds that the best fishing takes place just below the dam, especially when they let out the water.

Monte Burch has fished with Harold "Polly" Parratt, of central Missouri, who devised a catfish lure and bait that proved a killer for the channel catfish he likes to catch. Polly takes a plastic worm and cuts it into 3-inch sections. Then he ties a No. 4 treble hook to a monofilament leader and threads this with a wire needle through a one-inch square of soft foam rubber. The treble hook is buried in this foam rubber. Then, using the wire needle, he threads the mono line through the plastic worm. After which, he ties the mono leader to form a loop in front of the worm. To finish the lure, he adds some rubber legs by pushing them through the worm's body with a toothpick.

The lure is now finished and ready to be dipped in a special catfish formula, or stink. He makes this by taking a prepared commercial catfish bait to which he adds some cheese trimmings, minnows, or meat; the mixture is then ground in a meat grinder and allowed to "ripen" in the hot sun.

To use the lure, he dips it into the mixture, then casts it out into likely spots in a stream or river and lets it drift with the current into holes or snags or under sunken logs, where channel catfish like to hang out. When he gets a bite, he waits until he thinks the catfish has swallowed the lure before trying to set the hook.

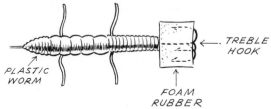

Catfish lure used by "Polly" Parratt

M. C. Hosmer recommends the following formula for catfish: Take equal parts by weight of hamburger meat, Limburger cheese, and flour. Add water to these and stir until the mixture becomes good and firm. Then you can form it into dough balls around a hook.

Robert Gilsvik fishes for catfish in the Mississippi River and the

St. Croix River along the Minnesota-Wisconsin boundary. He uses a sliding-sinker rig with a No. 2 hook. A split shot is added about 10 inches above the hook to act as a stop. He has used a variety of catfish baits, but his favorite is sharp cheddar cheese cut into 1-inch cubes. He uses a double hook to hold it more securely. But if he uses a single hook he wraps the cheese around the hook with thread.

Tony Moskunas, Jr., fishes for catfish in the Susquehanna River below the Conowingo Dam, and he is highly successful. He uses big minnows or small fish or fish strips for bait. He catches his own minnows or small fish on worms early in the morning, when the water is quiet below the dam. To hold the minnow or small fish, he uses a double hook and threads this through the bait's body so that it comes out at the vent with the shank buried.

The rig Tony uses for catfishing consists of a three-way swivel, with one eye tied to the line, another to the 3-foot leader with the hook, and the remaining eye on the swivel holding the sinker, which may range from 4 to 12 ounces. He uses salt-water rods and reels with 30- to 50-pound-test line to handle the rigs, heavy sinkers, and the bait.

Tony fishes by letting the rig and bait out into the current, where the water is rushing out below the dam. Then he lets the rig lie on the bottom in one spot for a while, after which he lifts the rod and sinker off the bottom and lets it move downstream a few feet and then lets it rest there awhile. He keeps letting the rig out and fishes it in several spots until about 200 or 300 feet of line is out. Then he reels in and repeats.

Sam Freel fishes for channel catfish in the streams and rivers of Missouri, and he claims that the best bait you can use for them is a soft-shelled crayfish. He fishes with this bait by wading in the water and casting it out across the stream in a run of fairly fast water and lets it drift along the bottom. He uses split-shot sinkers on the line to get it down deep enough yet allow the bait to move freely with the current. Then, when the crayfish is directly below him, he reels it in upstream very slowly, still keeping it close to the bottom.

Morris H. Shaw has a lot of fun catching channel catfish on lures in Florida when conditions are right for this fishing. He uses surface plugs and underwater plugs at night and finds that catfish will often hit them. The fishing is best when the catfish are looking for young shad below dams. But he has also caught them by trolling slow and deep with small jigs. And when the channel catfish are feeding on the surface on insects, he finds they will also take dry flies and wet flies.

Carlos Vinson also catches channel catfish on lures, in such waters as Center Hill Lake, Great Falls, and Dale Hollow, in Tennessee and neighboring states. He uses small red underwater plugs and trolls them slowly in depths of 6 to 10 feet. He also finds that trolling anywhere from 40 to 100 feet from shore, where the water is running slowly and is clear, is best. In murky water that is running faster, he fishes a greater distance from shore. Then he lets out 150 to 200 feet of line. And he finds that the catfish do not hit the plug very hard; they feel as if you've snagged the bottom. So he sets the hook at every indication of a strike.

Another angler who catches catfish on lures is Robert E. Price. He gets a lot of them in the Grenada Lake Spillway, in north-central Mississippi. And he catches them on jigs. He casts right into the turbulent water and lets the jig go down to the bottom, where it bounces along in the current. A catfish may grab it gently, so any nibble or hit calls for setting the hook. Catfish caught this way on light tackle and jigs put up a spirited fight in the fast current.

Russell Tinsley fishes for most game fish, but he enjoys catching channel catfish too, especially on light tackle. He may use a No. 2 hook tied directly to the end of his line and add a clincher sinker above it. Or he will use a sliding-sinker rig. For bait he'll try the usual worms, minnows, insects, or prepared baits, but he also finds that frozen salt-water shrimp tails work very well. Russ looks for catfish in slicks or pockets in a riffle, behind rocks and logs, in eddies, holes, and pools, and alongside undercut banks below riffles. He usually wades in the stream and casts his bait out so that it is drifted naturally into such spots.

Hank Bradshaw fishes for channel catfish in the rivers of Iowa, and he learned early that these fish can be fussy at times: you have to present your bait in the right spots to get action. He claims that channel catfish are sluggish and slow on hot days and won't move far for a bait. Fishing is usually better on the cool, cloudy, or rainy days. But if he presented the bait where the catfish could see or smell it, they would often take it even when conditions weren't ideal. So Hank makes sure that his bait drifts right into catfish hangouts such as logs, snags, brush, fallen trees, and roots. He also found that catfish like to lie behind a boulder or rock, in the quiet pocket there.

Hank Bradshaw holds a string of channel catfish caught in the Little Sioux River, Iowa. Catfish this size provide fine sport and great eating. (*Henry E. Bradshaw photo*)

So he casts his bait close to the rock and lets it be carried by the current past it and into the pocket where the catfish is lying.

Gene Doran, who lives in Corinth, Mississippi, has a reputation for catching catfish in the Tennessee River below Pickwick Dam. He uses a two-hook rig 15 inches below a foot-long dropper holding a 4-ounce sinker. The two hooks are baited with shad entrails. The hooks are hidden in the bait so that it hangs naturally. He drifts in a boat and lifts his rod up and down as the bait moves just above the bottom, to avoid hanging up in the rocks. He finds the catfish usually grab the bait as he lifts his rod. The fishing is best in these waters from May to the end of September.

George Fast fishes for channel catfish in the shallow rivers of Kansas and uses a method that works well for him. He wades downstream in the middle of the river and stops a short distance above the spot he wants to fish. Then he lets his bait—usually a preserved minnow—drift on a cork or plastic float toward the deep hold or catfish hideout. He makes about four or five drifts in each spot and then moves on to the next one.

Abner Self, of Tennessee, spent a lifetime fishing for catfish, and his favorite was the flathead cat. He believed that the fishing was best during the dark-of-the-moon period, when the catfish left the deep water to cruise around gravel points and shallow water. He used two big night crawlers on a hook and added a few drops of vanilla extract on the worms. He believed the extract makes the worms wiggle more and also attracts more catfish.

When you think of channel catfish, you usually think of some midwestern or southern river. But these active members of the catfish family have also been stocked in many other rivers throughout the country. Dick Pryce found this out when he fished the Delaware River in New Jersey.

Dick uses a light spinning rod and a bottom rig with a bell sinker and an 8-inch snell with a 2/0 hook. He baits this most of the time with night crawlers but will also use shrimp, live minnows, and cut fish. The best fishing usually takes place below dams or riffles with fast water and toward dusk and during the night. Dick finds that few anglers fish for catfish here, even though the Delaware River and the canals along it are close to such big cities as Philadelphia and New York.

Dwight R. Schuk fishes for bullheads early in the spring in such rivers as the Klamath, in Oregon. He finds that as soon as the water warms up above 50 degrees they become active. And since shallow water warms up faster than deep water, that is where he starts his early-season fishing for bullheads. He also finds that the water is usually warmer during the middle of the day in the spring.

Francis E. Sell fishes for bullheads with a 9-foot fly rod and 10-pound-test monofilament line on his reel. He adds a light sinker to the end of a 14-inch dropper and a small hook on a 10-inch dropper. For bait he uses either worms or a mixture made from cheese and blood. The blood-and-cheese bait is used on a "basket hook," which has a wire spiraled around the shank to hold the soft bait securely. Sell believes in chumming a pool or spot he is going to fish. He puts some of the blood and cheese in small bags and lowers them to the bottom. This is best done at the head of a pool, so that the bullheads will follow it upstream to the spot he is fishing.

11

PANFISH

In this chapter we cover the so-called "panfish," which will include the bluegills, crappies, yellow perch, white perch, white bass, and rock bass. These fish are caught by millions of fresh-water anglers and are easily the most popular fishes in this country. Although these fish bite well most of the time, there are also conditions and times when they can be hard to find or difficult to entice to the hook. Especially the bigger specimens of this group. The following anglers offer good advice and tips on how to catch them.

John Weiss feels that in order to locate and catch the bigger bluegills you have to approach this fishing the same way you do black-bass fishing. So he relies on electronic depth-sounders, a temperature gauge, and topographical or hydrographic maps of the lakes he plans to fish. He uses these to study the bottom structure and to find the spots where the big bluegills hang out.

John has found that in the very early spring or late fall, the big bluegills will be found along deep, steep shorelines. They'll migrate short distances to bars, reefs, or points that border deep water. Later in the season the bluegills will move into coves and bays prior to spawning but will still hang out in deeper water along drop-offs or channels. Then he looks for the beds or bluegill nests close to shore and fishes in the deeper water near by.

John Weiss uses a homemade lure created by Bill Gressard. He takes a beer or soda can made of aluminum and cuts a ½-inch by ⅝-inch rectangle, which is then folded around the shank of a No. 10 long-shanked hook and trimmed to form a half circle. Then he paints a blue stripe along the back of the aluminum lure and adds a yellow or black eye.

This lure is best fished with a fly rod and a tiny plastic bobber on the leader, which can be adjusted to the depth being fished. When cast out, the metal lure flutters as it sinks slowly and is often taken on the way down. But most of the strikes will come when the lure reaches the right depth, usually somewhere between 5 and 15 feet.

Bill Phillips locates the bluegill or "brim" beds by smelling them. The scent is comparable to that of oil of anise, he says. He also looks for the bluegills along steep walls with vegetation, around trees that have fallen into the water, in the white water below falls, and in the tailrace below a dam. In this moving water he uses a small plastic float, and 3 feet below it he ties on a small jig. He casts this into the current and backwash. He even catches bluegills at night on small poppers fished close to shore when the water is calm.

Frank Sargeant uses a simple plastic worm lure created by his friend Jim Modica for bluegills; he claims it outfishes any other lure he has used. All he does is get a small, slender white or pale-green plastic worm and cuts it into sections from ⅜ to ¾ inch long depending on the size of the hook (usually from No. 8 to 14). Then he gets some hump-shanked hooks and threads the plastic worms on the shank. The worms must be heated so that the plastic congeals around the hook.

The tiny plastic worms can be fished with a fly rod and in deep water are allowed to sink to the bottom, then are twitched to obtain strikes. In shallow water you can use a floating-type worm and fish it on top or just below the surface.

Vic Dunaway uses a special rig he developed to catch bluegills when they are down deep. He ties on a ⅛- or ¼-ounce sinker on the end of his spinning line. Then, about 2 feet above the sinker, he attaches a 12-inch dropper and ties a No. 6 or 8 cork-bodied popping bug with rubber legs. He casts this out until the sinker hits bottom and then activates his bug with light twitches of the rod.

When Charles K. Rawls, Jr., wants to locate bedding bluegills, he looks for bubbles on top of the water. These bubbles rise to the surface from the spawning beds when the bluegills are fanning the nests. Then he approaches the spot with care and fishes with bait or flies or panfish bugs.

Charles A. Barnes gathers his best bait for bluegills long before he uses it for fishing. Soon after the first frost, he breaks off the stems of goldenrod plants but only those having a gall, or swelling, on the stem. He keeps them in his garage, and when heavy ice forms on the lakes in his area he splits the pods, or galls, and removes the tiny white grubs, or larvae, found there. When fishing for the bluegills through the ice, he usually puts two or three of the grubs on a single hook or adds a grub to a tiny spoon or ice fly.

Art Dey also fishes for big bluegills through the ice, in the lakes near Pontiac, Michigan, and he usually catches his limit every time he goes out in January and February. He uses a very short rod and tiny reel, but his real secret is to attach a few inches of spring wire by taping it to the tip of his rod. The line runs through an eye on the end of the limber wire. This way he can detect even a light bite by watching the wire bend down. He finds bluegills bite very lightly in the winter, and it is hard to tell if you have a bite when using the regular, stiff rods.

Art uses a tiny, weighted ice fly and adds a goldenrod grub on the hook. He brings along flies in various colors. To bring bluegills to the spot he is fishing, he uses an attractor consisting of a series of hookless spinners rigged one above the other. He lowers this through the hole and jigs it up and down to attract the bluegills under him. Then he brings in the attractor and lowers his ice fly and grub into the depths. He usually gets immediate action.

Dave Goforth, of Greensboro, North Carolina, developed a lure that works for bluegills, crappies, and other panfish. It appeals to the fish's sight, hearing, taste, and smell, and works when other lures or baits fail. He takes a No. 1 Indiana spinner blade and adds a hook with a small, fiberglass body shaped like a tiny minnow, behind it. A short length of heavy monofilament is imbedded in this body to act as a weed guard.

Then Dave takes any fish he has caught and cuts a strip 1¼ inches long and ¼ inch wide and adds it to the hook. Finally he adds two small split-shot sinkers about 3 inches apart on the leader, about 8 inches in front of the spinner. Dave uses an ultra-light 5½-foot spinning rod, small reel, and 4- or 6-pound-test line to cast this lure, which he calls the "Meatgetter."

He casts the lure close to the brush for crappies and lets it sink until the line goes slack. Then he reels it in very slowly and deep. When he hooks a crappie he doesn't reel it in immediately but lets it struggle in one spot for a while. This brings other crappies to the scene, which are caught later.

Dave Goforth and his son show a string of bluegills caught on the lure Dave designed for these and other panfish. (*Dave Goforth photo*)

Dave Goforth's panfish rig

When crappies are on the spawning beds, Jack Connor uses a small streamer fly such as an all-gray or all-white tied on a No. 4 or 6 hook. He usually adds a tiny spinner ahead of the fly and a tiny, fly-rod-size pork rind on the hood of the streamer. He casts this out and lets it sink to the bottom over a crappie bed. Then he retrieves the lure very slowly, just enough to work the spinner and give the lure some action.

After the spawning is over, the crappies leave the beds and move around in search of food. Then Jack rows slowly or drifts with the wind and lets his lure out about 40 or 50 feet behind the boat. The lure should travel about 5 or 6 feet below the surface. When he gets a hit or catches a crappie, he quickly anchors the boat and starts casting all around the spot.

Dave Hickman lives in Winter Haven, Florida, and has fished for many fresh- and salt-water species in that state. But he gets a lot of fun catching crappies, too, for which he uses a fly rod. However, he finds that streamers up to 2 inches long are best, and he catches just as many crappies on them as others do on minnows or other bait. He likes streamers that have long, saddle hackle tails and marabou shoulders. He casts these big flies into weed beds with open pockets in the bottom. The main trick in using these flies is to cast them into the pockets and let them sink; then move the flies to give them some action but let them stay in one small spot as long as possible.

Ralph Morton catches a lot of crappies in Tennessee impoundments. He uses an electric motor to avoid frightening the fish and trolls a minnow or crappie lure very slowly. Ralph claims that crappies do not care for sunlight and come into shallow water only in the early morning and late afternoon and evening. Fishing is even better at night, when they come closer to the surface. In midday Ralph looks for deeper water, up to 30 feet or more, and fishes there. He also looks for old channels, river beds, ledges, drop-offs, and sunken brush or trees, and does his slow trolling there.

John Nansen uses small lures for crappies and likes tiny white or yellow bucktail jigs. He also uses small spinners but makes sure that they revolve when retrieved slowly. He also uses pork-rind strips, either alone or together with the jig or spinner. His best fishing takes place in the late afternoon and evening.

Don Woolridge finds that crappies can be caught even during the winter months in Missouri's Lake of the Ozarks. So he fishes during

These two fine strings of crappie were caught in Bull Shoals Lake, Missouri. Crappie usually run best in the spring, when they come in close to shore to spawn. (*Photo by Walker-Missouri Commerce*)

February, using a ⅙-ounce crappie jig and letting it down to the bottom in depths up to 60 feet. After hitting bottom with the jig, he starts bringing it up very slowly. At this time of year crappies hit very lightly, so he sets the hook at the slightest indication of a hit. If he catches a fish or two in a spot, he stays there and usually gets more. Once he locates the best crappie spots, he returns on other days and catches more fish from these favored locations.

According to E. Philip Rice, who wrote all about panfish in his book *America's Favorite Fishing,* if you want to catch big yellow perch you should fish in deep water. Except for brief periods in the spring and fall when the big perch may come into shallow water, most of the time you will find them in depths from 20 to 50 feet. And he claims that the best fishing periods are from 10 A.M. to 2 P.M. and again from 4 P.M. to 6 P.M.

When Don Shiner wants to catch some yellow perch through the ice during the winter months, he uses ice flies. He ties his own flies by getting a No. 10 IX long hook and ties a few hackle feathers of bright yellow or orange around the shank. Then he clamps a large-size split-shot sinker at the head of the fly just behind the eye of the hook. He usually paints the split-shot sinker a bright, light color. To use the jig, he gets a short stick and lowers it to the level where the perch are and starts jigging it up and down.

Ice fly for yellow perch

John O. Cartier fishes for yellow perch in Lake Michigan, and he has found that these fish have changed their habits and are now apt to be found almost anywhere in the lake. To locate the perch, he often resorts to drifting until he gets a bite. Then he anchors, casts out a small gold spoon, lets it sink to the bottom, and then jigs it back. He also uses worms and soft-shelled crayfish for bait. These are used on a rig with a dipsey sinker on the end and a hook on a short snell about 6 inches above the weight. Another hook on a snell can be tied about a foot above the first hook. John finds he gets most of his yellow perch in water from 10 to 35 feet deep.

Jack Woolner fishes for yellow perch in Massachusetts, and he likes to use a fly rod and reel but puts 4- or 6-pound-test monofilament line on the reel instead of the regular fly line. Then he baits a No. 6 hook with a worm or a tiny minnow. He strips off several coils of the mono line and casts his bait out about 30 or 40 feet. If he is fishing over a weed bed, he may add a bubble float above the hook to keep it away from the vegetation. Jack also finds that two or three grass shrimp on a hook make a good bait for the yellow perch. Other times, he may use a small red-and-yellow streamer fly.

Lester C. Boyd fishes for yellow perch in New England and gets plenty of them. He doesn't use worms or minnows, as most perch

Yellow perch can be caught throughout the year but are especially popular with ice fishermen in our northern states. (*Wisconsin Conservation Department photo*)

fishermen do, except to catch his first small perch or sunfish. Then he cuts a narrow, one-inch strip from the belly of the perch and puts it on a No. 6 or 8 hook. He fishes the strip by adding a split shot on the leader and then drifts over perch water in his boat. As the boat drifts slowly, he twitches his rod to give the bait some action and flutter. Or he may raise and lower his rod to make it rise and sink. If he catches a pickerel, he'll cut a strip from its belly and use that instead of the yellow-perch or sunfish belly. He finds it is thinner and has better action.

Ray Estes fishes for big yellow perch through the ice in New York State lakes. He uses a short jigging rod and small silver jigging spoons, and baits them with an oak-leaf bug, maggot, or May-fly nymph.

Woodie Wheaton, who earlier showed how he catches smallmouth bass, also fishes for white perch in the lakes of Maine. To locate these fish he looks for gulls; they usually indicate that white perch are chasing baitfish on the surface. He uses worms to catch the first white perch and then cuts it up into strips and uses these for bait.

Joel S. Fawcett also fishes for white perch in Maine, and he uses a fly rod with dry flies, wet flies, and small streamers and bucktails. He locates the fish by looking for the tell-tale ripple on the water that they make when in compact schools. Other times, he looks for the white perch near the mouths of streams, along drop-offs, and in the deeper channels and holes. He finds they come closer to shore toward sundown, when fishing can be fast and furious. September is a good month for this fishing, because the water is cool and the white perch come close to shore to feed heavily.

Biologist Stephen H. Taub made a study of the white perch in Quabbin Reservoir, in Massachusetts. He found that late spring was the best time to catch them, when they come into shallow water especially near the mouths of tributary streams. During the summer months the white perch move into deeper water, and there he found the best fishing was at the 15-foot level in water 30 feet deep. He drifted with a single worm behind a spinner and caught most of his fish at that level.

Richard W. Gross, of the New Jersey Fisheries Laboratory, claims that white perch are present in many of the tidal rivers of that state and in some lakes, but not too many anglers seek them. He says that the white perch prefer open water, away from vegetation, and are usually found over muck, sand, or gravel bottoms. They also tend to feed at night in shallow water, and return to deeper water during the daylight hours. But they will bite better during the daytime in tidal rivers and creeks, which have darker, discolored water.

Because white perch travel in schools, the big problem is to locate the fish and stay with them. Richard tells of one way some anglers do this. First they catch a white perch from the school and then tie a small inflated balloon with a long line to its tail. Then they release the fish, which joins the school, and all they have to do is follow the balloon and fish in the area.

Don Vetter fishes for white perch in many of the lakes and tidal creeks on Long Island, New York. He uses a light fly rod and wet flies such as the Yellow Sally, White Miller, and McGinty. Or he uses small streamers such as the Mickey Finn, Silver Darter, and White Marabou. He retrieves the flies in short strips with pauses in between. Don finds that the late-afternoon and evening hours are the best time to use the flies.

When the white perch are down deep in tidal streams during the cooler months, Don uses a white or yellow bucktail jig or shad dart and works it slowly near the bottom with his spinning rod. He also finds that white perch will take live grass shrimp and bloodworms fished on the bottom in brackish waters.

More and more anglers are fishing for white bass these days, especially on our larger lakes and impoundments, where these fish have been stocked or were naturally present. Hope Carleton, who works for the Kentucky Fish and Wildlife Resources Department offers some excellent advice on catching these fish in his state. He finds that the best fishing occurs in the spring, when they spawn and move up such rivers as the Dix and the headwaters of the Cumberland and Dale Hollow reservoirs. Then you can use tiny spoons, spinners, and jigs. The white bass will lie in certain spots in the river, and you have to cast your lure so it reaches them. He finds that eddies and the quiet spots behind boulders are good. Pools and deep holes can also be fished. You have to let your lure sink all the way down to the bottom, then bring it back slowly in short jerks.

Carleton finds that the fishing is best on cloudy, overcast days, when the water is slightly discolored. On bright days and when the

He's holding an average-size white bass. This fish is becoming more and more popular especially in our larger impoundments, where they are often caught in large numbers. (*Tennessee Conservation Department photo*)

water is clear, he advises fishing around daybreak and in the evening, before dark. Fishing for white bass is also good later on at night in the lakes. Then he hangs a lantern over the side of the boat and nets some small shad and minnows with a dip net. He hooks one through the lips or back, lowers it to the bottom and reels in very slowly. When he gets a bite he stops reeling and lets the fish swallow the minnow, after which he sets the hook.

Hart Stilwell started to fish for white bass in Texas soon after they were introduced there in such lakes as Buchanan, Texoma, Travis, and similar impoundments. He found that the most exciting way to catch them was by "jump fishing," when they surfaced to chase gizzard shad or other small fish. He would race the boat over to the school of feeding fish and cast spoons or plugs into them. Hart found that this fishing was best in the spring or early summer and that the period just before dark was the best time of day.

Clifford Farmer fishes for white bass in the lakes of Missouri, Arkansas, Oklahoma, and Texas. He likes to use polar-bear-hair jigs in yellow and black, which he casts in the fast water below dams. He also trolls with plugs and spoons when the white bass are down deep during the summer months. For this deep trolling, near the bottom, he uses a special trolling rig: He takes a 5-foot length of leader and ties a small barrel swivel on one end and an underwater plug on the other. Then he ties a 12-inch dropper with a jig about 2 feet above the plug and another 12-inch dropper with a jig about 15 inches above the first one. The plug, when trolled, gives the jigs action and looks like a small fish chasing the jigs. He finds that a yellow plug and yellow jigs work best most of the time, but he will also try a black plug and black jigs.

Emmett Gowen looked where shad minnows were thick, usually below dams, and used a splasher rig for white bass. He took a white surface plug and tied an 18-inch leader to it and then added either a spoon, a spinner, or a small jig on the end. He would cast this out and bring it back with loud, splashing jerks.

When it comes to catching rock bass, or "goggle-eyes," Bill Scrifes is an expert in the creeks and streams of Indiana and other waters. He uses an ultra-light 5-foot spinning rod or a fly rod to catch them with. One of his favorite lures is a $\frac{1}{16}$-ounce black jig with a worm on it. He also uses tiny minnows, crayfish tails, hellgrammites, and worms at times. Bill looks for rock bass in the same creeks and streams where smallmouth bass are present. Those with rocks, gravel, or sand bottoms are best. He fishes the riffles, potholes, undercut banks, logs, and brush in such waters.

Rich Zaleski also fishes for rock bass; he uses jig heads with 4-inch plastic worms for these fish. He casts these in spots with rocks, and when a fish grabs the lure he lets it run with it for a second or two before he tries to set the hook. He also uses Tail Spinners and the $\frac{1}{8}$-

ounce Mud Bug for the rock bass. His biggest fish are caught along rocky drop-offs in fairly deep water.

William Herrod catches rock bass, or "redeyes," in Tennessee's Stones River and other streams in that state. He uses a fly rod with a hook on the end of the leader and baits the hook with a small crayfish, about 1½ to 2 inches long. He keeps the crayfish alive in a minnow bucket, which is attached by a string to his belt. Then he wades in the river and drifts the crayfish toward likely spots. He tries to sink the bait along the edge of a submerged rock shelf or ledge. The crayfish usually goes down to the bottom and starts crawling under the rock. That's when a rock bass usually grabs it.

Bob Cary finds that during the hot summer months rock bass will often hit bass bugs about the same size as those used for smallmouth bass. He finds that the best time to use them is from dark to about 10 P.M. He casts the bugs into the riffles or the slick water just above them. He also drifts in a boat and casts the bass bugs into the shadows around the pilings of docks. Bob retrieves the bugs slowly with short pops at regular intervals.

12

OTHER FRESH-WATER FISHES

This chapter will deal with some of the other fresh-water fishes caught by anglers in various parts of the country. Some of these are not too plentiful or have too limited a range to be really popular. Still others require special fishing tackle or techniques, or are difficult to catch. But the following anglers do fish for them and pass on their knowledge and techniques here, for other anglers to use.

The largest of these fish caught in fresh water is the sturgeon, which is found in some rivers of this country. I say "some" because at one time they were plentiful in many rivers, but pollution, dams, and overfishing have taken their toll, and today only a few rivers provide such fishing. Even in the famous Snake River, in Idaho, fishing has fallen off drastically and big sturgeon have become scarce. In fact, the law states now that sturgeon cannot be kept but have to be released immediately.

When sturgeon were more plentiful, Willard Cravens fished for them with heavy surf rods and big spinning reels filled with 40- or 50-pound-test line. He used smelt for bait on big 6/0 or 7/0 hooks, and sinkers up to a pound to hold the bait on the bottom in the fast current. He found the best fishing in the deeper pools and backwaters in the spring and summer around the time of the full moon. Fishing this way, he caught a sturgeon going 360 pounds.

Bill Clem and his partner Bill Curtis also fished for big sturgeon in the Snake River, using lamprey eels, night crawlers, and pieces of meat for bait.

Sturgeon are still fairly plentiful in Florida's Apalachicola River, below the Woodruff Dam, and Robert Burgess fishes for them there. He uses a boat or a rubber inner tube and heavy spinning or conventional tackle with reels loaded with 60-pound-test line. His bottom rig

Garnet Ginther, with sleeves rolled up, loads a 265-pound sturgeon into his trailer. He has caught much bigger ones in the Fraser River, in British Columbia, Canada. (*Herb Williams photo*)

has a 3-ounce bell sinker and an 18-inch, 50-pound-test leader with three 6/0 hooks on the end spaced about 6 inches apart. He baits these hooks with large clumps of river moss or green algae, which he gathers from rocks in the water. He finds that the best months for this fishing in the Apalachicola River are August and September.

One specialist who has taken some of the biggest sturgeon ever caught on rod and reel is Garnet Ginther, who fishes for the giant fish in the Fraser River, in British Columbia, Canada. He has caught many, ranging from 200 to 640 pounds! The 640-pound monster was 11 feet long and took an hour to bring to the boat, three and a half miles from where it was hooked.

Naturally, to catch such big sturgeon you need husky tackle, and Garnet uses heavy salt-water rods and big reels filled with 80- to 100-pound-test line. He baits big 9/0 hooks with small live lamprey eels, putting several on one hook. And he uses 16-ounce sinkers to hold his bait on the bottom. The sinker is attached to a weaker line so that it breaks off after a fish is hooked. Garner fishes mostly during the incoming tide from low-water slack to high-water slack and does most of his fishing at night. He finds it is very important to give the sturgeon plenty of time to swallow the bait. A sturgeon swims along the bottom sucking up the food found there. It takes a bait slowly and gently and may play with it for several minutes or more before it finally swallows it. When the line starts to move off steadily, Garnet Ginther sets the hook.

Another giant fresh-water fish is the alligator gar, which may reach 10 feet in length and a weight of over 300 pounds. Johnnie M. Gray fishes for them in the White River, in Arkansas, and has caught them up to 230 pounds. He uses a salt-water rod and star-drag reel filled with 70- or 80-pound-test line. He also uses a 4-foot wire leader and attaches a husky, 6/0 treble hook on the end. Above the hook, he adds a 2- to 4-pound sinker. Then he baits the hook with a piece of fish such as the buffalo.

Johnnie gets the bait out to the middle of the river and lets it sink to the bottom, then puts his rod in a forked stick on shore. He leaves the click on so that he can hear a bite. He also ties a piece of tissue paper on the line about two feet from the rod tip to indicate when he has a bite. Then he sits and waits for a gar to pick up his bait—which could take a long time. When he does get a bite he lets the fish run with the bait awhile before trying to set the hook.

After the fish is hooked, his friend comes up to him with a boat and Johnnie gets in to fight the gar from the craft. A fight with a big gar may take an hour or more before it is brought close to the boat. Then it's a good idea to weaken or kill the fish with an ax, bow and arrow, or a revolver or rifle.

John T. Bickmore was fishing for other fish when the big alligator gar moved into Thompson's Bayou, on Florida's Escambia River. He got mad and decided to catch some of the monsters, using his salt-water rod and reel and 60-pound-test line to do battle with them. He fashioned a wire loop about a foot in diameter and suspended a mullet head in the center of this loop. About 4 feet above the loop and bait, he added a float and let this out in the river in a spot where he could see the alligator gar just below the surface or where they were disturbing the water. When an alligator gar grabbed the bait, John let him run with it for 20 or 30 yards. Then he came back hard with the snare to tighten the loop around the gar's upper jaw and the fight was on.

Johnnie Fox caught these two alligator gar, weighing 170 and 120 pounds, in an Arkansas river. Note the heavy, salt-water-type tackle used. They grow even bigger, up to 300 pounds or more and 9 feet in length! (*Arkansas Publicity and Parks Commission photo*)

There are many anglers who enjoy fishing for carp and have a lot of fun and sport at it. One such angler is Russell Tinsley, who uses light spinning tackle and a bottom rig with a sliding sinker and a small treble hook on the end. A bead or swivel on the line keeps the sinker from sliding down to the hook. Russ uses dough balls and canned-corn kernels for bait. He will often bait or chum an area he will be fishing by scattering cottonseed cake or meal over the area. Or he puts the cake or meal into a mesh bag and anchors it on the bottom.

When he uses a dough ball, he molds it around a treble hook to form a pear-shaped bait. With corn kernels, he uses a No. 4 or 5 single hook and strings several kernels on the hook point, bend, and shank—like beads on a necklace.

Russ finds that carp are slow about taking a bait. In order for them to do so, the bait must lie quietly on the bottom. When a carp starts to nibble Russ lets him play with the bait until he finally takes it for good and starts moving away with it. Then he sets the hook.

Russ Tinsley holds a big carp caught on light spinning tackle. More and more anglers are discovering that these fish provide great sport and are often a challenge to catch. (*Russ Tinsley photo*)

Charles S. Keefer, who fishes the upper Potomac River for carp, locates them by looking for mud streaks these fish make while rooting for food on the bottom. When he locates such a streak or patch of mud, he anchors his boat quietly 30 feet upstream and casts his bait toward the edge of the discolored water.

Alain Wood-Prince uses ulra-light spinning tackle for carp, stalks them in shallow water and casts to individual fish. He finds this fishing best in Illinois in May, June, and early July. That is when the carp root, feed, and spawn in the shallow water close to shore. By crouching and stalking the fish in the muddy water he can often approach very close to the fish and lob his bait right in front of a carp's nose; it is usually taken soon after. For bait Alain uses worms or dough balls made from bread.

Earl Pruden fished for carp in Paulins Kill Lake, in New Jersey, for many years and gained some valuable information about taking these often wary and slow-biting fish. In fact, he keeps detailed records of his carp catches, noting the size of the fish, weather, date, spot, time when hooked, and other vital information. He has found that carp fishing is best at night, especially during the hot summer months. But he doesn't use any light on the water, which would frighten the fish.

Unlike most carp fishermen, who fish from shore, Earl fishes from a boat carefully anchored, over the best spots, with two anchors. Before fishing he usually scatters some chum such as canned-corn kernels or dough balls. He uses short fly rods and fly reels filled with 6-pound-test monofilament. He may fish with as many as six fly rods at the same time. On the end of his line he uses two No. 6 bait-holder hooks spaced about 15 inches apart.

Earl uses dough balls for bait, which he makes with one cup of yellow cornmeal, half a cup of water, one cup of ground white cornmeal, two thirds of a small can of creamed corn, one teaspoon of instant coffee, and one third of a cup of sugar. He brings the water to a boil and then adds the other ingredients and keeps stirring them over a low heat until the consistency is right.

After baiting his hooks with the dough balls, Earl takes his fly rods and strips line from the reels onto the deck of the boat, then flings the baits out into the water in various directions and at various distances until all six lines are in the water. Then he sits and waits quietly for a bite. He leaves the click on his reel on and when he hears a carp moving off with the bait he sets the hook.

Although most anglers use dough balls and other baits for carp, Jim Rutherford has found that there are times when you can catch them with a fly rod and lure. When insects such as cicadas or locusts are falling on the water, carp feed on them and hit a bass bug. He ties his own deer-hair bugs on No. 4 hooks to resemble the locusts.

According to Jim the best fishing takes place from a boat. He recommends that you look for carp cruising just below the surface and taking the insects on top. Then you cast your bug in front of the fish and wait until the carp gets interested in the offering. For best results, he finds, you shouldn't activate the bug but let it lie still. When a carp grabs the bait, wait a second or two, until the fish gets it in its mouth, before trying to set the hook.

Herman Daley, of Frederick, Maryland, was catching more carp than anyone else, so Lefty Kreh asked him what his secret was. He told Lefty to mix some strawberry gelatin in with the dough when making dough balls. Lefty tried it and caught a 34-pound carp in the Potomac River on the bait. He found that the strawberry gelatin, when cool, makes the dough more gummy and soft, but tough. And it gives off a scent that attracts carp.

Daley's formula is to mix a cup of flour with two cups of cornmeal in a bag or other container but leave it dry. Then bring a pint of water to a boil over a stove and turn the heat low so that it just simmers. Now add a tablespoon of vanilla, two tablespoons of sugar, and a small package of strawberry gelatin to the water and stir these constantly. Ladle the dry flour-and-cornmeal mix on the surface of this water until it is covered. When the bubbles come through, cover the spot with more mix. When other bubbles appear, cover them, too, until all the mix is used up. Now stir everything for two minutes. The bait is now ready; when it cools, remove it from the pan and roll it into a ball. It can be stored in a refrigerator until used.

Fishing for shad has become very popular in the rivers along the Atlantic coast, and also along the Pacific coast, where this fish was introduced many years ago. James Douglas has fished for these shad in many waters, and he likes the combination spoon-and-jig rig. In clear water he uses a white jig with a silver spoon and a white feather. In murky waters he uses a yellow jig with a gold spoon and a yellow feather. He attaches a ⅛- to ½-ounce keel sinker between his line and the rig.

Jim trolls only to locate the shad. After he catches one or sees a school, he beaches or anchors the boat and casts in the area. In shallow water he'll often get out of the boat and wade in the water to fish. When he sees shad surfacing, he may change to a fly rod and use a yellow bivisible fly on a No. 8 hook. He also uses wet flies tied in gaudy colŏrs on No. 6 hooks.

But, most of the time, the shad are found on the bottom, so Jim reels the spoon-and-jig rig slowly and bounces bottom every so often. Casting with a light spinning outfit and 6- or 8-pound-test line gives you the feel of a fish's gentle strike and you can play a hooked fish without losing too many.

Don Jay uses fly rods and spinning rods for shad too, and he advises experimenting at various depths until you find the one the fish are hitting at in the waters you are fishing. Don finds that shad feed most actively when the water temperature is around 50 degrees. So

He's netting a shad from the Delaware River on the New Jersey side. When these fish run, during the spring months, they provide great sport on light tackle. (*Harry Grosch photo*)

he advises bringing a thermometer along and taking a reading when looking for shad. He also finds that the best shad fishing is below dams and falls, where the fish congregate in large numbers.

Larry Green fishes for shad in such California rivers as the Yuba,

Trinity, Feather, Sacramento, and Russian, in the northern part of the state. He prefers to catch them with a fly rod with shooting head sinking lines and 20-pound-test monofilament backing on his reel. He uses weighted shad flies, sizes No. 2 to 8. One of his favorites has a silver tinsel body with sparse white hackle, a red chenille collar, and a pair of bead-chain eyes.

Larry tries to get the fly down near the bottom, and while shad will often hit the fly while it is drifting dead, he also retrieves it in short jerks. He finds that the shad are apt to hit anytime during the day, but he has one trick up his sleeve when fishing is slow. He takes one of the shad he has already caught up to the fast water above the pool he is fishing. Then, standing out in the water, he scales the shad so that the tiny, silvery scales float downstream. This often excites the shad and they start hitting again.

Francis H. Ames fished for shad in many Oregon rivers; he trolled a lure from a boat, or he anchored in a line of boats. When anchored he used a sinker just heavy enough to hold bottom but light enough to "walk" downstream when he lifted the rod. About a foot above the sinker he tied a short leader and the lure, usually a tiny spoon or a spinner. The lure is light enough so that it is activated by the current.

Ted Hensen knows he can catch shad in Florida's St. Johns River by trolling small silver spoons or shad darts, as most anglers do. But he prefers to catch the shad by casting small yellow jigs into holes and along undercut banks where shad stop to rest. He casts the jig out and lets it sink to the bottom. Then he takes up the slack, twitches his rod tip to lift the jig off the sand and lets it drop back to the bottom again. This up-and-down movement is repeated until he gets a hit.

John Culler fishes Georgia's Ogeechee River, and he catches some big shad when they run there, in March and April. He likes this river because it is still clean and not too crowded with other fishermen. About thirty miles of the river can be fished, between Richmond Hill and Blitchton. He trolls along the shore of the river with the lure traveling just above the grass on the bottom. He uses tiny spoons with yellow or white bucktail hair but finds that spinners and jigs also work. All these lures can be cast instead of trolled if desired.

Pete Elkins fishes for hickory shad in such rivers as the Mattaponi, in Virginia. These relatives of the white shad run here in April and

Hickory-shad rig

into May and provide top sport on light tackle. Pete locates the hickory shad by making up a trolling rig with a ⅛-ounce keel sinker about 4 feet above a tiny silver spoon, size No. 0 or No. 1. He trolls with this until he gets hits or catches a shad. Then he stops, either anchors the boat or lets it drift, and casts with a double-lure rig. Then he attaches a tiny spoon on the end of the line and adds a shad dart on a short dropper about 2 feet in front of it.

When trolling, Pete finds that a low speed against the tide or current is best. He finds that the hickory shad swim deep and a light sinker may be needed to keep the lures down. He also uses a light, 4- or 6-pound-test line, which brings more hits than a heavier line. When casting the lures, he casts upstream or upcurrent, lets them drift deep and then reels them back slowly.

Jack Randolph also fishes for hickory shad in the rivers of Virginia, and he feels that this great fishing is neglected or overlooked by many other anglers. Jack uses an ultra-light spinning outfit and 3- or 4-pound-test line. He ties either a single or a double shad dart on the end of his line. He likes the ¼-ounce size, with white, yellow, and orange the favored colors. Those painted with fluorescent paint are usually most effective.

Jack casts his dart or darts across and downstream, or he casts across and upstream. Then he retrieves them very slowly, with occasional twitches. He finds that most strikes occur when the line begins to straighten and the dart starts to rise.

C. Boyd Pfeiffer fishes for hickory shad in Maryland, and he uses a light 7½- or 8-foot fly rod and shad flies. Boyd has found that hickory shad are apt to lie at the tail end of a pool, and this is where he wades and casts across and downstream. As the fly completes its swing in the current he gives it a few twitches and lets it hang there for a while. Then he retrieves it, with some rod action all the way in. He has had his best fishing at daybreak and at dusk.

Hickory shad, like this one, are scrappy fighters on light spinning tackle or fly rods. They'll hit small spoons, shad darts, spinners, and flies. (*North Carolina Department of Conservation and Development photo*)

Some anglers like to fish for whitefish, and one of these men is Jack Parry, who has sought them for many years in Minnesota and Canada. He looks for whitefish near shore when they are feeding on hatches of flies. Then they dimple the water and will rise to an artificial fly. He uses a small black, brown, or tan dry fly tied on a No. 14, 16, or 18 hook. He finds that the fish are usually found rising where the fast water meets the slow-moving water, so he casts upstream and lets the fly drift with the current. He also finds that you have to set the hook lightly when a whitefish rises or you'll rip the hook out of its tender mouth. The same is true when the fish runs —Jack lets it take line with very little pressure being applied.

Ted Trueblood fishes for whitefish in our western rivers, and he finds that early in the spring, soon after the ice breaks up, they bite best on natural stone-fly nymphs. He puts one of these on a No. 10 or 12 hook and uses it on a drifting rig with a pencil sinker. He uses a fly rod with an enclosed spinning reel and 5-pound-test line on it.

Ted casts out and lets the rig and nymph sink to the bottom and move along with the current. To do this properly he reels in all the slack line and follows the drift downstream with his rod tip. He keeps taking in line or letting it out to keep the sinker bouncing along the bottom at all times.

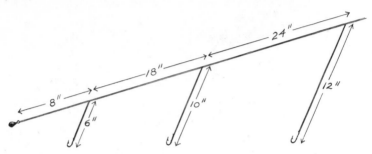

Sucker rig used by Ray Beck

Some anglers may look down their noses on sucker fishing, but not Ray Beck. He enjoys fishing for them and says that they are not always easy to catch and can provide top sport on light tackle. He uses worms for bait and finds that you should cover the hook point completely with the bait. Otherwise the sucker will feel the point in its mouth and expel the worm. He fishes the worms on a three-hook rig spread out 4 feet above the sinker. The first hook, on a 6-inch snell, is tied 8 inches above the sinker. The second hook, on a 10-inch snell, is tied 18 inches above the first hook. And the third hook, on a 12-inch snell, is tied about 2 feet above the second hook.

Ray casts this rig out from the bank and tightens the line when the bait reaches and lies on the bottom. He fishes mostly in the spring and early summer, especially after a warm rain. That is when the suckers are apt to bite best. And instead of casting into the deep pools or holes, he finds suckers bite better in water 5 feet deep close to shore where a steep underwater slope levels off at the bottom.

13

STRIPED BASS

There are more experts and specialists fishing for striped bass than for any other single fish found in salt water. These men spend hours, days, weeks, months, and even years casting, trolling, live-lining, bottom fishing, and surf fishing for the highly prized striper. They are always developing new lures, finding new baits, and perfecting techniques that will catch more and bigger striped bass. Today you'll find thousands of such skilled anglers fishing for striped bass in the ocean, surf, bays, tidal rivers, and even fresh waters where these fish are naturally present or have been stocked.

One of our earlier striper specialists was Charles B. Church, who caught a 73-pound bass back on August 17, 1913. In twenty-eight years of fishing around Cuttyhunk Island, Massachusetts, he caught many big stripers, and most of them were taken on live eels. He carried a bait can of live eels in his small boat, which was rowed by his brother-in-law or another angler. He would hook an eel through the lips and cast it into likely spots near shore and then reel it back just fast enough to keep it from getting into the rocks. When he got a strike he didn't try to set the hook immediately but let the line go slack so that the fish could mouth and swallow the bait.

Charlie Church died in 1932, and his method of fishing with live eels was all but forgotten. Then it was revived, about twenty-five years ago, by Captain Dick Lema, who ran a bass boat and a charter boat out of Galilee, Rhode Island. He started using live eels on his bass boat during night trips. In one season, anglers who chartered his boat caught a total of 731 striped bass. The average weight of the fish caught was 38 pounds, and there were twenty-three stripers going 50 pounds or more!

Dick Lema knew almost every rock, reef, hole, and other striper hangout along the rocky Rhode Island coast, and especially favored the waters off Charlestown Breachway and Beach, along the south shore of the state. He would drift or anchor over the spot to be fished and the anglers in his boat would cast out their eels and let them head for the bottom. But if the eel reached the kelp or rocks, Dick advised lifting the rod tip slowly to free the eel. When drifting or anchoring didn't pay off, Dick would often troll the live eel slowly near the bottom, using lead-core or weighted lines.

Another striped-bass fishing guide who favors live eels is Captain Alan Anderson, who also gets a lot of big striped bass for his clients in Rhode Island waters. He uses husky spinning rods and big surf spinning reels loaded with 20- to 30-pound-test monofilament line. In front of the line he ties a 2-foot leader testing 40 to 60 pounds. He recommends a hook no larger than a 6/0 Eagle Claw or O'Shaughnessy; make sure it's needle-sharp.

Anderson drifts off the rocky shores or sandy beaches in depths from 10 to 30 feet, swimming the eel close to the bottom. He advises keeping just enough tension on the line so that you can feel the eel swimming. Too much slack will enable the eel to dive into the kelp or rocks and hang you up. When a bass grabs an eel and moves off with it, he lets it take about 15 to 20 feet of line, then waits until the line tightens, and sets the hook.

Frank Daignault also uses live eels, and he often fishes with them from shore or the beaches. He likes a 9/0 Eagle Claw hook on a 50-pound-test mono leader with a barrel swivel on the other end. The eel is hooked by running the point of the hook an inch into the mouth and out on the underside. Frank likes eels from 14 to 18 inches long for casting from shore. He casts his eel out and lets it go down to the bottom, then reels in slowly. When a bass grabs his eel, he counts to ten before setting the hook. Frank finds his best fishing on nights when the surf is rough, and he keeps reeling in his slack line with each wave to maintain contact with the eel bait.

Jack Meehl also uses live eels from Rhode Island's breakwaters or jetties; he lets the eel out in the current on an outgoing tide in an inlet or river mouth, thumbing the line lightly. When the line stops vibrating or starts to move out faster, he gets ready to set the hook.

John Kardys, of Cromwell, Connecticut, likes to use small, shoe-string eel from 6 to 8 inches long in the bays and inlets and when fishing under bridges for small and medium-sized stripers. He hooks

Frank Daignault drags a striper caught in the surf at night with a live eel. Some of the biggest striped bass are caught on live eels from beaches, rocky shores, jetties, and boats. (*Frank Daignault photo*)

an eel through the jaws or eyes and casts it out and reels in slowly. He also fishes with live eels on the bottom, using a fish-finder or a sliding sinker rig. He hooks the eel through the tail, because this makes the eel swim away from the rig and there is less chance of tangling around the line or leader.

Milt Rosko, who wrote the book *Secrets of Striped Bass Fishing,* does a lot of fishing for these fish from his favorite rock jetties along the New Jersey coast. He uses mostly spinning tackle, with light outfits favored for small and medium-sized fish and heavier rods and reel with 20-pound-test line for the cow bass. He also believes in using big lures for big stripers, and one of his favorite jetty lures for lunkers at night is a rigged eel with a small metal squid head. He rigs the 12-to-15-inch eel on this action head and reels it slowly, speeding up at times and trying various depths.

Milt also uses big swimming-type plugs, which move on top, and he finds these especially effective on calm nights. He works the plug slowly at night, feeling it wiggle and speeding up as a wave pushes it forward, slowing down when the backwash pulls on it. In a strong rip or current, he may barely move the plug, letting the tide give it action.

Milt works a jetty by covering it completely on both sides and at the extreme end. He starts near the beach on one side and makes a few casts, then moves toward the end about ten feet and casts again and so on, until he reaches the end. Then he fans the water in front of the jetty in an arc and starts working his way back on the other side of the rock pile until he is back on shore. When he stops to cast in a spot, he casts at various angles so that he covers most of the water around the jetty.

Clair Paul, of Massapequa, Long Island, New York, is extremely successful when fishing for striped bass with clam chum and bait. His technique is to squash the clam bellies into the water to let the juice form a slick in the tide. Then he tosses the rest of the clam into the water, baits a hook with two clam bellies and a piece of the hard section of the clam on the point and barb and lets it drift out in the current. Or he cuts or grinds the clams up into tiny pieces and throws these overboard every minute or so. Then he baits a hook with a piece of the hard part of the clam and lets it drift out in the chum slick.

Clair finds that the tide is very important in this clam chumming and fishing. Usually, one and a half hours before and one and a half hours after either high or low water is the best time to chum and fish. And, of course, you have to fish the holes, channels, drop-offs, and other spots where stripers feed and lie. He has his best fishing around bridges in inlets and bays.

Frank Woolner, editor of *Salt Water Sportsman* magazine, fishes for striped bass along Cape Cod in the ocean between Provincetown and North Truro. Big stripers often move in there during August and feed along the outer bars and in the sloughs. Frank launches a cartop aluminum boat in the surf and heads out to those spots. He uses

Frank Woolner holds a surf-caught 49½-pound striped bass. He also catches them from a small boat launched in the surf with live mackerel for bait. (*Frank Woolner photo*)

surface and underwater plugs, plastic eels, rigged eels, and other striped-bass lures, but he finds that you can't beat a whole live mackerel for the big cow stripers during the summer and early fall.

Frank likes to use a conventional outfit with a revolving-spool reel filled with 30-pound-test mono line for this fishing. But the rods he uses have extra-large ring guides to enable the algae, which are often present in the water, from clogging the ring guides and stopping the line when it is being reeled in. He hooks a mackerel about a foot long with an 8/0 hook through the back just ahead of the dorsal fin. On the other rod he will often hook a dead mackerel and lower this to various depths or even let it lie on the bottom. The live mackerel is allowed to swim around freely. When a bass grabs the bait, Frank lets it swim off about 50 to 100 feet. Then the bass will usually stop to swallow the fish. When it moves off again he sets the hook.

Ted Keatley has caught a lot of his stripers by trolling a Turkey Bone lure in western Long Island Sound. This is a white plastic tube about 3 inches long with two 6/0 hooks behind the tube. He puts two or three sandworms on the hook and trolls the lure and bait about 50 feet behind his boat at night. He trolls close to shore in shallow water, just fast enough to keep from hanging up on the bottom.

Bob Pond has designed many popular and effective striped-bass plugs, such as the Striper Atom and Striper Swiper, and has spent a lifetime using these lures from Maine to the Carolinas. Bob emphasizes the importance of bait in the water. He looks for mullet, herring, menhaden, silversides, sand eels, and mackerel, and finds stripers feeding on them sooner or later. He uses popping plugs in the daytime and swimming plugs at night and finds that the popping plugs work best when there is a ripple on the surface, while swimming plugs are most effective in a tidal rip over a reef or bar. Bob likes to use plugs for striped bass during the last of the outgoing tide and the first of the incoming tide. He feels that at this time both the fish and the bait are concentrated and easy to locate.

Stan Gibbs also makes fishing plugs and often tests and uses them along the Atlantic coast. When using popping plugs, he recommends reeling in and jerking the rod at the same time. Then you should stop, let the lure drift back a bit, and start popping it again. Stan suggests reeling slowly, then speeding up. Other times, the plug should be worked more gently so that it doesn't cause too big a commotion.

With swimming plugs, Stan casts across the current and reels them in slowly, especially if the tide is strong. When the tide is slow, he speeds up the reeling. He also pops it every so often so that it makes a splash.

With darting-type plugs Stan reels in slowly with short, strong jerks, creating an erratic action. Then he stops reeling, jerks the plug a few more times, reels in a few feet, jerks again, and so on. He feels that the more varied the action of the plug, the better. At night he works a darter more slowly; working it on top just enough to create ripples or a wake is sufficient to bring strikes. In fact Stan advises working all lures more slowly at night than in the daytime.

Walter K. Grossman is a real pro at fishing for striped bass around the bridges along the South Shore of Long Island, New York, in the bays, creeks, and inlets. And he has caught plenty of stripers, up to 50 pounds, in these waters. To stop and turn and hold a good-sized striper, he uses a stiff 7-foot rod with a conventional surf reel filled with 40- or 45-pound-test line. For lures he likes a white bucktail jig weighing 1½ ounces, with a strong 6/0 hook. Or he might use an eelskin jig or underwater plugs at times. But one of his favorite lures is a plastic eel tail with a jig head.

Eel jig

Grossman finds that the best spot to catch striped bass under a bridge is just inside the shadow line. The bass lie in the shadow close to the edge and wait for baitfish, crabs, shrimp, or other food to be swept by the tide into the dark area where the bass grab it. Grossman tries to cast about 10 to 15 feet above the shadow line and lets his lure be swept into the dark area. He finds that the best fishing usually takes place during the last half of the outgoing tide, and he does most of his fishing at night from about 1 A.M. to daybreak.

Jack Fallon finds that drifting with a seaworm can be a deadly method of catching striped bass, especially in New England waters, where he does most of his fishing. He does this drifting in tidal creeks, rivers, and bays along drop-offs, meadow banks and sand and rock bars, and over submerged rocks and deep holes. He hooks his worm on a 4/0 bait-holder Eagle Claw hook about a third of the way down the worm's body. Jack adds or removes split-shot sinkers on the leader above the hook, depending on the strength of the tide and the depth he wants to fish. As he drifts, he raises and lowers his rod slowly every minute or so to fish various levels and give the worm added movement.

Captain Don Zboyan fishes for striped bass off Sandy Hook and other sections of the New Jersey coast. He sails out of the Atlantic Highlands marina in May, June, and early July, when big stripers are feeding in those waters. He finds that live bunkers, which he obtains from commercial fish-trap operators or snags himself and keeps alive in water-circulating plastic cans, are a top bait then. He hooks a live bunker with a 2/0 or 3/0 treble hook by running one point and barb through the roof of the bunker's mouth and out on top.

Don usually adds a 2-ounce drail weight between his leader and line to take the bunker down in the strong tide. It is important that the bunker swim close to the bottom. He lets out about 100 feet of line and puts the reel in free spool with the click on. If a striper picks up the bunker, he lets it swim off with anywhere from 100 to 200 feet of line before trying to set the hook.

Nick Karas, who wrote *The Complete Book of the Striped Bass,* also uses bunkers, but his are often dead. He hooks the bunker through the eyes with a 5/0 or 6/0 hook and then runs close to the beach or a jetty and drops the bunker into the water. Then he puts his reel into free spool and lets all his line come off the reel while he runs the boat out into deeper water. Next he stops the boat and slowly reels in the bunker along the bottom until it is all the way in. He keeps repeating this in various spots until he gets fish.

Al Reinfelder, who together with his partner Lou Palma created the deadly "Alou" plastic eel, was also one of the top striper anglers along the Atlantic coast. The plastic eel comes in various colors, weights, and lengths from 8 to 14 inches for small and big stripers. Al recommended using the eel in several ways: The basic action was a slow, snakelike movement like that of the naturally swimming eel. You reel at the lowest speed to bring out this action. Other times, he suggested you try speeding up your reeling so the eel moves faster. This is especially true when the tide is slack or when you're reeling with the current. To give the eel an erratic movement, you can raise your rod every few seconds. And when using the eel in a strong rip tide, Al suggested reeling in very slowly or even no reeling at all, just let the flow of water activate the eel.

When fishing in the surf, Al would speed up the reeling when a wave brought the eel in and then slow it down when the backwash pulled on the eel. In other words, he tried to maintain a constant "feel" of the lure working.

When trolling an "Alou" eel, Al ran the boat just fast enough to bring out the action of the lure and would try the eel alongside the boat before letting it out. He trolled eels on monofilament lines when fishing in water from 10 to 20 feet deep. In deeper water he used lead-core or wire lines. While trolling he would slowly raise the rod and then slowly drop it back at regular intervals.

Al Reinfelder also developed the Bait Tail, which has a jig head and a plastic tail, and he claimed it was an extremely versatile lure for many fishing situations, especially when used for striped bass. He would reel it just fast enough to keep it above the bottom. Or he would keep it above the bottom and jig it with his rod. Or he would bounce it along the bottom. When bass were on top, he would reel it fast with sweeps of the rod tip to make it rise and sink.

Spider Andresen, who fishes for striped bass in New England, especially on Cape Cod and around the islands off Massachusetts, has a couple of tricks up his sleeve when stripers are playing hard to get. He takes a whole bunker and cuts off the back and backbone. Then he hooks it through the upper lip with a treble or single hook. He casts this out where he sees stripers chasing bunker and lets it sink several feet. If a bass hasn't grabbed it by then, he lifts his rod, then lowers it again to let the bunker sink once more, and keeps doing this a few times.

When Spider trolls for striped bass with a surgical tube he adds one or two sea worms to the hook. Then he trolls the lure very slowly on a wire line. To hook more fish on this tube-worm combination, he advises letting a striper nibble on the worm a few seconds before trying to set the hook.

Captain Joe Renzo sails out of the Highlands, in New Jersey, and many striped bass are caught from his boat. One of his favorite lures is a surgical or plastic tube from 15 to 18 inches long. This is usually rigged with two hooks and has one or two curves in the tube to give it the best action. Joe will experiment with tubes of various sizes and colors, and at various depths and trolling speeds, to find out what the stripers want. As a general rule, the tube lures work best at low speeds while traveling close to the bottom. This usually means trolling them with wire line or trolling weights or both.

Al Urban owns and operates the bass boat called *Duke,* at Montauk Point, New York, and he takes parties out to fish from it. His method is to move in close to the rocks or beach, usually along the South Shore near the Point, and cast toward likely spots. He fishes the so-called "middle grounds," between the breaking surf and the rips in deeper water. There the depth usually varies from 5 to 15 feet and there are sand bars, rock bars, reefs, boulders, mussel beds, depressions, and strong tides where baitfish get trapped and tossed around and stripers move in to feed.

Al's favorite lure is a big swimming plug such as the Striper Atom, which he reels in slowly so it travels on top, creating a wake or a ripple. Every so often he may pop it or pause in the reeling or try an erratic action. Al likes to use this plug in the late afternoon and evening until dark. If he stays after dark, he will cast a rigged eel or plastic eel. Or he will try trolling the eels or other underwater lures.

Al Urban scans the South Shore of Montauk Point, New York, for spots where he can cast that big surface-swimmer plug to catch striped bass.

Captain Ronnie Leper, who owns and runs the bass boat *Kim* out of Atlantic Beach, New York, catches a lot of big stripers for those who charter his boat and services. He uses all kinds of lures and baits, depending on the time of year and the kind of baitfish in the water. In the spring and fall, when stripers are feeding on menhaden (bunker) or other good-sized fish, he uses the big "bunker" spoon, especially in the daytime.

Ronnie uses a spoon with a weighted keel in front and a 6/0 treble hook attached to the big single hook in the spoon. He finds that spoons painted white are the most consistent producers. The best action in a bunker spoon, according to him, is a snappy side-to-side wobbling movement but without spinning. He holds the spoon in the water alongside the boat and makes sure the action is right before letting it out. Once he has the spoon all the way out and working at the right depth, he watches his rod tip all the time and can usually tell by its action whether the spoon is working properly. He likes soft-action trolling rods and reels filled with 300 feet of Monel wire line for the bunker-spoon trolling. Captain Ronnie Leper feels that the average angler would catch more stripers if he had more time to fish and was patient. He feels that many anglers leave before the tide is right or the bait moves in or the fish start hitting.

When George Heinold fishes sandy beaches for striped bass, he looks for the obvious signs such as birds working, fish breaking, bait leaping, or other surf anglers catching fish. But when these are lacking he also looks for sand bars, sloughs, holes, drop-offs, and rips, and that is where he casts his lure or bait. He also finds good striper fishing at the mouths of inlets or rivers emptying into the ocean.

Charles R. Meyer, like most striped-bass fishermen, finds that these fish can be hard to fool and hook when phosphorescence lights up in the water and glows around his lure, line, and the wake of the boat. At such times stripers tend to shy away from lures and baits and do not hit at all or only halfheartedly. He offers some good tips to overcome this handicap. First, he recommends that you reel as slowly as possible. Swimming plugs are better than poppers for this. Rigged eels and plastic eels that glide silently through the water are better than other underwater lures, which have too much action. Live eels or natural baits are even better for this fishing. He also recommends fishing in the daytime or just before dusk or after daybreak. If

George Heinold holds a nice striper caught on light spinning tackle. George has caught many stripers during a lifetime of fishing along the Atlantic and Pacific coasts. (*George Heinold photo*)

you must fish at night, he says, you should choose a bright one, when the moon is shining, since the phosphorescence is less noticeable then.

Dick Mermon trolls sandworms and bloodworms in Long Island Sound, New York, for striped bass and finds them particularly effective in the shallow water along rocky shores. Although he trolls the worms at times with spinners such as the June Bug and the Willow Leaf, he finds that the plain worm is usually best for this fishing. He hooks the worm by running the point into the worm's mouth and then out about ¼ inch below the jaws. If a second hook is used, it impales the worm's tail. The worm is trolled slowly anywhere from 30 to 100 feet behind the boat without any weight.

One of the most successful striped-bass anglers in Maine is Bob Boilard, of Biddeford, who has fished the Saco River for many years and averaged twenty-two fish per trip! Trolling from a boat is Bob's

Sandworm on two-hook rig

favorite and most productive method. For this he uses light 7- or
7½-foot popping-type rods with level-wind salt-water reels holding
20-pound-test line. For lures he favors a 7-inch plastic eel or worm
such as Burke's Jig-A-Do. Although the plain, unadorned lure will
take stripers, Bob likes to sweeten it by adding a 3- to 4-inch section
of sea worm to the tail hook.

Bob trolls these lures with two rods at the same time—one heavy
lure, which rides deep, near the bottom, on a long line, and the
other, somewhat lighter lure, on a shorter line, which travels about
mid depth. He often gets two fish at the same time when passing over
a hot spot. And there are plenty of such hot spots along the irregular
bottom and holes and off the points of the short stretch of the Saco
River from Biddeford to where it empties into the sea.

In recent years Bob Boilard has been fishing in Saco Bay and the
ocean with live mackerel anywhere from one hundred to one thousand yards off the rocky shoreline. Here he usually anchors in water
12 to 15 feet deep and lets out the live mackerel on a free line. Bob
has caught stripers up to 40 pounds or more, fishing in this manner

Captain Don Imbriaco, of the charter boat *Fiesta II,* sailing out of
Neptune, New Jersey, catches a lot of stripers every year, and he
favors bucktails or jigs for this fishing. He likes a stiff rod and hard
metal guides and roller tip-top. The reel is filled with 30- or 40-
pound-test line, and on the end he attaches 150 feet of 30- or 40-
pound-test wire line. Don uses white or yellow bucktails from 1 to 3
ounces in weight. He uses the lighter ones in shallow water and
the heavier ones in deeper water.

Don does most of his trolling close to shore over rocky bottoms in
the morning and toward evening. It is important to have the jig traveling close to the bottom. And jigging constantly, making sweeps
with the rod from the stern toward the bow at the rate of forty to
fifty strokes per minute, will result in the most strikes. You have to
establish a certain rhythm, Don says, and you also have to experi-

ment with the jigging motion, trying short strokes and long ones and combinations to see what the stripers want on a particular day.

Roy Seher uses a diamond jig for striped bass off Montauk Point in a strong rip known as the "Elbow." He uses a fairly stiff rod and a 3/0 reel filled with a 30-pound-test monofilament line and ties a 6-ounce diamond jig directly to the line. Then he moves very slowly in his boat along the edge of the rip and lets the jig out as quickly as possible so it heads for the bottom. When the jig hits bottom, he engages the reel and starts reeling in slowly for about twenty turns of the reel handle. If there is no hit or fish hooked, he reels in quickly and lets the jig go down to the bottom again and repeats the process. He finds that the diamond jig is most effective at Montauk in late May and early June and again in September, October, and November.

Jack "the Professor" Frech catches a lot of stripers in the waters around Long Island, New York. He makes many of his own plugs, and one of these is a light-weight popping plug, about 3 to 4 inches long, made from white pine. He adds two or three treble hooks to this but no extra weight, so that it will be buoyant and float high. Jack uses a light rod and 8-pound-test line to fish this plug and finds it most effective on quiet, calm nights. He reels it very slowly, making a couple of turns of the reel handle, stops the plug, then twitches or lifts the rod tip. After the plug pops, he lets it lie still for a while. Then he moves it slowly again. The strike usually comes at this time.

Copp McNulty, of Norwalk, Connecticut, fishes for striped bass with a fly rod on Long Island Sound. He uses the standard salt-water flies such as the poppers, streamers, bucktails, Honey Blondes, shrimp flies, hair bugs, and Lefty's Deceiver. But he has also created his own flies for special conditions. One of these is the Worm Fly, which is used when stripers are feeding on cinder worms. This fly is tied with red, pink, or orange marabou feathers for daytime fishing. Another one of his creations is the Dark Night Fly, which is tied with brown and black marabou and black bucktail on a 3/0 keel hook. It is up to 8 or 9 inches long, and he uses it for night fishing near the bottom with a sinking line.

Like most expert striper fishermen, McNulty knows his waters and looks and fishes for stripers at various spots, according to the time of year. He also looks for birds working, fish breaking, and bait jumping. He does most of his fly fishing at daybreak or dusk in the summer and early fall. But in the spring and late fall he often finds good fishing even in the middle of the day.

Lou Tabory also uses a fly rod for striped bass, but he fishes for them in Great Bay, New Hampshire. There, even in July and August, he locates small schools of stripers feeding during various times of the day. When the sandworms are spawning, early in July, he uses a small pink or green bucktail on a No. 4 hook tied to look like one of the worms.

Art Hansen has fished the Cape Cod Canal, in Massachusetts, for several years and has caught many striped bass in the fast-flowing waters of the "Big Ditch," as it is often called. He particularly enjoys fishing there in late June, when big stripers do surface feeding and chase the whiting and squid. This "spot casting" requires dropping the plug close to a feeding bass and then working the surface plug so that the fish takes it. Art uses conventional surf tackle for this fishing and finds plugs such as the Gibbs Pencil Popper and the Reverse Atom best for this fishing. He casts the plug out and works it in a whipping action while reeling fairly slowly. Fishing in this manner, he has caught many big stripers in the 30- and 40-pound classes and even one going 50 pounds. Art finds that early-morning east tides are most favorable for this fishing.

Larry Green fishes for striped bass in many waters along the Pacific coast. He often casts plugs, metal squids, and Hopkins lures into the surf for the bass. But he finds that this fishing is usually limited to the "bass busts," when the stripers are actually feeding and chasing baitfish near or in the breakers.

Other times, Larry fishes from a boat and either casts or trolls for stripers. Casting plugs, metal lures, and jigs is often very effective when birds are working or fish are chasing bait in the early morning or late in the evening. Larry also trolls, often using a spreader rig, which has two arms. The longest, 6-foot leader usually has a plug or spoon, while the shorter, 3-foot leader holds a jig. Larry trolls in shallow water without any weight, but in deeper water he may add a cigar-shaped trolling weight in front of the wire spreader. He usually sets up a trolling pattern, moving back and forth or zigzagging until he has covered the best water.

When going after striped bass, Larry enjoys fishing with light spinning tackle or fly rods best. He does this fishing in San Francisco

Larry Green is shown fishing the Pacific surf for striped bass. He's using a long spinning rod, which is popular with surf anglers in that area. In recent years they have been catching more and more stripers on lures from the beaches in California. (*Larry Green photo*)

Bay in the spring and the fall and finds the fastest action when stripers are on the shallow flats chasing baitfish. He likes the last of the incoming tide in the late afternoon and evening. During the flurries when the stripers are feeding, Larry finds that the lure you use should match the baitfish closely in size and shape. So he picks a plug, spoon, jig, or fly that matches the baitfish. Most of the time you have to be very quiet and cast the lures so that they don't land with too big a splash. But there have been times when Larry deliberately splashed around in the water and found that stripers often moved in to investigate the commotion; he often got hits from those fish.

Denny Hannah runs a fishing camp at Lakeside, Oregon, and fishes for striped bass in the Coos Bay area. He especially favors the Umpqua River, which has good runs of stripers from May to October. In May and June he looks for striped bass feeding on top and finds that surface plugs can be effective then. Later on and when fishing at night during the summer months, he favors underwater plugs and lures. One of his most consistent fish getters is Burke's Jig-A-Do plastic eel in the 14-inch size. Denny looks for striped bass in the channels, along the ledges and gravel and sand bars, in holes, eddies, and tidal rips, and around underwater obstructions. At times, he also sees the bass themselves either swimming or feeding in shallow water close to shore, usually on an outgoing tide. Then he casts lures toward them.

Dick Wadsworth also fishes the Umpqua River, and he has caught stripers from 30 to 50 pounds on a fly rod! He fishes with his buddy Gary Dyer, who also uses a fly rod, and between them they have caught hundreds of striped bass in the Umpqua and Smith rivers and in nearby estuaries. Dick uses an 8½- or 9-foot fly rod that can handle a No. 10 or 11 line. He uses a high-density shooting-head line most of the time. Then he adds one hundred yards of 40-pound-test monofilament behind it, followed by two hundred yards of 18- to 27-pound-test braided Dacron as backing. He tapers his 8½- or 9-foot leaders from 40-pound- down to 15- or 10-pound-test and adds a 20-pound-test shock tippet on the end.

Dick uses divided-wing bucktail flies created by his partner, Gary Dyer. Colors may be white, red, or yellow in the back and white, yellow, blue or green in the tail. The bodies have silver or gold tinsel.

Wadsworth fishes hard up to eight and twelve hours a day for about three months, from May 1 to August 1, when stripers can be

Denny Hannah, fishing guide and striped-bass expert, gaffs a striper for Harold Folkert. They are fishing in the Umpqua River, in Oregon, using a plastic eel as a lure. (*Al Bonenko photo*)

Gary Dyer striper streamer

seen swimming or feeding in the Umpqua River. Then he casts the fly to them. But, most of the time, he casts the fly blind to spots where he knows big bass have been taken in the past. He finds that they move in with the tide during the last half of the incoming and the first half of the outgoing. He usually finds the stripers around the mouths of sloughs. Here there is usually a shallow delta, and the bass lie where the edge of the delta breaks off from the deep water of the main river. He also looks for big bass along the cliffs, rocks, and banks next to deep water. Then he shuts off the motor some distance from the spot and rows over quietly and either drifts or anchors while casting.

Russell Chatham also uses a fly rod for striped bass, but he catches them the hard way: right in the Pacific surf, where he fights the waves and has to make long casts to reach the fish. He uses a fly rod that can handle a No. 10 line, which may be a floating-, sinking-, or shooting-head. The shooting line is usually one hundred feet of soft 30-pound-test mono, backed with enough 30-pound-test Dacron to fill the big fly reel. He finds that the best flies for stripers range from 5 to 8 inches in length. In a rough surf he uses the larger flies, but in clear, calmer water he uses smaller flies. In murky water he finds that a black fly works best. He created such a fly, called the Black Phantom, which is usually tied about 3 or 4 inches in length. He feels that such a black fly is also more visible at various depths than light-colored or fluorescent flies.

Like most striper anglers, Chatham fishes various spots depending on the season, time of day, and the time of the tide. He generally chooses spots that have the strongest tides and rips at daybreak or dusk.

14

CHANNEL BASS AND
BLACK DRUM

The channel bass, like the striped bass, has many enthusiasts who would rather fish for the big red drum than for any other fish. But anglers seek these fish mostly along the shores of our Southern States, from Virginia to the Gulf of Mexico. There they are caught in the surf, inlets, bays or sounds, and lagoons, as well as in tidal rivers. The biggest channel bass are caught in Virginia and North Carolina, and this is where most of the "pros" and other regulars fish.

One of the old-timers who achieved a reputation for catching big channel bass was Captain Bernice R. Ballance, of Buxton, North Carolina. For many years he was in the U. S. Coast Guard, then he retired and acted as a channel-bass guide and continued fishing right into his eighties. He died in 1973 only a few days before his ninetieth birthday. During most of those years he fished for channel bass from the surf, one of his favorite spots being the Point, at Cape Hatteras. He caught thousands of them, including the 75½-pound channel bass that held the world's record for several years.

When asked which months he liked best for big channel bass in the surf, Captain Ballance replied, "Give me October and November for big drum. You can't beat the late fall for the big ones, although April and May are also good some years." And this is borne out by the fact that he caught his 75½-pounder on November 29, 1941.

Although Captain Ballance caught his big channel bass on a metal squid, he usually fished with fresh or salted mullet on a bottom rig. He fished the sloughs (troughs) at the half tides and low water, and the sand bars at high tide. He found that the fishing was best early in the morning, in the evening, and at night, especially just before and after the full moon.

When it comes to choosing a present-day channel-bass angler, I would say that Claude Rogers, of Virginia, is one of the best. He is director of the Salt-water Fishing Tournament there and has caught many big channel bass both in the surf and from boats. He has also helped to develop rods, lures, rigs, and baits to catch these fish. Claude fishes from the surf along the beaches of Virginia's barrier islands, which have to be reached by a small boat. This surf fishing is best during the spring and fall months.

Head of a spot hooked for channel bass

Claude likes to use conventional surf rods and reels most of the time, and for bait he takes a small spot and cuts it in half diagonally. Then he runs a No. 8/0 or 9/0 Sealey Octopus hook through the nose of the bait. Claude claims that this bait lasts longer on the hook than a section of the softer flesh from a baitfish. And with the point and barb exposed it hooks a channel bass more readily.

When seeking channel bass in the surf, Claude looks for a good trough. This should have an entrance in the outer bar and should be deep even at low tide. He likes the outgoing tide for many of these sloughs, but others may be productive at the last of the incoming tide or at high tide.

Claude Rogers also helped to pioneer small-boat casting for channel bass in Magothy Bay, Virginia. There he wears Polaroid glasses and searches for the drum during the incoming and high tides. When the tide falls, he heads for the inlet and cruises off the beaches looking for the schools of channel bass. Claude has found that locating the channel bass can be easy on some days and difficult on other days. He finds that the sun helps greatly by shining on the water and

Claude Rogers is shown casting from a boat for channel bass in Magothy Bay, Virginia. Claude has caught hundreds of big channel bass from boats and the surf. (*Claude Rogers photo*)

revealing the presence of the fish. Channel bass are hard to spot on overcast or cloudy days. Likewise, finding them is easier when the water is calm and clear than when it is rough and murky.

Claude finds that the channel bass may appear as patches of white, gold, copper, bronze, or purple. Or the surface of the water may be slightly ruffled or rippled. These signs are all investigated, but Claude never gets too close to the fish. He stops within casting distance and then casts his metal lure toward them. He has found that for this casting the Hopkins lure with a big single hook is most effective.

Another angler who has spent a good part of his life seeking channel bass is Karl Osborne, of Vero Beach, Florida. He has fished for them from the surf and boats from Virginia to Florida and has caught them in all sizes from the "puppy" drum to the 50-pounders. At one time he found good fishing at Sebastian Inlet, in Florida, in August, September, and October, fishing at night from the first quarter to the third quarter of the moon. Then he found the last two hours of the incoming tide and the first three hours of the outgoing tide were best for this fishing. He cast from the jetties when there was a moon and from the beaches nearby with lures or bait. But this fishing has declined in recent years and Karl usually heads for Virginia or the Carolinas to do his channel-bass fishing.

Osborne likes Ocracoke Island, in North Carolina, and there he finds thirteen miles of beach he can work. He looks for the sloughs, with deep water close to the beach, that have a passage, or break, in the outer bar. Two good spots to fish there are North Point and South Point. He likes the outgoing tide and the early flood tide at South Point. At North Point he finds the period from two hours before high tide through the first two hours of the outgoing tide best. He likes to fish the hours just before and after sunset, and at full moon night fishing can be good. For best results the surf should be moderate and the water fairly clear. The best months for Ocracoke Island fishing are from early April to mid-May and during October and November. However, he finds that the spring run is more dependable than the fall run.

Karl Osborne also does a lot of fishing from boats, casting Hopkins lures at schools of channel bass he sights in bays, along grassy banks, in inlets, and along the beaches. He will also fish with mullet, menhaden, spot, or crab baits on a bottom rig in many of these spots.

Ken Lauer, fishing guide who operates out of Buxton, North Carolina, takes anglers out to fish for channel bass along the Outer Banks. In the early spring he starts fishing about a mile north of Ocracoke Inlet, at False Point, at Hatteras Inlet, and in the rip at Cape Hatteras Point. Then the channel bass spread out and are caught from many of the sloughs along the beaches. In the fall Ken starts looking for channel bass at Cape Point and the sand lumps just north of Hatteras Inlet. At this time he finds night fishing at full

Ken Lauer, fishing guide along North Carolina's Outer Banks, is shown fishing for channel bass. He fishes for them from April to December, but the spring and fall runs are the best. (*Nick Karas photo*)

moon very good. And he tries to avoid shining any lights into the water, because this tends to spook the red drum.

Ken advises using a light spinning outfit with 14- to 20-pound-test line when the surf is light and you can hold with 3 to 4 ounces of lead. In a rough surf and strong tides he likes a conventional surf outfit with 36-pound-test Dacron line. This will handle the 6- to 8-ounce sinkers and big baits needed for this fishing. He uses a modified fish-finder rig with hooks from 5/0 to 9/0 depending on the size of the fish running and the baits used. In the spring Ken uses squid or salt mullet for bait. In the fall he uses finger mullet, cut fresh mullet, or spot. He also uses metal lures such as Hopkins when channel bass can be seen feeding on top.

Ernest Hudson and the members of his fishing club discovered good fishing for channel bass in Pamlico County, North Carolina, where the Neuse and Pamlico rivers run into Pamlico Sound. Ernie runs a supermarket and tackle store in Cash Corner, but he fishes every chance he gets. He finds April and May the top months for this fishing and claims that it is best when the wind blows and the water gets rough and muddy. He likes to fish a shore where the wind is blowing from the water toward him. He also likes to use as many rods as possible, usually up to twenty heavy surf rods spread out with the lines and baits in the water. Naturally, he can't handle all these rods himself, so he usually invites other anglers to participate in the action.

Ernest Hudson finds that big chunks of natural squid make the best bait. He uses this bait on a regular surf bottom rig with a 7/0 hook on a 16- or 18-inch plastic-coated-cable leader and a 4-ounce pyramid sinker. He finds that the best fishing for channel bass usually takes place in the late afternoon. If the day is cloudy or overcast, however, he may fish earlier in the day. The channel bass he catches average about 40 pounds, and some run over 50 pounds.

Joel Arrington also fishes for channel bass in Pamlico Sound, but he does it from a boat and during the summer months. Up until recently, most of the fishing for big channel bass was done in the spring and fall. But when the big schools of red drum were discovered on the shoals in several places in Pamlico Sound, a whole new summer fishery was opened up for the red drum. A good way to locate these schools is to have a light plane fly around, and when it spots the fish it can direct the anglers on the boats to the area. Joel

Karl Osborne, left, and Ernest Hudson admire a channel bass caught from shore in Pamlico Sound, North Carolina. Both men are highly skilled channel-bass fishermen. (*Photo by Joel Arrington*)

Arrington finds that the channel bass will hit Hopkins lures or large Mirro-lures when they are cast into them.

Tommy Collonna, a fishing guide at Wachapreague, Virginia, often takes out parties in his boat to troll for the big channel bass found in his area. He uses big spoons and big jigs, lets them out on long lines and swings them toward a school of fish spotted on the surface. Or he trolls blind in an area where he feels they are present.

But when channel bass are reluctant to hit lures, Tommy tells his anglers to fish on the bottom with bait. Then he uses a fish-finder rig with a big, 8/0 or 9/0 hook baited with a peeler crab, squid, or fillets or chunks cut from such fish as mullet, spot, or whiting. To bring the channel bass near the boat, Tommy often chums with big clams, cracking them and throwing them overboard. He feels that the juices and meat will create a streak of scent and a slick that will attract the big red drum to the spot.

Vernon Stevens pioneered the catching of channel bass from the piers at Virginia Beach, and he uses regular long surf rods, big reels, and menhaden, mullet, or spot baits for them. He finds that the fishing is best in late September and October, during the northeast storms. And the best tides to fish are usually around high water and low water.

Bob Hutchinson does most of his channel-bass fishing from the beaches of Virginia and North Carolina, but he also fishes from the piers, especially those on Hatteras Island, North Carolina. He finds that the drum can be caught during the spring and fall runs but that the autumn months are most productive. The fishing usually starts in September after the first big storm and may continue into November.

Bob likes to use a sturdy, conventional surf outfit for the channel bass. He uses a fish-finder rig and a 60- to 80-pound-test monofilament leader to hold the big, 9/0 hook on the end. He prefers the mono over wire, because he doesn't want to waste time fighting a big shark. He'd rather have the shark bite through the leader, so that he can resume fishing for channel bass. He baits the hook with the head section of a spot or mullet. Bob finds that pier fishing is best for channel bass during the night, or early in the morning just before daybreak.

Tom Goodspeed likes whiting (called kingfish up North) and mullet for channel bass in the surf. But if he can't get these or runs

This world-record, 90-pound channel bass was caught by Elvin Hooper from the Hatteras Island Pier, at Rodanthe, North Carolina, in November. The fall months are usually best for the big red drum. (*Aycock Brown photo*)

out of bait he will use almost any piece of fish or whole small fish he has on hand. He once cut up a bluefish he caught, put some on a hook, and caught a 48-pound channel bass!

Hall Watters, who worked as a spotting pilot for a commercial fishing fleet seeking menhaden, was also an ardent channel-bass angler with rod and reel. He would strap his spinning rod and reel to his light plane and then fly along North Carolina's beaches. If he saw channel bass in the surf, and if the tide was low and he had room, he would land near by. Then he would grab his rod and start casting small plugs at the fish. He would often catch one or two before he had to go back and start spotting menhaden again for the fishing fleet.

Charlton Marshall fishes for channel bass near Crisfield, Maryland. There the channel bass show up, in the Chesapeake Bay backwaters and marshlands, from June to September. He finds that they will move in on a flood tide and feed on the flats and in the shallow water along the marsh banks of the shores and islands. Tangier Sound is especially good for this fishing. He finds that the fishing is usually best in the late afternoon and evening, especially around the time of the full moon. He uses a bottom rig with a 2- to 3-ounce sinker and a 6/0 or 7/0 hook baited with a peeler crab cut in half or in quarters.

Captain Sam Crayton fishes for channel bass from his boat, out of Georgetown, South Carolina. There he finds that the fishing for big channel bass is best in May and June and again in October. He catches smaller ones from April to November. During the fall months he can almost guarantee good fishing for these fish. The Winyah Bay entrance is one of his favorite spots for channel bass. He uses cut mullet for bait with bottom rigs and finds the incoming tide best. Weather doesn't influence the fishing there too much, according to Captain Crayton. In fact, he catches them even if the water is rough and murky.

A. C. Becker, Jr., has caught thousands of channel bass in more than thirty-five years of fishing and has written the only book devoted to this fish. It is called *Big Red—Channel Bass Fishing* and is published by A. S. Barnes & Co. He does most of his fishing in the surf along the Gulf of Mexico and in the lagoons and bays just behind the beaches. He finds that the best fishing in the surf takes place in October but fish can be caught from September to November. He uses a spinning or conventional surf rod, and when fishing in a strong current along a beach he uses the special Surf Weight sinker. This has four wire tines that bend easily but dig into the sand and hold the bait in place. Then, when you reel in, the tines straighten out and release the weight from the sand.

Becker uses mullet, shrimp, and squid for bait. If the mullet are under 6 inches he uses a whole one. Larger ones are cut into chunks. He believes in burying the hook inside the bait, because, he claims, a channel bass will feel the point and eject the bait. He chooses days when there is some surf and the water is somewhat discolored, to do his fishing. Clear water makes for poor fishing along the beaches in this sector. But if the surf is too rough he finds that the channel bass will hang out in the deeper water, from three to ten feet, just behind the first line of breaking waves. He likes to fish about two hours before high water to about an hour or so after it turns to go out.

Forest Peek fishes for the smaller channel bass, or "reds," on the flats of Laguna Madre, in Texas, and he gets a lot of them. He uses a light spinning outfit and casts 3-inch plastic worm tails on a ¼-ounce jig head. He finds that the yellow or white jigs with black spots and the pink- and red-colored jigs are most effective. According to Forest, the channel bass bite best during the very high tides, when they come into water only a foot or so in depth. He looks for them over solid bottoms, near eel grass, and along drop-offs. He finds that channel bass are nearsighted, so he casts his lure and works it slowly, close to the bottom, in front of the fish's nose, where it can be seen.

Ed Bell also fishes the flats in Texas, in such spots as Matagorda Bay and Powderhorn Bay, using a small, No. 6 treble hook on which he impales a live shrimp. This is then fished under a cork or plastic float. He adds a light sinker on the leader about 8 to 10 inches above the hook to keep the shrimp near the bottom in the shallow water he likes to fish. He fishes mostly on days when it is windy and stormy and the water is somewhat muddy. He claims he catches more channel bass then than when the water is calm and clear.

Bob Rinerman is a fishing guide who operates out of Bud n' Mary's, in Islamorada, in the Florida Keys. He does a lot of fishing for small channel bass, or "redfish" as they are called there. He finds some of the best fishing on the flats in Florida Bay and in the Everglades. The reds are spotted by poling just as you would for bonefish or permit. But Bob finds that the redfish are less wary or spooky than the bones or permit. He claims that the redfish usually feed into a falling tide along the edges of the flats and that it is best to approach them with the sun and wind at your back.

A jig tipped with a piece of shrimp is the most effective lure for the redfish, but they will also hit surface plugs, underwater plugs, spoons, and plastic jig tails. You have to cast your lure right in front of the fish's nose for him to see it. But if you fail to connect on the first cast you can usually make other casts.

Phil Ford fishes for channel bass around Pensacola, Florida, during the fall and early-winter months, when this fishing is best. He drifts in his boat in the inlets and bays and fishes with a bottom rig and sinker. He uses a small, live pinfish for bait and hooks it through the back or lips, then lowers it to the bottom. When he gets a bite he lowers his rod and lets the fish take some line before setting the hook.

We told about how Claude Rogers catches channel bass earlier in this chapter, and now we'll tell how he catches black drum—a close relative of the red drum. Claude fishes for them often off Virginia and finds that May and June are good months for these fish. He looks for them just off the beaches and surf and up to a half mile offshore. He has been keeping records on these fish for years, so he can predict their movements with uncanny accuracy. He usually knows which spots to fish at various times of the season.

Claude usually uses clams for bait when going after the black drum. He threads the meat up on the hook and covers the point with a tough part of the clam. He may also make a "sandwich" by adding a piece of peeler crab on the same hook with the clam. Claude recommends that you keep a tight line all the time and reel in a foot or two every so often to take in the slack. If you feel a nibble, you should set the hook quickly, because black drum will steal the bait off your hook in a hurry.

Claude also finds that when black drum are schooled and near the surface they will hit lures either trolled or cast into them. He has taken black drum over 40 and 50 pounds on the Hopkins "Shorty" metal lure off Chincoteague and Fishermans Island and at the entrance to Chesapeake Bay. July is a good month for these areas. He finds that locating the schools is easier when the water is clear and the sun is bright. The black-drum schools resemble the channel-bass schools, and a hooked black drum fights as hard as the red drum

Claude Rogers caught this 65-pound black drum on a Hopkins "Shorty" metal lure, from a school off Chincoteague, Virginia. Most of these fish are caught on clam or peeler-crab baits, but when in big schools, they will hit a metal lure. (*Claude Rogers photo*)

when hooked on a lure. However, Claude finds that you usually have to cast three or four times into a school before you get a hit on the lure from a black drum.

Hopkins "Shorty" for channel bass and black drum

Boyd Tyler fishes for black drum in Delaware Bay, off Cape May County, in New Jersey, from April to June, when these big fish come in there to feed on clams. Some of the black drum run up to 80 or 90 pounds, and even the "smaller" ones usually run from 30 to 50 pounds. Boyd looks for clam beds to fish over, and one good spot, called the "Green Shanty," discovered by his father back in the 1930s, is still productive.

Boyd uses a fish-finder rig with an 8/0 or 9/0 hook for this fishing and baits it with skimmer clams or shedder crabs or a combination of the two. The meat from a whole big clam makes the right-sized bait for the big drum. This should be lowered to the bottom from a boat, and black drum will follow up the clam-juice scent and find it. Keeping the bait on the bottom most of the time is the best method.

Boyd finds that the fastest fishing usually takes place at dusk, especially during the top of the flood tide. He also likes a southeast or northwest wind for this section of Delaware Bay. The strong tides of the new moon or full moon provide the fastest fishing.

Rick Cox catches black drum on lures near Suwannee, Florida. He uses mostly sinking and deep-running plugs and casts them with spinning or bait-casting outfits. Silver mirror-sided plugs seem to work best for him. The secret in this fishing is to locate a school of black drum on the flats and then cast into them, letting the plug sink or run deep. Then reel in very slowly.

15

BLUEFISH, WEAKFISH, AND SEA TROUT

In recent years, we have been enjoying fabulous bluefishing up and down the Atlantic Coast from Maine to Florida and in the Gulf of Mexico. These hard-fighting fish have provided top sport and food for many salt-water anglers. When plentiful and hungry, bluefish can often be easy to catch. But when they are playing hard to get, they can be as exasperating and difficult to hook as any other wary, unpredictable salt-water fish.

One angler who has made a lifetime study of the bluefish and enjoys fishing for them is Henry "Hal" Lyman, publisher of *Salt Water Sportsman* magazine. Hal has fished for bluefish in many parts of the world and wrote a book about them called *Successful Bluefishing*. He particularly enjoys catching blues from the surf along the beaches of New England. There he looks for gulls and terns wheeling and diving, fish breaking, or bait leaping. If these obvious signs are lacking, Hal looks for a clash of currents or tides, especially where rivers and inlets empty into the ocean.

When fishing a strange beach, Lyman visits it at dead low water and notes the offshore bars, cuts or breaks in them, holes, deep sloughs, and underwater obstructions. Then he makes a mental note of the best spots and returns when the tide is up or more favorable.

He uses most of the popular bluefish lures in the surf such as surface popper and swimmers, underwater plugs, metal squids, heavy spoons, bait tails, and jigs.

Hal Lyman finds that the blues will often feed in a rough surf if the water is clean. But when it gets brown and dirty the blues will leave or not show up. And they are more likely to show and feed in

Nick Karas holds a bluefish he caught from his small boat. Nick catches bluefish by all the methods of casting, trolling, and jigging, mostly in Long Island Sound. (*Nick Karas photo*)

the surf early in the morning and in the evening than during the middle of the day.

Nick Karas fishes for bluefish in the New York waters of Long Island Sound. He locates the blues as most anglers do, looking for birds working, fish breaking, and bait scattering. But, most of the time, he uses his electronic fish-finder to pick up any blues beneath his boat. He also tries to locate the drop-offs, holes, reefs, and rips and does his casting or trolling there. He usually trolls slowly, with spoons, jigs, or tube lures. He tries to avoid trolling through a school of feeding blues but circles around the edges. Other times, he may drift over the fish and jig with a Scotty rig made up of a diamond jig and a series of feathered hooks on the leader, above the weight.

Nick Karas finds the bluefish is most consistent at Plum Gut, at the eastern end of Long Island Sound. There during the summer and fall blues from 6 to 16 pounds or even heavier are caught almost every day. The tides and rips are strong there, and you have to get down to the bottom in water from 80 to 120 feet deep. So, fairly husky tackle is needed: a stiff rod and reel holding two hundred yards of 30-pound-test monofilament. Nick uses a bottom rig with an 8-ounce sinker, a 2-foot wire leader, and the hook. This is baited with a piece of mackerel, butterfish, or other fish. He lowers this rig to the bottom until he feels the sinker bounce, then reels in the slack as the boat drifts with the tide. He tries to keep contact with the bottom as often as possible to make sure his rig and bait is deep enough.

Other times, Nick looks for blues on top chasing baitfish, with gulls and terns in big flocks working over them. Then you can cast and let the bait or lure sink and you will often get hits close to the surface.

Ted Keatley also fishes Long Island Sound, at its western end, where he catches big bluefish on live bunkers. He looks for schools of the bunkers swimming on top and snags a few. He keeps them alive in a 15-gallon pail, which he keeps floating in the water with an inner tube around it. Ted uses a two-hook rig to hold the live bunker: He takes a single 7/0 hook and attaches it to the end of the wire leader. Then he attaches a second hook above the first one. This hook is run through the bunker's back, while the other hook is held in place at the tail of the bait with a small rubber band. This way he hooks more bluefish (many of which try to bite off the tail part of the bunker) than he would with a single hook.

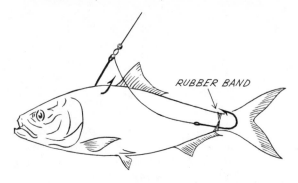

Two-hook bunker rig for big bluefish

Peter J. Frederikson says that many anglers fail to catch their share of bluefish from party boats and private boats, because they do not pay attention to small details and tricks that pay off. He fishes the New York and New Jersey grounds for bluefish, where chumming is usually practiced. He finds that when the bluefish are wary or fussy, a No. 4 short-shank hook buried in the bait should be used. Then the butterfish or bunker bait is taken readily. He attaches the hook to a dark wire leader at times but finds that tying it directly to a 60-pound-test monofilament shock tippet or to the 30-pound-test mono line itself will get more strikes, or pick-ups, from the bluefish.

Pete also finds that it is very important to let the bait out in the chum slick as naturally as possible and keep it moving all the time. So he strips off a foot or two of the line from the reel and continues doing this until a bluefish takes or he reaches the end of the drift. Then he reels in and repeats.

Jeff Dane caught a 17-pound 7-ounce bluefish on a fly rod while fishing from Captain Eddie Nelson's boat the *Early Bird* off Virginia, fifteen miles southeast of the Chesapeake Light Tower. He used a red-and-white streamer with Mylar strips on the sides to make it flash and look like a silvery baitfish. The captain ran the boat over to a school of blues feeding on top and shut off the engine so Jeff could cast. He cast the streamer a couple of times and hooked the big blue. After a tough fight he boated it. His friend Billy Thigpen caught a 16-pound 8-ounce blue on a red-and-yellow popping bug a short time later.

Fred Luks, who fishes for bluefish in Long Island Sound, finds that they can be very temperamental about the lures they want on a given

Jeff Dane holds the big, 17-pound 7-ounce bluefish he caught with a fly rod and a streamer fly off the coast of Virginia. (*Jeff Dane photo*)

day. So he carries a good assortment of lures, and experiments until he finds what they want. He notes that on cloudy days the blues prefer light-colored and fluorescent lures.

Fred also has a lot of fun and sport fishing for the smaller blues, or "snappers," with a fly rod from July to October. He uses a 9-foot fly rod and a No. 9 forward-taper line. His favorite fly is a polar-bear-hair streamer with silver tinsel body tied on a No. 1/0 or 2/0 hook for the bigger snapper blues. For the smaller snappers, he ties the fly on No. 4, 5, or 6 hooks.

Fred fishes for the snapper blues during the daytime when the tide starts to move out. He usually finds them in bays, harbors, creeks, and shallow stretches. He often sees them splashing on the surface or swimming just below it. He also tries chumming at times, using ground herring and oatmeal. This attracts baitfish, which in turn draw the small blues. Once the fish appear or are located, he casts the fly into the school and retrieves it in a series of fast twitches.

Jim Guy, who has fished a lot for bluefish in Long Island Sound off Connecticut, tells about one trip when he had trouble catching bluefish on his regular-sized lures. So he looked through his tackle box and came up with a small fresh-water goldfish-type spoon he had often used for mackerel. He cast this out, let it sink several feet, and started a slow retrieve. He hooked and boated a 10-pound and, later, a 15-pound bluefish on the small lure!

Captain J. T. Haley, who fishes for big bluefish off Virginia, finds that trolling with a natural balao, or ballyhoo, is highly effective for these fish. He often adds a plastic skirt over the ballyhoo's head for such trolling.

Nugent Brasher, Jr., fishes for bluefish at night near the oil rigs found in the Gulf of Mexico off Louisiana. He finds that a strip of Spanish mackerel on a hook and a 3-ounce weight on the leader is a good way to catch the blues there. He casts out and lets it sink to the bottom. He lets it rest there a second or two, then starts to retrieve it toward the surface, working his rod tip up and down to give the bait some action. Or he will add a mackerel strip to a jig, let it sink to the bottom, then reel it back toward the surface.

In recent years the northern weakfish, or gray trout, has been making a comeback and is now being caught in many of its former haunts from Rhode Island to North Carolina. In the old days most of this fishing was done by chumming with grass shrimp and then drifting out a sandworm, or two or three of the grass shrimp, on a hook. Nowadays, with light spinning tackle and a lot of new lures on the market, many anglers have been taking plenty of weakfish without resorting to chum. One angler who catches his share of weakfish is Dr. William A. Muller, who fishes for them in many parts of Long Island, such as Peconic Bay and Great South Bay.

Doc Muller likes the Tri-Fin Whiptail, which has a lead head with a keel and a split surgical-tube body. He uses the all-white one and adds a strip of squid or pork rind to the hook. He casts this out, lets it settle on the bottom and then retrieves it slowly. He experiments to find out what action the weaks want on a particular day. Sometimes a gentle twitch is all that is needed. Other times, you have to jig the lure more. And on still other days, all you do is reel in the

Tri-fin whiptail lure used for weakfish

lure steadily with no rod action. Doc also uses bucktail jigs, instead of the plastic jigs, in the same way.

To catch big weakfish, Doc Muller recommends that you fish at night with a high-leader rig and use sandworms or squid for bait. Another good way to catch the big tide runners, according to Doc, is with small bluefish, or snappers, from 5 to 8 inches long. Hook one of these through the back with a No. 1 or 2 treble hook, add a float a few feet above it, and let it out to swim around until a big weakfish grabs it.

Doc Muller finds that early in the season, when the water is still cold, the weakfish tend to feed on the shallow flats. Later on in the summer, when the water warms up, you will catch them better in the deeper holes, channels, and inlets. Fishing is also better at night during the summer months. He finds that fishing is usually poor during slack water but picks up soon after the tide changes. And because weakfish tend to feed at a certain level, it is important to present your lure or bait at this level.

Captain Bob Schavel also fishes Long Island for weakfish and uses the usual lures and baits for them. But his ace in the hole when fishing is slow is a combination rig he makes himself. He ties a plastic shrimp or a bucktail jig on the end of his line and then adds a white streamer fly about 18 inches above it. He uses this from a drifting boat by lowering it to the bottom and jigging it up and down. If he is anchored he casts the rig out and lets it sink to the bottom, then retrieves it while raising and lowering his rod tip. He finds he gets most of his hits and fish near the bottom, but some fish will also follow the lures and hit them close to the boat.

Al Reinfelder used his Bait Tail jig for weakfish by letting it sink deep to the bottom and then bouncing it along so that it kicked up a puff of sand on each lift. This imitated a shrimp or small crab and attracted the weaks. Al liked the ¼- or ½-ounce Bait Tails for small

Dr. William Muller holds a weakfish he caught in Long Island, New York, waters. These fish have made a great comeback in recent years and provide sport for thousands of anglers along the Atlantic coast. (*Dr. William Muller photo*)

or medium-sized weakfish and larger Bait Tails, up to 2 ounces, for the tide runners.

When Charlie Peacock lived in Wildwood, New Jersey, and fished the jetties there, he caught plenty of big weakfish. He found that he had the best fishing with jigs and long strips of pork rind or small rigged eels. ·

Claude Rogers catches weakfish in Virginia waters with a small Hopkins lure or plastic tail jig. The plastic tail jig is often sweetened with a piece of peeler crab. This is cast out and allowed to sink to the bottom and then reeled in slowly.

One of the top anglers for the southern weakfish, or sea trout, is Gary Bennett, of Cocoa, Florida. Through the years, he has caught many big "gator" trout, going from 6 to 12 pounds, in the Indian River, Banana River, and other nearby waters. Gary liked to use long, needlefish-type plugs and found that the sea trout bite best during the last two hours of the outgoing tide and the first hour of the incoming tide. The peak fishing usually occurs during the winter months, with April also very good. He finds that the best period is from the new moon to the full moon. And he catches most of his big sea trout at night, early in the morning, and in the evening toward dusk.

Jim Martenhoff fishes for sea trout in Florida waters and enjoys catching them from a boat on ultra-light spinning tackle. He does a lot of his fishing in Florida Bay, especially during the spring months, when it is usually best. He finds that the fishing is most effective when there is enough breeze to move the boat at a slow but steady pace. Then he lets out his live-shrimp bait so it follows the drifting boat. In a brisk breeze he may have to add a light weight on the leader to keep the bait down.

When using lures such as plugs, jigs, and plastic tails, Jim casts as the boat drifts. He looks for "muds," or patches of marl and silt stirred up by the feeding fish. Then he runs the boat upwind and drifts through the muddy spot and casts around it. Other times, he does his drifting over grassy spots where he has caught sea trout in the past. Once he gets hits or fish, he makes repeated drifts over the same spot.

Ed Reddy, of Palm Beach, Florida, catches big sea trout in his area. He claims that the best fishing will occur during the "spring tides," from about three days before to about three days after the full moon and new moon. That is when the sea trout like to move in on the grassy flats to feed on shrimp and baitfish. Reddy likes to do his fishing when the weather is calm early in the morning and late in the evening. He prefers high tide about two hours before slack water to two hours after. He uses mostly surface plugs such as the torpedo or cigar shapes, which can be worked erratically on top.

Chuck Pettit fishes the West Coast of Florida for sea trout and catches a lot of these popular fish. He uses a spinning outfit with 10-pound-test line and a popping float. He attaches the float to his line, then adds a 2-foot, 20-pound-test leader and a 2/0 hook. He uses a live shrimp on the hook most of the time but will also use a mullet strip occasionally. But, unlike most sea-trout anglers, he doesn't do

Gary Bennett has fished the Indian River and the Banana River, near Cocoa, Florida, for many years and has caught many big sea trout in those waters. (*Florida State News Bureau photo*)

much drifting. Instead he likes to anchor his boat in a good spot and cast his float and bait all around the boat in an arc.

Claude Rogers often locates sea trout in Virginia by drifting and then casting ahead or to either side of the boat in an arc. Claude uses bucktails, plastic tail jigs, and plugs for his sea-trout fishing. He claims that the smaller, lighter jigs and plugs usually outfish the larger, heavier ones. He also likes his bucktail jigs to be lightly dressed. Claude feels it is very important to present the lure at the proper depth, where the sea trout are at rest or feeding. So he lets his lure sink to various levels and down to the bottom and retrieves it, until he finds the right level. In rocky areas or on bottoms with snags Claude will cast out and then start counting as the lure settles. When he gets a hit or a fish, he will then know at which level they are hitting and he'll wait until this depth is reached in subsequent casts before starting his retrieve.

Doyle Wells, of Port Isabel, Texas, is a fishing guide who takes his parties out on Laguna Madre. This big body of water separates Padre Island from the Texas mainland and is noted for its sea-trout fishing. Doyle depends on live shrimp for most of his fishing, so he brings plenty of this bait with him. He uses the shrimp on a popping float rig. To make it he ties a small swivel on the end of his line. Then

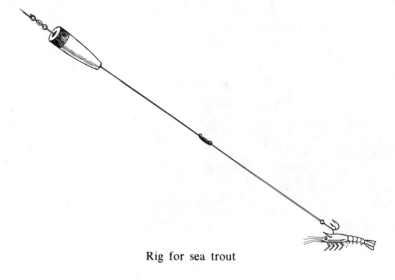

Rig for sea trout

he takes a 3-foot, 30-pound-test leader and ties it to the swivel. Just below the swivel he adds a popping float. Next he adds a small clincher sinker at the middle of the leader, ties a No. 4 treble hook on the end and hooks a live shrimp in back of the head. Doyle uses a long, medium-weight rod to cast this rig as far as he can. Then he pops the float two or three times and lets it rest, then pops again and lets it rest, and so on until it is near the boat. He finds that this popping will attract sea trout even in the murky water often encountered in the shallow lagoon.

Jim Ericson also fishes for sea trout in Laguna Madre, but his method is to drift in a boat until he runs into a school of sea trout. Then he anchors the boat and gets out and wades. He feels that wading is quieter and a fisherman is less likely to be seen or to frighten the fish in the shallow water. He likes to use a fly rod with an orange-and-red bucktail. Other times, he uses a spinning outfit and casts surface plugs such as the torpedo-shaped floaters. These he finds are especially effective for the big sea trout. But he will also use underwater plugs, spoons, and jigs and work them below the surface.

Sam DiVincezo has found that sea trout along the sea wall at Corpus Christi, Texas, bite best during December and January when cold fronts move in. But the fishing is usually poor when the cold northers are blowing. He finds you have to wait until the wind dies down and the sun begins to shine before the sea trout start hitting again.

16

BONEFISH AND PERMIT

Bonefishing really didn't become popular until after World War II, when a few anglers pioneered the sport and worked out the lures, methods, and techniques that proved successful. The development of salt-water fly fishing and spinning tackle helped along these lines because it enabled an angler to present the small, light lures without frightening the wary, spooky bonefish. Now there are many bonefish experts, specialists, and guides, who seek them in the Florida Keys, the Bahamas, Bermuda, the Caribbean, and other places where these fish prowl the flats.

One of the early pioneers who helped make bonefishing popular was Joe Brooks. He spent many years fishing for bonefish and liked to use a fly rod for the "gray ghosts," or "phantoms," as he liked to call the elusive bones. When Joe was seeking bonefish, he liked to stand as high as he could in a boat so that he could spot the fish before it saw him. Or he waded quietly and looked for groups, pairs, or single bonefish. He tried to fish with the sun at his back so he could see the bonefish more easily. Conditions for this were usually best in the morning, from 9 A.M. to 2 P.M., which is when he did most of his stalking. He also fished on a rising, or incoming, tide, because that is when the bones swim up on the flats looking for food and they are bolder than when the tide is going out.

Joe looked for bonefish "tailing," or showing their tails above the water, when they were in very shallow water. Other times, he looked for them "mudding," i.e., sending up puffs of mud and discoloring the water while feeding and rooting on the bottom for shrimp or crabs. Joe found that bonefish rarely hit or stayed around long, once they spotted an angler. So he felt that the first cast was the most important; you rarely got a chance to make a second cast. Timing

Joe Brooks is shown grabbing a bonefish caught on a fly rod. He was one of the first anglers to fish for them on such tackle and did a lot to popularize the sport. (*Joe Brooks photo*)

was all-important and he presented the fly accurately, dropping it the right distance beyond and in front of the bonefish so that it would pass where it could be seen and taken.

Joe Brooks used small flies in shallow water, because they sank slowly and didn't catch on the bottom readily. In deeper water he used bigger streamers and bucktails. He liked flies with some white in them, either in the wings or the body. He also used the brown-and-white, red-and-white, and the Phillips pink shrimp.

Stanley M. Babson wrote the first book dealing only with the bonefish. *Bonefishing* tells of his experiences and his views on this fish, which he has pursued for more than thirty-five years. When using spinning tackle and a "wiggle" jig he recommends making it jump off the bottom in short hops so that it imitates a shrimp trying to escape. He side-casts the lure and lets it drop about 7 to 10 feet ahead of a bonefish. Stan feels the side cast makes the lure hit the water more quietly than a high, overhead cast. For the same reason, he likes the lighter lures, weighing no more than ⅛ ounce.

When using a fly rod, Babson casts about 5 feet in front of a fish, because a fly lands more softly and doesn't scare the fish as much as the heavier lures. He likes flies with small, light wire hooks, which do not make the fly sink too fast. Babson also feels that to be a good bonefisherman you have to learn how to spot fish underwater or see the "tails" and "muds" they create. You should also know the tides, the winds, and the temperature of the air. You should be able to cast accurately and know how to present and manipulate the lure. You should also know how to play the fish after you hook it.

Duke Ducette, who specialized in fishing for bonefish on Andros Island, in the Bahamas, would bring along a sack of land crabs, crush and crack them and then toss them into the water around the boat as chum to attract bonefish.

Lee Cuddy caught hundreds of bonefish on fly tackle, spinning tackle, and bait-casting tackle. When he uses a bait-casting outfit, he puts 8- or 10-pound-test monofilament on it and ties the lure directly to the line. His favorite lure is the "wiggle," or "skimmer," jig with a chrome head and blue-and-white tail feathers. He finds this works best in water 2 feet or more in depth. In shallower water, when bonefish are tailing, he uses a fly rod and bucktails or streamers.

Cuddy does most of his fishing between Miami and Key Largo. Instead of using a push pole he uses a regular outboard motor to get to the fishing grounds and then switches to a small electric motor powered by a battery. This doesn't frighten the bonefish and he can get close to them. He claims that any cast over 75 feet is too far for bonefish; most of his fish are caught at distances of less than 50 feet from the boat.

One of the most successful bonefish guides in the country is Cap-

Captain Bill Curtis helped actress Frances Fong catch this bonefish in Biscayne Bay, near Miami, Florida. Captain Curtis is one of the top bonefish guides in that area. (*Florida News Bureau photo*)

tain Bill Curtis, and the amazing thing is that he gets most of his fish near Miami. He fishes the Cape Florida flats, Soldier Key, Sands Key, and Elliot Key. Curtis, of course, knows his waters and all the paths followed by feeding bonefish intimately. He anchors his boat

in such a spot and then starts chumming with pieces of shrimp. He
does this over a light-colored bottom close to a nearby channel or
drop-off. The bonefish pick up the scent and follow it up to the light-
colored spot. For most of his customers, he recommends using live
shrimp on a 2/0 hook. But first he pinches off the tail of the shrimp
to prevent it from spinning in the air during the cast.

Other anglers who can use a spinning outfit or a fly rod use lures
such as jigs or flies and cast to the bonefish in the chum slick. Bill
Curtis lets them use two flies he created—one called the "Blue Tail
Fly" and the other the "Golden Getter." They are highly successful
in the Biscayne Bay waters he fishes.

Lefty Kreh, who has caught many bonefish on fly tackle and spinning tackle, recommends a spinning rod 7 or 7½ feet long that can
be cast with one hand and is able to handle lures weighing ⅛ to ¼
ounce. The spinning reel should hold 200 to 250 yards of 4- to 10-
pound-test monofilament line. And the drag should be set very light
—no more than 2 pounds, and even a pound, to cope with the fast,
long runs of a bonefish. When using a "skimmer" jig, Lefty finds that
adding a small piece of shrimp to the hook will often make it more
effective.

Bonefish rig with piece of shrimp

Bob Reineman is a top bonefish guide who operates from Bud n'
Mary's, in Islamorada, in the Florida Keys. He says that October is a
good month for this fishing but that the biggest ones are caught from
March to May. For lures he recommends bucktail jigs in the ⅛- and
¼-ounce sizes. He also uses a plain jig head with a small strip of
pork rind on it. He casts these anywhere from 8 to 10 feet in front
and beyond the fish and works them in short hops but not too fast.
On windy days or when the water is muddy, Bob anchors in deeper
water than usual and chums with small shrimp and fishes with live
shrimp.

Warren Freeman, of Miami, has caught several thousand bonefish
since he began specializing in this fishing, soon after World War II.

He gets most of them near Miami, on the flats within sight of the big city. Naturally, after years of fishing he knows the best spots and varying tides and weather conditions and how they affect the fishing. He can often predict to the minute when the bonefish will appear at a specific spot.

Warren uses a light spinning rod and ties a No. 2/0 Eagle Claw hook on the end of his line. He baits this with one or two live shrimp, depending on their size, and then casts either from his boat or while wading. He casts to fish that he sees in shallow water, but he also knows deeper spots where bonefish travel or feed, and will often cast the shrimp blind and let the bait settle to the bottom and then wait for a bite.

More and more bonefish guides, such as Cal Cochran, of Marathon, in the Florida Keys, are starting to fish for them at twilight. They find that as the sun goes down and it starts to get dark the bones are apt to move in to feed on the flats. And they are not as wary or as easily frightened as in the daytime. In this fishing you should look for bonefish tailing and cast a live shrimp in front of the fish.

Phil Francis discovered years ago that bonefish will take a pork frog, or pork chunk, and found that these lures are very effective on the shallow, grassy flats. He puts the pork chunk on a No. 1/0 weedless hook. The pork chunk should be heavy enough to cast with a spinning rod and should have a wiggly tail or two. Phil fishes for the bonefish when the tide is low and just starting to come in. When he spots a feeding bonefish, he casts the lure a few feet beyond and in front of the fish. Then he starts to retrieve it slowly with some rod action to make it look alive. When a bone heads for the lure, he waits until the fish takes it and turns away. Then he sets the hook.

Alain Wood-Prince found that plastic worms will take bonefish. He trims these to about four inches or a bit shorter and uses a No. 1/0 hook with them. He finds that no weight is needed to cast the worm except on windy days or when long casts are required. Then he may add a split-shot sinker a few inches above the worm. The big advantage of using the plastic worm is that it doesn't sink as fast as most lures and can be worked at any level—a real boon in the shallow water where bonefish do most of their feeding.

Permit are even harder to find and more difficult to hook than bonefish, since they put up a longer, tougher fight. Only a small number of men have caught these fish on a fly rod and fly; a somewhat greater number have taken them on lures, but most of them are caught on crab baits. When Bob Stearns uses a crab, he advises casting it about four feet ahead of the fish and slightly beyond its path of travel. Then he slowly reels the crab in so it ends up in front of the fish's nose. When the permit goes for the bait, Bob drops his rod tip and lets the crab sink toward the bottom. The permit thinks the crab is trying to hide in the grass and grabs it before it can get away.

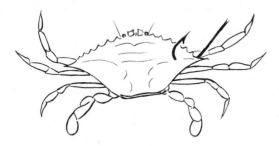

Hooking crab for permit

When using lures such as a tan-colored skimmer-type jig weighing ¼ or ⅜ ounce, Bob Stearns casts it well ahead and beyond the fish. Then he reels it in so that it passes in front of the fish where it can be seen. Once the fish sees the lure, Bob lets it sink to the bottom. Permit will usually follow it down and often grab it even when it is lying still on the bottom.

Bob finds that the best fishing for permit takes place in water from 2 to 4 feet deep. He finds that in water less than 2 feet deep they can often be seen "tailing"—their black tails waving back and forth above the surface of the water. The best flats, according to Stearns, are those with deep water near by.

Bob Montgomery is a fishing guide in Key West, Florida, who specializes in catching permit in that area. And he has been very successful in getting these fish for his customers. He recommends a rig consisting of a light spinning rod and reel and 10-pound-test line. He ties a No. 3/0 or 4/0 hook directly to the line; this holds the small crab usually used for bait.

Montgomery often fishes the Marquesas Keys in his 20-foot boat *Blue Runner,* and he knows where permit will be feeding during various stages of the tide. Permit like and need somewhat deeper water than do bonefish, but they show up on the same flats day after day on an incoming tide. And they leave soon after the tide starts to drop. Permit are often difficult to see, but using Polaroid glasses and looking for the dark tail often protruding above the water helps in spotting them.

When the flats fail to produce, Bob Montgomery's "ace in the hole" is a wreck in deeper water. He often finds schools of permit in the vicinity, and he picks them up on his fathometer or fish-finder. He finds that permit are present and are caught around Key West most of the year but, for peak fishing on the flats, the period from late April to mid-June is best.

One of the biggest permit caught on rod and reel was taken while fishing one of the wrecks found in the Key West area. It was a 50-pound 8-ounce fish caught on 16-pound-test line by Marshall Ernest on a live-crab bait. He cast to a fish he saw swimming in the water and hooked it. Then the permit almost stripped his reel and fought for seventy minutes before it was finally boated.

Tom Paugh, salt-water fishing editor of *Sports Afield* magazine, claims that the permit is the rarest, wariest, smartest, and most invisible fish caught on light tackle. He knows permit can be caught more easily around wrecks and reefs on heavier tackle, but he prefers to stalk the fish in shallow water on lighter tackle. He finds that the best fishing usually takes place in Florida during the spring and summer months.

Tom Paugh says that one of the best spots for permit is in Belize (British Honduras). There he has seen permit swarming on the flats in greater numbers than anywhere else. The only problem seemed to be that the flats where permit were plentiful were also covered with sharp coral, and a hooked permit usually cut the line soon after being hooked. Finally Tom and his companions came up with a solution and succeeded in boating permit in those waters. As soon as a fish was hooked they chased it with the boat so it ran into deeper water, where they could fight it with less danger of being cut off.

Captain Johnny Cass spent many years in the Florida Keys as a guide, and his specialty was catching the wily and elusive permit. He averaged seventy to eighty permit a season for his clients, while most anglers consider themselves fortunate to hook and land one or two of these fish in a year. Naturally Johnny knows where the permit feed,

Tom Paugh holds a husky permit caught on spinning tackle. Most of these fish are caught on small crabs, but they will also hit a lure at times. (*Tom Paugh photo*)

and can put you in a spot where you'll see permit sooner or later. He uses Polaroid glasses and can spot an individual permit or a school quicker than anyone else. He looks for swimming fish, and the telltale signs of shadows, dorsal fins, and tails when the fish are moving along or feeding.

Like most permit guides, he uses small crabs for bait, because they get quicker and better results than artificial lures. This is especially true when baiting a single fish or a pair of them. He finds that when permit are in schools they are apt to hit lures better than single fish. Then there is more competition and they are more likely to chase a properly presented lure. Johnny tells his customers to set the hook hard, as many as a half dozen times, to drive the point and barb of the hook into the tough mouth of the permit.

Al Pflueger, Jr., caught two permit—one weighing 12 pounds and the other 14 pounds—on a fly rod in one day! Most anglers fish for years and fail to hook their first permit on a fly. Al fished the offshore wrecks where big schools of permit are present or are swimming by. But he claims that conditions have to be just right to catch them. The tide should be slack and the water calm; a school of permit has to appear near the surface and you have to get them into a feeding or at least a striking mood.

17

TARPON

The high-leaping and tough-fighting tarpon has been a favorite fish with skilled salt-water anglers from just before the turn of the century. These early anglers traveled to Florida from many parts of the country and even from England to fish for the "silver king," as the fish was often called. Their fishing tackle was heavy and strong and they usually fished with bait, although a few anglers were beginning to use spoons and plugs.

Then, in the 1930s, Dave Newell and others started to use light tackle such as bait-casting outfits to take tarpon on plugs and other lures. Dave fished mostly in the Florida Everglades and the mangrove country. He claimed that in these waters the tarpon did not stay put but moved with the tides and traveled the bays, channels, creeks, and rivers in search of food. The tarpon usually gave themselves away by leaving a trail of bubbles or patches of foam. And of course they also rolled on the surface.

When Newell fished in narrow creeks and rivers, he approached the fishing spot quietly and with caution. He usually rowed or drifted toward the fish or fishing spot. He liked to use surface lures such as the torpedo-shaped plugs, or else red-and-white and silver underwater plugs.

Hart Stillwell was another early tarpon fisherman, who spent a lifetime fishing for them in Texas and Mexico. He looked for big tarpon in inlets, passes, around the ends of jetties, and in ship channels and the big bends of rivers. There he found tarpon lying in the bends, where the current shifted from one side to the other. At first Hart tried surface plugs and shallow running lure, but he got few strikes from them. Then he started using sinking plugs and other lures that could be worked along the bottom, and he began to get some real action. His favorite technique when using a sinking plug was to let it go down and rest briefly on the bottom; then he'd move it a bit. He also found that tarpon hit a slow-moving lure much better than a fast-moving one.

After World War II, more and more anglers began going after tarpon with light tackle, using bait-casting outfits, spinning tackle, and even fly rods. One of these men was Jerry Coughlin, who fished for big tarpon with a bait-casting rod and reel and then, later, a fly rod, in the Florida Keys. He took many tarpon over 100 pounds on this light tackle and won many tournaments and contests.

One of Jerry's secrets was to pay close attention to his rods, reels, lines, lures, hooks, and knots. In addition, he hired a top-notch fishing guide such as Jimmie Albright to help locate the tarpon and handle the boat. Jerry believed in the quiet approach when stalking tarpon, especially on the flats. He found that a gentle ripple on the water was better than a flat calm. Jerry liked to use a ¾-ounce topwater plug with silver sides when bait casting. He would cast this plug about 5 to 6 feet in front of a fish and retrieve it slowly.

Jimmie Albright is a fishing guide operating out of Islamorada, in the Florida Keys, who has helped many anglers to catch their first tarpon or to catch them on light tackle. He claims that the best months for this fishing are from March to August, with June a prime month. He looks for tarpon on the flats in water from 3 to 6 feet deep and in the strong tides near bridges and claims that the best way to catch a tarpon is with a live mullet or other small fish at night during an outgoing tide. When fly fishing for tarpon he recommends using a 5-inch streamer on a 5/0 hook with long feathers that breathe. Yellow and orange flies are usually most effective for tarpon, he finds.

Another fishing guide who has caught thousands of big tarpon for the anglers who used his services is Bill Hunter. He does most of his fishing in Boca Grande Pass, on Florida's West Coast, where the fishing is best during May, June, and July. Bill knows the pass and waters like his back yard and drifts, in depths from 40 to 60 feet, over rocks and ledges.

Hunter uses fairly stiff salt-water rods with a 4/0 reel filled with 50- or 60-pound-test line. He uses a 5/0 Sobey hook on a bottom rig with an egg sinker attached lightly with soft wire so that it comes off after a tarpon is hooked. You need this heavy tackle when fishing at Boca Grande in order to fight a big tarpon in the deep water and

Tarpon caught at Boca Grande, in Florida, require fairly heavy tackle, because they are taken in deep water with bottom rigs. (*Florida News Bureau photo*)

strong current with other boats around and to bring it up to the boat for release.

Bill Hunter usually baits the hooks with a small live crab, but he will also use squirrelfish or mutton minnows or some other small fish. These are let down to the bottom and the sinker bounces along until a tarpon grabs the bait. Then the rod bends into a big arc and you set the hook immediately.

If you hire Bill Hunter and want to use lighter tackle, he'll take you out into the Gulf along the beaches, where you fish in shallow water. There you can use a small, live fish for bait under a cork or plastic float and have a better chance to land a tarpon on light tackle.

One highly skilled angler who catches big tarpon the hard way —on a fly rod—is Stu Apte, who fishes for them mostly in the

Florida Keys. He caught one tarpon going 154 pounds on a fly rod off Key West and others going over 100 pounds. Stu's real vocation is being a pilot for Pan American World Airways, but he has also been a fishing guide and he fishes almost everywhere for fun and sport.

Stu pays close attention to the minor but important details of his rod, reel, line, leader, lures, and hooks. He makes sure his hooks are extra sharp and he triangulates the point of his hook so that it has three cutting edges rather than just a conical point. He carries a small whetstone in his pocket and touches up his hooks often.

When Stu casts his streamer fly to a tarpon, he tries hard to present it the correct distance from the fish. He has found that you have to drop the fly in front of the fish close enough so that it can be seen but not so close that it will spook the fish. He fishes with a light drag on his reel and applies tension with his fingers when needed. When a tarpon hits the fly, he sets the hook three or four times in rapid succession.

Once a tarpon is hooked, Stu keeps the pressure on the fish all the time, keeping the fish as close as possible during the fight. He believes that "bowing" to the tarpon is necessary when it leaps. This is done by lowering the rod and pointing the tip directly at the fish. He feels that you lose fewer fish this way by having the hook pull out, and there won't be a taut line when the tarpon falls back into the water.

Captain Johnny Brantner, who runs the boat *Fiesta* out of Marathon, in the Florida Keys, is a top tarpon guide who has caught hundreds of big tarpon from his boat for his clients. He fishes mostly under the bridges along the Overseas Highway, so he uses fairly heavy tackle for the tarpon. Sturdy salt-water rods and 3/0 or 4/0 reels filled with 50- or 60-pound-test monofilament line are needed to fight and boat the big fish.

Johnny's favorite bait is a live mullet, which he hooks through the upper lip with a 6/0 Sobey hook. He will often cripple the mullet by pinching its gills to make it bleed and act disabled. He then lets it out under a cork or plastic float toward the bridge or a likely spot. Johnny recommends striking soon after the tarpon picks up the bait, rather than waiting.

Vic Dunaway, editor of *Florida Sportsman* magazine, is also a fine all-around angler who fishes for big tarpon in Government Cut, situated at the south end of Miami Beach. There, from spring to early

Stu Apte, master angler, admires the huge, 155-pound tarpon he caught on a fly rod at Sugarloaf Key, in Florida. This is the fourth tarpon over 150 pounds that he has taken on a fly rod. (*Bernice Apte photo*)

summer, big schools of tarpon are usually present. The best fishing for them takes place on an outgoing tide early in the morning, in the evening, and at night. Most of the fishing is done during the high tides near the jetties guarding the entrance to the cut or inlet. Then, as the tide drops, you can fish the channels and markers in the ocean in front of the jetties. You'll often see the tarpon rolling and can fish in that spot.

Vic uses such lures as the bucktail or plastic tail jig weighing about 1 ounce, and he fishes them from a drifting boat. He lets the jig sink to the bottom, then reels in a couple of turns and starts working his rod up and down gently. He finds that a tarpon will usually hit the jig as it is tumbling down. You can also catch tarpon there on live baits such as shrimp, mullet, blue crabs, and pinfish by letting them drift out on a free line.

Bob Trotter fishes for the big tarpon that show up during some years on the flats along Florida's West Coast from Crystal Bay to just south of Chassahowitzka Bay. There schools of big tarpon may show in shallow water during May or June. Bob caught one going just over 200 pounds in those waters.

This is sight fishing: you stalk the tarpon quietly until you get within casting distance and can cast a plug in front of a school or an individual fish. Bob says it is best to cast beyond the fish and then reel the plug in in front of them. The strike is savage, and if the fish is hooked there are plenty of wild leaps in the shallow water. As anywhere else, however, most of the tarpon are lost early in the fight.

When tarpon refuse to hit lures, Bob O'Hara finds that the gaff-topsail catfish makes one of the best baits for these fish. He hooks the catfish through the back with a big, 8/0 or 9/0, hook and lets it down to the bottom on a sliding sinker rig, then waits for a bite. When a tarpon picks up the catfish, he lets it run with the bait. Then, when the tarpon stops, he waits again, until it starts moving off once more, before setting the hook.

FIN CUT OFF

Gaff-topsail catfish hooked for tarpon

Cal Cochran is a fishing guide in the Florida Keys who takes his anglers out for tarpon during the so-called "off season," in the winter, when they are hard to locate and catch. He concentrates on the mangrove-lined islands and shores in the Keys and finds that the smaller tarpon hang around these mangroves, and can be caught, most of the time except during cold fronts, when they may leave for a short period.

Most of the tarpon Cal catches are taken by casting a live shrimp or lures close to the mangroves. He approaches the spot to be fished quietly and shuts off his motor at least three hundred feet away. Then he poles or drifts toward the mangroves. He also advises the anglers in his boat to be quiet and not bang anything around. If he does happen to frighten the fish he waits for fifteen or twenty minutes before fishing so that the tarpon get used to the presence of the boat.

However, Cal has also found that tarpon are curious, and he has one trick that often draws them out of the mangroves for a look. He poles up to the mangroves and hits the water with the push pole where the mangrove roots touch the water. He calls this "bush-whacking," and it often draws tarpon out from under the mangroves so you can cast to them later.

Captain Bob West is a fishing guide who runs the boat *Sea Dancer,* at Key West, Florida. He catches a lot of big tarpon, over 100 pounds, for his clients. He gets most of them by trolling slowly along the edge of the ship channel in Key West Harbor. He uses underwater plugs on fairly heavy salt-water rods and reels with 30- or 40-pound-test lines.

Captain Mike Montella says that the best time to catch tarpon in the ocean or along the beaches on Florida's East Coast is when they are chasing mullet. Then you can use a weighted snag hook to foul-hook a mullet and let it sink toward the bottom. Or you can hook the mullet through the lips or back and cast it out and let it swim around. He finds that tarpon will also hit big plugs, spoons, and jigs when they are feeding on the mullet.

Scott Boyd, who owns a tackle store in Fort Lauderdale, recommends that when fishing for tarpon in that section of Florida you use a "Trout Tout" weighing about an ounce and a quarter. This is a jig with a plastic tail, and he finds the white body and red head very effective. Once you locate a school of tarpon, you cast the lure, let it sink to the bottom, and then jig it up. Night fishing is usually best, with the period around the full moon especially productive.

Roger Cavallo fishes for tarpon from the bridges in the Tampa, Florida, area and he catches many. He uses a live baitfish such as a greenback minnow, small ladyfish, pinfish, or mullet. When using a pinfish, he cuts off the sharp spines on the dorsal fin. Roger finds that the last of the incoming tide at night is a good time to fish for tarpon from bridges. Then he looks for baitfish under the lights and for tarpon hanging around in the shadows. He tries to cast his baitfish about 4 to 6 feet in front of a tarpon.

When a tarpon takes the bait, Roger gives him some slack line and then sets the hook. As he doesn't apply too much pressure or drag, the tarpon will usually move away from the bridge and run and jump in open water, where it will use up most of its energy, becoming easier to handle and land later.

Ray Howerton fishes around Fort Myers, Florida, for tarpon from April to September. He finds that the best fishing takes place on nights around the time of the full moon. He uses the head part of a big mullet and hooks it through the lips. Then he lets this bait out in the tide on a sliding-sinker rig.

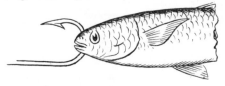

Mullet head used for tarpon

Ed Corlett waits until the sea worms called *Leodice* start hatching on the flats in the Florida Keys. This usually occurs in May or June during the full moon. Then he heads for these flats and finds tarpon by the hundreds feeding on the worms. He casts a streamer fly toward the feeding fish and usually gets fast action.

John O'Neil catches a lot of tarpon in the Fort Lauderdale, Florida, area. He uses such plugs as the Rebel, Sea-Bee, Cisco Kid, and Mirro-Lure. He casts and trolls these lures at night using a fairly stiff rod with a bait-casting reel filled with 25-pound-test line for most of this tarpon fishing. And like most tarpon fishermen, he keeps the hooks on his lures needle-sharp.

Marion Huston catches big tarpon from the surf along Virginia beaches. This kind of tarpon fishing offers plenty of thrills and sport; but this is the hard way to catch them. It calls for a heavy surf outfit to do the job: Marion uses a 10½-foot surf stick with a revolving-spool reel filled with three hundred yards of 36-pound-test braided nylon line. He adds a 100-pound-test shock leader in front of his line. With this outfit he can cast up to 6- and 8-ounce sinkers and fish bait, usually a big piece of spot or mullet. Huston looks for tarpon rolling near the beach and then casts his bait out in that spot. He finds this fishing is best during the summer months.

18

SNOOK

The snook, in southern waters, is the closest counterpart to the striped bass in northern waters. Their actions, feeding and other habits are very similar to those of the striped bass. They are highly selective most of the time and, like the striped bass, are unpredictable and temperamental. When conditions are right they'll feed like crazy for brief periods and hit lures and baits. But when they go on a hunger strike they'll drive you nuts trying to fool them with a bait or a lure. So, like the striped bass, they are not an easy fish to catch and offer a challenge that many Florida anglers can't resist. Many of these anglers become snook specialists, fishing only for these fish and spending hours haunting the spots where they are present or apt to show.

One such specialist is Earl Downey, who has spent a lifetime fishing for snook in many parts of Florida and who wrote a small book called *How to Fish for Snook*. He catches most of his snook from piers and bridges and uses a stiff rod from 6 to 8 feet long and a salt-water reel that holds 150 to 200 yards of 30- to 50-pound-test line.

Downey uses a live shrimp on a bottom rig with a sinker, lowers it under a bridge and fishes it at various levels but usually close to the bottom. He hooks the big shrimp through the head. When he wants to cast a live shrimp with a spinning outfit, he takes a long-shank single hook and ties a big yellow feather near the eye of the hook. Then he hooks a live shrimp through the head on this feather hook, casts it out, and retrieves it slowly with some rod action.

Downey also uses lures such as jigs for snook. He likes the 1-ounce jig with a yellow head and white nylon body, which he bounces along the bottom. Or he reels faster to keep it at the level at

which the snook are feeding. He also uses plugs such as the Mirro-
lure and the underwater Pikie. He varies his retrieve with these
plugs, trying slow, normal, and fast reeling with rod action.

Earl Downey likes to fish for snook during the high tides in most
places. He feels that you have more spots to fish then and the snook
are apt to be feeding rather than moving or cruising. He finds fishing
is usually best in the evening from just before sunset to midnight.
Then, again, in the early morning from before daybreak until an
hour after sunrise. He likes an incoming tide in the evening and
morning and finds the period from the first quarter of the moon until
the full moon the most productive. He catches most of his snook
in Florida from May to August.

Jean Crooks pioneered the fishing for big snook seen cruising in
the canals in Florida. He found that if you use a fly rod and a small
white or yellow streamer tied on a No. 2/0 hook, you can often
make a snook seen cruising on top hit this lure. You have to keep
abreast of the moving fish and cast your fly in front and beyond the
snook and then retrieve it so that it passes in front of its nose.

Rocky Weinstein was a well-known fishing guide who also fished
for snook in the canals and Everglades of Florida. He advocated
light tackle, often used a fly rod himself and liked customers who
did. He tied many of his own flies with long hackle feathers, which
would breathe in the water. And he retrieved them in short jerks and
pauses that brought this action out to the utmost. When fishing in canals such as the one along the Tamiami Trail, he used a fly tied to
resemble the tiny mud minnows that the snook would feed on in
those waters.

Ted Smallwood, who guided and fished in the Florida Everglades
for many years, had one trick that he often pulled on the snook. He
found that the snook would usually lie well back in the roots under
the mangrove trees at high tide. So he would cast and deliberately
hang up in a mangrove tree, then pull and shake it hard. A snook
would then come out to see what all the fuss was about and Ted
would cast a lure toward the fish and often hook it.

Herman Lucerne also fished the Florida Everglades for many
years, and he knows the best spots and techniques for snook. He'd
usually head into the maze of bays, rivers, lagoons, creeks, and
islands that few other anglers fished since he would rather fish for
wild snook that haven't been seen by any other humans. And he

Jean Crooks fished in Florida's canals and caught many big snook like this one on a fly rod with tiny bucktail or streamer flies. (*City of Miami News Bureau photo*)

didn't waste much time fishing a spot. He'd make a few casts and then be off to try a new spot.

He liked to fish the passes, points, and small creeks where there is a runoff. He found the mouths of rivers and creeks best on the outgoing tide. A prime spot is the upcurrent side of an oyster bar and the point of an island where the current splits to go in opposite directions.

Still another snook expert who fishes the Everglades and has caught thousands of snook is Oscar Jenkins. He lives in New Jersey but spends the winters in Florida in a trailer near his fishing grounds. He likes the Ferguson Bay and Ferguson River area and does most of his fishing there. He uses a spinning rod with 12-pound-test line for most of his catches, since the snook range from 2 to 18 pounds in weight. His favorite lure for these fish is a light jig, varying from ¼ to ⅜ ounce. When bigger snook are around he would use a heavier outfit, with plugs.

Of course, having fished the small region he has for so many years, he knows all the best spots, such as the mangrove-lined shores, points, holes, channels, drop-offs, eddies, rips, and creek junctions, where snook hang out. And like many snook experts, he doesn't waste much time fishing these spots. He stops in a spot for five minutes and casts to all the best water. If he gets no hits and sees no signs of fish, he moves on to the next spot.

Frank Haverstick waits until the mullet run in the surf along Florida's East Coast and then fishes for snook from the piers. This usually happens in the fall, when northeast storms lash the coast and the surf turns rough. Then he often has good snook fishing even in the middle of the day. He finds that jigs and plugs make good lures at this time, and your best chance of getting a strike is to cast where the snook can be seen chasing the mullet.

Captain Andy McLean has fished for snook in the Florida Everglades country for many years. He takes anglers out in his boat the *Snook Dust II* from Chokoloskee Island. After years of fishing these waters, he knows the best spots, holes, channels, and tides for each area. Andy McLean publishes a fishing guide called the *Fishing Mate,* which comes out every year; it has maps of the Everglades National Park showing the best spots to fish for snook, tarpon, redfish, sea trout, and snappers.

Captain Andy McLean is a great believer in the quiet approach in snook fishing, and he feels that most anglers speed too much through the narrow creeks and waterways where snook are found. When the tide starts to ebb, he fishes in the passes and rivers, along the shore-lines at deep bends, around oyster bars, drain-offs, and dead trees, and at the mouths of creeks. He also looks for spots where two currents meet. He finds that during the winter months the creeks offer the best fishing for snook. There he fishes the sharp bends, the places where two creeks converge, and the entrances to bays. He drifts with the tide and casts jigs or plugs.

When the water is muddy, Andy will often troll a No. 4 Reflecto spoon about 60 feet behind the boat to locate and catch the snook. Once he catches a fish or two, he may stop, and start casting in that spot.

Butch Cameron is a guide who fishes around Marco Island, in the Ten Thousand Islands area of Florida. One of his favorite spots is the rip off Cape Romano. There the deadliest method of fishing is to anchor in the tide and fish with a live pinfish. This bait is fished on fairly stout tackle and reels filled with 20- to 30-pound-test line. A sliding-sinker rig is used with a 2- to 3-ounce weight and a 6/0 or 7/0 hook. The hook is run through the lips or eyesockets of the pinfish, which is then let out in the current. Usually the best fishing takes place when the tide is going out and running at a good speed. The best months in this area are May, June, and July.

Snorky Ryan finds fast fishing for snook in Florida from April to June, when fresh water pours into tidal canals, bringing baitfish such as small shad into the ditches. Then the snook move in to feed in these canals and rivers.

Vic Dunaway has fished for snook in about every good spot in southern Florida from the beaches, piers, and bridges, and in the bays, rivers, and canals. But one of his favorite ways of catching them is to use a casting rod and reel and flip a plug into or close to the mangrove roots. For this he uses a yellow darter plug and drops it as close to the root as possible or even inside a small opening in the mangroves. He then pops the plug two or three times and starts to reel it in fast. He finds he gets most of his hits after the plug dives and starts darting underwater. Vic recommends casting to the same spot three to four times before moving on to the next one.

Bob Whitaker fished around Marco Island for many years using the standard snook lures. Then, one day, he hit on the idea of using

a cardboard lure for these fish. He cuts a 4-inch-long strip tapering
to a point at each end and runs a No. 4/0 Eagle Claw hook through
one end of the paper lure. He uses this simple lure at night from a
boat and drifts it down with the current toward the feeding snook.
You can also use the paper lure from a pier, dock, or low bridge at
night when snook are lying and feeding near the lights. Then it's a
good idea to move or swish it around on top to give it some action.

Cardboard lure used for snook

Jack McCrea, of Cape Coral, Florida, fishes for snook with a live
shrimp below a popping cork or float similar to the rig used for sea
trout. And he fishes it almost the same way: by casting the rig out,
then jerking it to pop the cork, and then waiting to see if it attracts a
snook.

Ed Buckow also enjoys the challenge of fishing for snook in Florida. He favors inlets such as those at Palm Beach and Jupiter, and
St. Lucie Inlet, with the best time being from June to September. He
fishes the inlets on an outgoing tide and uses live pinfish, small
croakers, or mullet. He prefers a light boat rod with a revolving-
spool reel or a medium salt-water spinning rod for this fishing, with
lines testing from 15 to 25 pounds.

Ed finds that when snook are feeding they will cruise along shorelines, sea walls, and jetties, and over bars, oyster beds, and sand
flats. At times, they will chase baitfish on top. Then he uses live
baits fished just below the surface or casts surface plugs at them. But,
most of the time, he finds, snook will be lying and feeding on the
bottom, and the lures and baits have to be presented at that level.
When fishing from a bridge, Buckow uses a live shrimp or a lure
and casts upcurrent so that the offering sweeps back under the bridge.

There are a lot of snook specialists fishing the bridges in the Stuart area of Florida, and they get some big ones from time to time. One of these men is George Hopkins, who favors the bridge over the St. Lucie River, where he has caught snook up to 44 pounds. Unlike most snook experts, George Hopkins prefers to fish in the daytime. He uses live mullet, which he catches with a cast net. Then he hooks the mullet through the back just behind the head with a big, 8/0 or 9/0 hook. This hook is attached to a 4-foot stainless-steel wire leader, which in turn is tied to 150 yards of 60-pound-test monofilament line on a salt-water revolving-spool reel.

According to George, the best fishing takes place when the mullet are moving under the bridge. He finds that big snook are lazy, so he cripples his mullet a bit, making it easier to catch. Other times, Hopkins may fish in the surf from a beach during the late-spring or early-summer months. Then snook will often come in to feed on baby turtles, which hatch in the sand and head for the water. There he uses a regular surf bottom rig with a mullet head for bait. He casts out the mullet head and lets it roll around on the bottom, and big snook often mistake it for a baby turtle.

Bert Fania also fishes the Stuart area for snook, but he does it from a boat, using whole rigged eels. He used to use the rigged eels up North for striped bass, then decided to try them for snook in Florida waters. They were an immediate success, and since then he has caught many big snook on them. Bert uses eels about 12 to 14 inches long and adds a small block-tin squid with a hook weighing about 1½ ounces at the head to give the eel action. He adds another, 9/0 hook to the hook on the jig and ties it to the neck of the eel.

Bert uses husky tackle for his snook fishing, because he trolls near bridges and other obstructions and has to hook and hold or turn a big snook. So he trolls with a salt-water rod, 3/0 reel, and 60-pound-test line, and he tightens the drag on the reel so that the line barely pulls off the spool. He checks the eel next to the boat to see if it has the correct swimming action and then lets it out 35 to 40 feet when trolling next to the bridges. In more open waters he may let out 70 to 75 feet of line. Most of the snook caught on the rigged eels run from 15 to 40 pounds.

Jim Branch is a charter member of the "Jetty Conchs," a club of anglers who fish for snook from the rock piles when the mullet run in September and October along the surf in the Palm Beach, Florida,

The Ten Thousand Islands area of Florida contains many snook, which are caught there among the mangroves. They can be caught the year round, but fishing is best in the spring and early summer. (*Florida News Bureau photo*)

area. He uses a stiff rod and a reel filled with 30- to 50-pound-test line. On the end of the 5- to 6-foot wire leader he adds an 8/0 hook and a ¼-ounce weight. Then he tries to snag a live mullet, hooks it through the lips, and casts it out where snook are feeding.

Doyle Doxsee is a guide who does most of his fishing around Marco Island. He finds that the most dependable combination for snook is a white or yellow jig with half of a small shrimp on the hook. The jig with shrimp should be cast as close as possible to the mangroves or other snook hot spots. After making a few casts in a spot, Doyle moves on to a new spot, and he knows plenty of them in the mangrove country.

Herbert Houghton fished for many years from Florida's Inland Waterway bridges on the East Coast, and he caught plenty of snook. He used a 20-foot husky cane pole and attached 20 feet of No. 8 stainless-steel wire line to the pole and a strong hook on the end of this leader. He baited it with a live shrimp hooked through the head. Then he flipped the shrimp into the current and let it sink toward the bottom as it was carried back toward the bridge and under it. He found that most of his snook took up positions in an eddy or dead spot in the current. Or they would hang back in the shadows thrown by the bridge lights. He would drift the shrimp a few times in such spots and then move on to another one.

Half a shrimp on hook for snook

Carl Garrettson and his wife, Millie, are snook specialists who also fish from bridges, but in the Florida Keys, and they catch many of them from November to March. They get most of these snook on bucktail jigs, which Carl makes and sells. His favorite is a red-and-white bucktail weighing ½ to ⅝ ounce. They have their best luck at night, casting into the current during the last of the outgoing tide and retrieving the jig close to the bottom. Most of their strikes come as the jig nears the bridge.

Jerry Klink lives in Mexico and fishes for the so-called "black snook," of Baja California. They are closely related to the Florida species but reach a larger size. Two top spots for this fishing, according to Jerry, are Puerto Chale and the Mulege River. He finds that the snook at Puerto Chale hit jigs and shrimp, while those in the Mulege River like underwater plugs and live finger mullet. You need strong tackle for these snook, because they run for the mangroves and foul your line or cut you off, every chance they get.

Carlos Barrantes owns and runs a fishing camp in Costa Rica and fishes for snook from the Caribbean beaches there. He finds this fishing is best during the fall months, especially during September and October. The fish come into shallow water then and cruise just beyond the breakers. Carlos picks a spot along the beach and just casts until a snook or a small school of them come by. The most effective lure is a darting-type plug in red-and-white or yellow. He casts these with a spinning outfit with 8- to 12-pound-test lines. And he catches snook up to 20 or 30 pounds there.

19

SWORDFISH

The first swordfish was taken on rod and reel by William Boschen back in 1913 off Catalina Island, California, and weighed 355 pounds. Since then, fewer than two thousand have been caught by sportsmen. When you add up the total of years, months, days, and hours spent by thousands of anglers, the gas and diesel fuel burned up, and the millions of dollars invested in buying, outfitting, and maintaining sport-fishing boats and for fishing tackle just to catch swordfish, you begin to realize that this is a sport for a select few.

Swordfishing will never be a sport for the casual angler who fishes for them once in a while. To catch a swordfish you have to make it your prime goal. Anglers seeking swordfish don't waste much time on other fish during the height of the season. They pass up opportunities to fish for marlin, tuna, sharks, and other species because they want to use every available minute to locate and bait a sword.

And not every angler is physically or mentally suited to be a swordfisherman. You really have to have determination, patience, fortitude, and dedication to keep you going in the face of all kinds of disappointments and frustrations—and the odds against seeing, baiting, and hooking a swordfish. There are many cases on record of anglers fishing ten, twenty, and even up to thirty years without boating a single swordfish! During this period they may have sighted, baited, and hooked dozens of fish and lost them all. One angler, George C. Thomas, baited one hundred fifty swordfish and didn't get a single strike! He hooked and lost sixteen in fights ranging from five minutes to eight hours before finally catching one.

Zane Grey fished for every major game fish in the ocean, and he wrote that swordfishing "takes more time, patience, endurance, study, skill, nerve, and strength not to mention money of any game known to me." In eight years of fishing he caught only two swordfish. He tells of fighting one swordfish for eleven hours and then have the hooked fish start feeding on a school of flying fish. Then his luck changed or, rather, his skill and know-how increased and he finally wound up catching a total of twenty-four swordfish.

Zane Grey believed in using large baits for swordfish, because he felt that they were more readily seen by the fish than small baits. He concentrated on swordfishing in Pacific waters for several years and fished two to three months each year for them. He would cruise and search and present his bait to swordfish wherever he thought they might be present. He was one of the first big-game anglers to install a crow's-nest, or platform on a mast, for spotting swordfish and for presenting the bait to them from a height. He believed that keeping as much of the line and leader off the water as possible resulted in more pick-ups, or strikes. He would make a big circle a good distance from the swordfish and swing the bait in front of it. This kept the boat away from the swordfish; his strikes increased dramatically and he began hooking more fish.

Oliver C. Grinnell caught the first rod-and-reel swordfish in Atlantic waters off Montauk Point, Long Island, in 1927. He hired Captain Walter Baker and Captain Billy Hatch as his crew, and they used whole mackerel up to 1½ and 2 pounds for bait. Mackerel are less favored as bait nowadays and most anglers use a whole squid, a favorite food of the swordfish and most likely the main reason why it dives at night to great depths to feed. But swordfish are hard to interest in any food while they are basking on the surface, so a new or strange bait of fish may prove more effective than their regular diet.

J. Charles Davis II fished for swordfish in Pacific waters for many years. He mentions running into a school of them once while they were feeding on skipjack. Then he had one of the swordfish take his bait while it was being trolled fast on top. Finding more than one or two swordfish in one spot and having them take a trolled bait blind are both unusual events in swordfishing. Most of the time, Davis would wait until he saw the fins of a swordfish before presenting the bait. If a swordfish took his bait he fed line off his reel by hand. He felt it was very important to do this so that the swordfish felt no resistance, otherwise it would drop the bait and fail to return.

Kip Farrington fished for swordfish in many parts of the world, and both he and his wife, Chisie, caught quite a few of them. Like Zane Grey, he felt that the "swordfish is the greatest sporting game fish of them all." Kip baited some swordfish as many as sixteen times before they submerged without taking the bait. He felt that if a swordfish didn't strike a bait by the fourth time it was presented, you might as well give up and look for another fish. According to Kip, the best swordfish to bait was one that was swimming steadily and slowly on the same course. And he learned that swordfish that breached, or leaped, rarely took a bait.

Kip Farrington would look for commercial harpooners and search for swordfish in that area. He would also look for birds and oil patches or fish floating on the surface. He found that swordfish surface mostly between 10 A.M. and 4 P.M. Because a swordfish is apt to take a bait that it doesn't usually feed on, Kip carried several kinds of rigged baits and presented these to the fish. And he always tried to avoid changing the speed of the boat's motor when approaching and baiting a swordfish.

W. E. S. Tuker, who pioneered swordfishing off Chile and caught many big ones in those waters, used a 4- to 5-pound bonito for bait and rigged it with two 14/0 hooks. He offset the hooks just a bit before putting them inside the bait. Tuker used to split the fish bait along the belly and remove the insides but leave the backbone in. After putting two hooks inside with their points facing the tail of the bait, he would sew up the belly. The cable leader emerges at the tail and is tied to it, after which the leader is brought up along the fish's back toward the head. Then it is tied to the line used to sew up the bait's mouth. The bonito is trolled head first, but when a swordfish hit, it would cut the line holding the leader to the bait's mouth. The bonito would then turn around and the swordfish would swallow it head first with the leader out of the way.

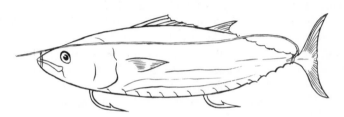

Tuker method of rigging bonito for swordfish

Tuker would let the bonito out about 200 to 250 feet behind the boat and present it to the swordfish underwater. He believed in giving the swordfish plenty of time to swallow the bait, so he let the swordfish take 100 feet of line and would often wait eight to ten minutes before the fish started moving off again. He would then let it take another 400 or 500 feet before setting the hooks.

Lou Marron also fished off Chile for swordfish, with his wife, Eugenie, and they both caught some of the biggest swordfish ever taken on rod and reel. Lou Marron caught the world-record, 1,182-pound swordfish in 1953 in one hour and forty-five minutes. He worked the big fish up to his boat eleven times before it was finally subdued. A couple of years later he caught two swordfish in one day, weighing 710 and 750 pounds, for a combined weight of 1,460 pounds! And Eugenie, who was a great advocate of light tackle, caught a 772-pound swordfish on twenty-four-thread line in one hour and fifty-five minutes even though one of her legs had been injured earlier.

Lou Marron usually tried to present the bait about twenty-five feet in front of a swordfish just below the surface of the water. He would let out about 150 feet of line while holding another 50 feet of slack line in reserve. When a swordfish hit the bait, he would throw the slack line into the water. Lou found that there was no set rule on how long a swordfish should be allowed to run with the bait before setting the hook. Each strike and each fish acted differently, and he set the hook when he felt the time was right. He also found that at times it was necessary to present the bait to the same swordfish two, three, or even four times before it was finally taken.

Captain Walt Gorman, who ran the boat *Explorer* for Lou Marron when he caught many of his big swordfish off Chile, claimed he could smell swordfish when they were around. And Captain Walter Budd, who handled the boat for Hans Hinrich when he fished for swordfish, looked for sharks swimming on top; he knew then that swordfish would also be found in the same waters.

Captain Frank Mundus, the shark-fishing expert, also found that this was true on many occasions while chumming for sharks from his boat the *Cricket II* off Montauk. He has had swordfish take such baits as whiting, butterfish, mackerel, and squid being fished for sharks.

Captain Walter Drobecker was a charter-boat skipper at Montauk

Point for many years, and he caught quite a few swordfish for his customers in those waters. But his greatest feat was catching a 400-pound swordfish all alone from a forty-three-foot boat! Usually, billfishing, especially swordfishing, is a "team" sport, requiring the close co-operation of the captain, mate, and angler in baiting, hooking, fighting, and gaffing one of these gladiators of the deep. But Walter Drobecker did it the hard way—all by himself. He was taking the big boat offshore along the south side of Long Island. But he had a rod, reel, and squid bait rigged and ready just in case he did see a swordfish.

Then, about eighteen miles south of Shinnecock Inlet, he spotted the tell-tale dorsal fin and tail of a swordfish. He made a pass toward the fish and dropped the squid bait in the water about fifty feet in front of the fins and let out some line. Then he saw the dorsal fin and tail fin on the sword quiver, and the fish went down below the surface. Drobecker peeled more line off the reel, then threw on the reel drag, ran up to the flying bridge and gunned the engines of the boat to set the hook. The rod bent sharply and the fish was on!

The swordfish ran three quarters of the line off the reel before it stopped and Walt could start regaining some line. The fish headed toward the boat and he had to take off the harness and run up on the flying bridge again to get the boat out of the way. Then he came down and got into the fighting chair again. But on several more occasions he had to leave the chair to handle the boat. Finally, after a battle of three hours and twenty-five minutes the swordfish was gaffed, lashed, and safely boated. Only one or two other anglers have ever succeeded in catching a swordfish on rod and reel alone in a boat.

Walter Drobecker used a Tycoon rod, 10/0 Penn Senator reel, and 80-pound-test line to make his catch. He believed in setting a light drag, of around 15 pounds, on his reel, as this would eventually exhaust the fish and reduce the chance of the hook's pulling out. He used a 15-foot cable leader and rigged a medium-sized squid with an 11/0 Martu hook. He had everything ready to go in the boat with his line in the port outrigger at the 100-foot mark. The squid rested in a bucket of ice and the slack line was coiled in the boat.

Drobecker always tried to approach a fish from the side, rather than from behind. He trolled at a low speed when he was near a swordfish, and he would free the line from the outrigger and swing the boat so that the bait passed twenty to fifty feet in front of the fish. But he didn't wait for a fish to slash at the bait. He would put the boat's engine into neutral and then let out enough slack line so that the bait sank. He believed that a swordfish found it easier to grab and mouth a bait that was 10 feet below the surface.

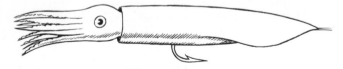

Squid rigged for swordfish

Frank Moss was also a charter-boat captain at Montauk Point, and he fished for swordfish there for many seasons. He says that the first big run of swordfish in June and early July at Montauk is the heaviest and produces the most action. After that, the action tapers off and is better farther north, off Massachusetts and the rest of New England, and off Canada.

Frank liked to use a good-sized squid rigged with a 10/0 or a 12/0 Sobey, Martu, or Sea Demon hook. The squid should be unwashed and fresh and kept in a plastic bag on ice until it is used. He felt that the natural oils and ink of the squid made it attractive to the swordfish and that it was more readily taken than a stale, washed-out bait.

Frank also believed that you should present the squid to a swordfish below the surface, letting it sink as a swordfish approached it. If the swordfish didn't take the bait or Frank lost sight of it, he would mark the spot with a buoy and then hang around and wait. He found that the swordfish will often surface again near by. Since swords usually travel in pairs or even small groups, Frank would also look around for another fish in the same area.

There have been cases in which swordfish have hit baits trolled fast for other fish and no drop-back or feeding of slack line was necessary. One such catch was made by Dr. Frank Black, the well-known conductor and musician, while fishing from Captain Ralph Pitt's boat the *Margaret III* off Montauk. He hooked and successfully boated a 307-pound swordfish, which took a rigged eel being trolled for school tuna.

Harry McGrotty is shown with a swordfish he caught on Captain Carl Darenburg's boat the *Tumult*. Captain Darenburg fishes out of Montauk for these and other fish. (*Frank Moss photo*)

Captain Carl Darenburg, another Montauk skipper, believes in presenting a bait to a swordfish with 150 to 200 feet of line out, and he swings the boat so that the bait passes in front of the fish. When a sword rises behind the bait and crosses over from one side to the other it usually means he's interested and ready to strike, and when he does, line is peeled out and a long drop-back is made. Then, when the swordfish stops, Carl waits until it starts swimming again before setting the hook. He doesn't believe in using the boat to set the hook, because it may take the bait too far away if the swordfish isn't hooked, and then you'll miss the chance to bait it again.

Darenburg also uses live baits such as mackerel, whiting, or sea robins for swordfish. Then he tries to drift down toward a swimming or surfacing swordfish and heave the bait close in front of it. The splash of the bait will often cause the swordfish to move in and pick up the live fish. Then, too, plenty of line is let out to allow the swordfish to mouth and swallow the bait.

Most swordfish are hooked on top or just below the surface, but some swordfish anglers believe more of these fish would be caught if you fished deeper for them. Catches such as the one made by Stuart Golden on Captain Harry Carter's boat the *Scamp* show that swordfish can be caught well below the surface. While fishing for sharks and chumming with ground bunker off Long Island, they drifted out a fresh squid, and when it reached a depth of 40 to 50 feet it was taken by a big fish. Stu fought the monster for two hours and fifty minutes and finally boated a 416-pound swordfish!

Most anglers wait until they see a swordfish before presenting a bait. This is fine if the water is calm and the visibility is good. But when the water is rough or the visibility is poor, it is difficult, if not impossible, to sight a swordfish. On such days Ted Lyman will troll blind for swordfish even though the odds are against a fish's seeing your bait, and against your hooking it even if it does.

One of the most successful swordfish anglers is Ed Gruber, who has fished from the boat *Nitso,* skippered by Captain Bill Holzman. He has taken as many as eleven swordfish in one year, and on several occasions he has caught two swordfish in one day. One of the reasons for their success is that they fish hard and range far and wide during the swordfish season, going out in all kinds of weather. Captain Bill Holzman feels that the "tuna" tower, or as he calls it, the "swordfish" tower, is highly important, since more than half of the fish they hooked were first seen underwater.

Bill Holzman finds that a small squid, about 12 inches long, rigged with two 12/0 hooks, works best for him. He hides the hooks inside the squid bait. But he will also carry and try other baits, such as mullet and eels. When a swordfish is sighted, Holzman tries to ma-

Most successful swordfish anglers use big, well-equipped boats such as this 42-foot tournament fisherman. They have to range far and wide in their search for the swordfish. (*Chris-Craft photo*)

neuver the boat so that the bait is presented on the end of 250 to 300 feet of line about 30 feet in front of the fish. Then he slows the boat down so that the bait sinks but still moves a bit.

If the swordfish takes the bait, Ed Gruber keeps feeding him slack line, and then, when he feels it is time, he puts the reel in gear, takes up the slack line, and sets the hook hard several times. Ed fights a swordfish with a very light drag on his reel but tries to keep the fish close to the boat as much as possible. But when a fish sounds, he will increase his drag and try to bring it up to the surface again. He never forces the fight too much and will always let a swordfish run if it is still fresh. Only when the mate grabs the wire leader and finds he can pull the fish in do they try to gaff it. If the fish can't be led and still shows signs of fight, Gruber lets it run out and continues the fight. This has payed off: Ed Gruber is one of the leaders in the number of swordfish successfully boated by a rod-and-reel angler.

Another highly successful swordfisherman is James French Baldwin, who has won many swordfish tournaments. He approaches swordfishing in a highly scientific manner and has even subscribed to a private weather service because he feels it is more accurate than the U. S. Weather Service. He keeps charts marked off to show where swordfish have been sighted, baited, hooked, lost, or boated. And he makes a note of the water temperatures, depths, dates, times, baits used, and the weather and water conditions.

Baldwin believes in using small baits, usually squid or whiting rigged on a single 12/0 hook sharpened to a needle point. He finds that he hooks more fish by using small baits, which are easier for a swordfish to swallow. He uses a 50-pound-test Dacron line on a 7½/0 reel. His drag is set at about 18 pounds.

If Baldwin sights a swordfish in a given area he usually goes back there the next day and often sees more. This payed off for him during one period of eleven days of fishing when he boated eight swordfish and caught doubles on two of those days! He also found that it pays to look for swordfish below the surface, because such fish are more likely to take a bait than those basking or cruising on top with fins showing.

Most of the anglers mentioned above caught their swordfish on top from big sport-fishing boats. But recently there has been a radical change in the swordfishing picture, and for the first time anglers in small, open boats from eighteen to twenty-four feet long have started catching these fish in large numbers. And in relatively short periods of time.

For years it was known that swordfish seen on top are not really feeding or interested in food. It was claimed that swordfish do most of their feeding down deep at night. Commercial fishermen often proved this in many parts of the world by hooking and boating swordfish on hand lines at night. Then some Cuban commercial fishermen in this country started long-lining at night for swordfish off Miami and began catching them regularly in large numbers.

Sports fishermen heard about these commercial catches, and on July 5, 1976, two cousins, Jerry and Jesse Webb, set out at night from Miami to try for swordfish. That first trip produced two swordfish, weighing 348 and 368 pounds. Other anglers got into the act, and by the end of that year forty-nine swordfish were caught on rod and reel at night.

Since then, several night-swordfishing tournaments have been held, and in almost all of them many fish have been caught. In one of these tournaments out of Fort Lauderdale, Doug Smith, fishing in a small, open boat, caught four swordfish in two nights, including one weighing 490 pounds! And he did it all the hard way: by fighting the swords while standing up.

Doug Smith and other Florida swordfish anglers are still learning about the best techniques, but quite a bit of information is already available. The fishing seems best along Florida's East Coast from Fort Pierce down to the Florida Keys, where the water is from 600 to 1,500 feet deep. Usually a run of ten to twenty miles offshore puts your boat in the prime waters.

Although swordfish are known to be present the year round off Florida, the best fishing has been from May through November, with the period just before and after the full moon being the most favorable.

The best bait for this night swordfishing is a natural squid about 10 to 14 inches long and rigged with two hooks in sizes 10/0 to 12/0. One hook has the shank buried in the tail end of the squid with the bend and point protruding. The other hook is inserted through the eyes or head of the squid. Some anglers also insert an egg-shaped sinker of 6 to 8 ounces inside the squid. Others attach the sinker with soft wire to the swivel above the leader so that it comes off when a swordfish is hooked. Mullet, mackerel, ballyhoo, or other fish are sometimes used for bait instead of the squid. Swordfish have also been caught on artificial plastic squid scented with fish oils.

The bait or lure is attached to a monofilament leader from 12 to 20 feet long testing from 200 to 300 pounds. And while these night swordfish have been caught on 50-pound-class outfits, most anglers favor 80- to 130-pound-class outfits.

Night swordfishing is done from a boat drifting with the tide, current, or wind, with anywhere from two to four lines set out at various depths from 50 to 200 feet. Swordfish feeding down deep at night aren't as fussy about taking a bait as those found on top or just below the surface during the daytime. They may play with the bait for a while but usually grab and swallow it before long. At the first indication of a pick-up of the bait by a fish, the reel is thrown into free spool and a long drop-back is given so that the swordfish can swallow the bait.

So, for the first time in history, swordfishing is within reach of the average angler. For years it had been practiced mostly by wealthy sportsmen who could afford the big boats, equipment, fuel, and captains and mates that were needed to catch even a few swordfish. This is no longer true; the small-boat angler of moderate means can now go out off Florida and stand an excellent chance of catching the mighty swordfish.

20

MARLIN

The various marlins are held in high esteem by most big-game anglers throughout the world. In fact, many of these anglers rank the blue marlin just below the swordfish as the greatest game fish. And even the smaller marlin, such as the striped marlin and white marlin, are spectacular fighters, often leaping out of the water many times before being subdued.

Through the years, Ocean City, Maryland, has ranked as the foremost fishing port for white marlin, and anglers who seek them make annual visits there during the summer months. It all began back in 1934, when Paul Townsend and his brother Jack started searching for white marlin offshore and located them in a place called the "Jack Spot." In 1935 they brought Captain Bill Hatch up from Miami and began fishing for them in earnest in August. In that one month alone they saw more than one hundred white marlin, raised sixty, and caught thirteen. They hooked so few fish because they didn't have outriggers on the boat. The following year, they started fishing earlier, in July, from a new boat with outriggers and began to hook and catch a lot more marlin.

Donald Leek is one sportsman who admires the white marlin and has spent many years fishing for them from one of the "Pacemakers" his company builds. He fishes long and hard, often putting in eight or ten hours a day, criss-crossing back and forth covering the best waters where white marlin are found. Don favors 20- or 30-pound-class outfits for white marlin. He likes a small squid for bait and rigs it with a small, No. 5/0 hook. He will also use ballyhoo and mullet at times. He fishes these baits on three lines—one on a flat line directly behind the stern and the other two on the outriggers. The bait on the

White marlin such as the one he's holding rarely run over 100 pounds, but they are one of the greatest light-tackle fish in the ocean. (*Florida News Bureau photo*)

flat line will be about 30 to 35 feet behind the boat. And the two outrigger baits will be about 50 to 60 feet out.

When a marlin rises behind his bait and knocks it off the outrigger but fails to get hooked, Don will reel in and lift his rod tip, taking the bait away from the fish. This often excites the fish and makes it hit. He has often taken the bait away from a marlin four or five times before the fish finally took the bait for good. Once the fish is hooked, Don likes to fight his white marlin standing up with the rod in a belt.

Don fishes almost everywhere that white marlin are found. During the summer months he fishes out of Ocean City, Maryland, or New Jersey ports at such spots as the Norfolk, Baltimore, and Wilmington canyons. He likes North Carolina waters during the fall of the year. And he also fishes off the Bahamas—at Bimini, Walker Cay, and Chub Cays.

Paul Mumford fishes for white marlin out of Ocean City. He helped to develop the saran teaser, and trolls two or three of them on short lines behind the boat. For bait he uses squid, ballyhoo, and eels, and trolls these anywhere from four to seven knots. Two of the baits are on flat lines and two more on the outriggers. When a white marlin follows a bait for a long time without striking, Paul teases the fish by raising the rod tip and jigging the bait. Or he reels in about 15 feet of line, lowers his rod and free-spools the bait back to the fish, then raises the rod and jigs the bait.

Captain Charles "Bob" Robinson also fishes for white marlin out of Ocean City, on his 47-foot boat the *Calypso*. He finds the best

Rigged eel with plastic skirt for white marlin

fishing is found at the Norfolk Canyon or the Baltimore Canyon. He likes to use eels from 12 to 14 inches long rigged with two hooks, and he usually adds a plastic skirt over the head of the eel. These are trolled on four or five lines at high speed. He also has a couple of teasers out just beyond the prop wash.

Captain Robinson prefers the rigged eels because they make tough, durable baits that can be trolled all day without falling apart. In fact, you can often catch more than one marlin on the same eel. He finds that the plastic skirt added at the head makes the eels weedless and also easier to see in the water. He uses green, yellow, white, orange, and blue plastic skirts.

Captain Robinson finds that the white-marlin fishing off Ocean City usually runs from June to September. Fishing will often be fast and furious early in the season. By July, the fishing tends to settle down, with the boats getting one to three marlin a day. Then it picks up again, in late August and September.

Dr. Irving Sussman has been an avid white-marlin fisherman for over twenty-five years and has helped to pioneer the fishing at the various offshore canyons. He made one trip with seven anglers on his boat the *Ripper* near the Baltimore Canyon, and that day they raised sixty white marlin, hooked and lost fifteen, and caught twenty-one! Of course, almost all these fish were released to fight another day.

The striped marlin has been a favorite with California anglers since way back in 1903. Later on, members of the Catalina Tuna Club began using light tackle and catching marlin up to 300 pounds on 9-thread and 6-thread lines. Harry Willey was one of those early anglers around Catalina Island and other Pacific waters. One of his tricks was to fill up several balloons with gas and use them to skip a bait on top of the water for the marlin. He also chummed the water around the boat with dog food and fish oil. He claimed that the chum brought around mackerel, which in turn attracted marlin.

One of the greatest light-tackle anglers for marlin is Andy Anderson, who caught over 323 striped marlin and twenty-two black marlin and even two swordfish on 12-pound-test line! Some of these fish ran over 300 pounds. One black marlin he caught went 381 pounds, but his line tested slightly more than 12 pounds, breaking test, so the fish was put into the 20-pound class.

Anderson trolls for his marlin with a flat line, holding the rod and reel in his hands with his thumb on the line, ready to let out line when he gets a strike. And once the fish is hooked, he and his captain try to keep the fish running and jumping all the time so that it gets tired quickly and can then be gaffed.

Harry Bonner fishes for striped marlin off southern California during July, August, and September. He swears by the artificial lures, such as plastic squid, flying fish, or mackerel. He especially favors the plastic squid called the Baja Killer, because it is so deadly in the Sea of Cortez, off Baja California. Bonner trolls these lures about 60 feet astern at speeds from three to five knots, depending on the wind and sea conditions. The lures should skitter and swim on top in a lifelike and attractive manner.

Al Zapanta is another light-tackle angler who has caught many striped marlin on spinning tackle. He does most of his fishing in Mexican waters and favors such ports as La Paz for his fishing. He rigs his flying-fish or mullet baits so that the hook is buried inside the fish. Then the marlin doesn't feel the hook when it swallows the bait. The fish is allowed to run with the bait freely so it doesn't go down deep. Then the hook is set and the marlin is fought with constant pressure so that it doesn't get a chance to rest. When the marlin does sulk or sound, the boat is backed down and line is gained for the next run. While fighting the marlin, the boat is kept parallel to the fish at all times.

Ernest Hemingway spent many years fishing for blue marlin in the Bahamas and off Cuba and caught many of these fine fish. He fished with and learned a lot from H. L. Woodward, who was one of the pioneer anglers for blue marlin off Cuba. H. L. Woodward often tried to drift baits deep, like the Cuban commercial fishermen in their small boats, but Hemingway looked down on this fishing and insisted on taking his marlin on the surface.

Hemingway was a husky, rugged individual who didn't believe in sparing himself when fighting a big fish. Part of this was due to the many sharks around Bimini, in the Bahamas, which would often multilate a hooked fish. So he tried to shorten the fights with marlin or tuna before the sharks got a chance at the fish. But he also believed that you have to show the fish who is boss, break its spirit early in the fight and take command. He never allowed any big fish to rest even a minute and applied pressure throughout the fight. He used to say, "You have to convince all big fish, and to convince them you have to be willing to suffer. Never give them a rest and never take one yourself. If you do, they get the equivalent of five minutes for every minute you get."

Kip Farrington fished in many of the best waters for blue marlin, which he often saw chasing a school of dolphin, so he liked to use these fish for bait. Many other blue-marlin anglers and captains like to troll along weed lines or patches of weeds or floating objects when seeking the big fish. Dolphin hang out under such flotsam, and this in turn attracts blue marlin to the area.

Don McCarthy, who helped promote the fishing in the Bahamas and fished himself every chance he got, says that the best months for blue marlin there are June, July, and August. His favorite grounds were the western edges of the Great and Little Bahama banks, in the rips and eddies of the Gulf Stream. He used a whole bonefish, mackerel, dolphin, bonito, or squid weighing from 2 to 5 pounds for bait.

Captain Tommy Gifford fished for all the big-game fish found in the ocean, but the blue marlin was one of his favorites. He played a big part in developing the fishing for blue marlin in the Bahamas at Cat Cay and helped catch the first ones there, back in 1933. He advocated light tackle for these fish as far back as 1939 and started using 16-ounce rods and 24-thread line for them. One of the anglers fishing from his boat with this tackle proved it was practical when he boated a 585-pound blue marlin with it. One day when fishing with Mike Lerner off Bimini they hooked a fish that fought for eight hours until it straightened out the 14/0 hook and got away. Tommy, who saw the blue marlin, which jumped twenty-five times, estimated its weight at 1,800 pounds.

Gifford spent the rest of his life seeking such big marlin off the Bahamas, Puerto Rico, and the Virgin Islands. He particularly liked the Virgin Islands, because blue marlin there ran big, were plentiful, and could be caught the year round. In 1969 he boated thirty-one blue marlin in two months of fishing! He felt that of all the marlins the blue marlin were the toughest fighters, because most of the fish over 1,000 pounds that are hooked get away.

Another blue-marlin master who likes the Virgin Islands and does most of his fishing there is Captain Johnny Harms. In fact, he was the one who told Tommy Gifford about the great fishing found there and invited him to come down to fish the area. Captain Harms in turn was approached by Laurance Rockefeller, who was developing Caneel Bay as a resort. He wanted an experienced fisherman to explore and develop the offshore fishing at this spot in the Virgin Islands.

Johnny Harms knew that currents bring baitfish and small fish on which the larger game fish feed. Since the Virgin Islands are the meeting place of such heavy currents, Johnny figured that this was a natural feeding area for the big billfish he was seeking. His beliefs were confirmed during the first year he fished there. He boated twenty-two blue marlin, thirteen white marlin, and many other spe-

Catching big billfish, such as this blue marlin being boated, is a team sport, in which captain, mate, and angler all pitch in to hook, fight, and boat the fish. (*Joel Arrington photo*)

cies. With such results, he thought so highly of the fishing potential that he moved to the Virgin Islands permanently in 1963 and started to take out fishermen on his charter boat. Since then, anglers on his boat have caught blue marlin weighing 814 and 845 pounds.

Johnny does most of his fishing along the 100-fathom curve, and he finds blue marlin the year round, with the biggest ones caught in July and August. One productive spot there is about eighteen miles north of Caneel Bay, along the drop-off, and another is the drop-off east of Virgin Gorda. Johnny looks for birds such as terns, boobies, and frigates working over schools of anchovies driven to the surface by bonito and blackfin tuna, which in turn attract the blue marlin.

L. T. "Leaky" Davis fishes for blue marlin off North Carolina and is very successful in catching these fish. He did a lot of his fishing on the boat *Pyramus,* out of Wrightsville Beach, owned by Captain W. John Craig. The fishing there is best from May through September. Davis likes to rig his bait Catalina style, with the hook outside, in front of the bonito, dolphin, or mullet. He feels that this is the best way to rig for blue marlin, because he believes the billfish takes the bait from the front, not from behind. And when he swallows the bait, the hook turns and snags him. He will also use a big strip bait cut from the belly of a bonito or skipjack. He shapes it like a fish, with points at both ends.

George Reed fishes strictly for blue marlin from his 31-foot boat *Marlin My Darlin.* He fishes off Florida and in the Bahamas for them but finds the most consistent fishing at Bimini, where they are present the year round, with the late-spring and summer months offering the peak fishing.

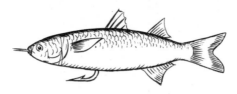

Big mullet rigged for blue marlin

George likes to use a 1½- to 2-pound mullet rigged with a single No. 12/0 Martu hook. The hook comes out on the underside just behind the head. He ties the gills down with light line so they stay closed. He usually trolls one mullet on a flat line just beyond the prop wash and two mullet on the outriggers about 150 feet out. If the marlin show behind the baits but refuse to take them, George will often speed up the boat to make the mullet leap out of the water; this often excites the marlin and makes them hit. He looks for blue marlin in tidal rips, along drop-offs and the edges of reefs, and in the deeper water of the Gulf Stream itself.

In recent years, more and more anglers have been discovering the great billfishing in the Gulf of Mexico. It started as far back as 1951 and 1956, when the Bureau of Commercial Fisheries conducted exploratory fishing surveys and caught blue marlin, white marlin, sailfish, and tuna on long lines fished in many parts of the Gulf west of the De Soto Canyon. Then, in 1964, Dr. Norman Vick, a director of the Bureau of Sport Fisheries and Wildlife in Panama City, Florida, teamed up with charter-boat captain Joe Knowles and made twenty trolling trips in the deeper water along the eastern rim of the De Soto Canyon. They caught nine blue marlin, eight white marlin, and numerous sailfish, dolphin, wahoo, and blackfin tuna. They raised a total of twenty-two blue marlin during those trips. Most of the blue marlin were found along the 100-fathom curve.

Now many boats leave from Florida, Mississippi, Alabama, Louisiana, and Texas ports to fish for marlin. In Florida, Destin, Panama City, and Pensacola are the top ports for this fishing, with charter boats available and berths for private craft. To reach the best fishing grounds, you have to run anywhere from thirty to seventy miles offshore, depending on which port you leave from. Most of the action takes place from May to November, with the summer months best for white marlin and the fall months for blue marlin.

Esteban A. Bird, a Puerto Rican banker who helped to pioneer blue-marlin fishing in his native land, has caught many of these great game fish in Puerto Rican waters. He did most of his fishing off San Juan and tried various months of the year to find out when the blue marlin hit best. He found that the biggest ones ran during the spring and summer months, and that more marlin were caught in September and October, though they were smaller then. The blue-marlin season runs from July to October. A few big ones are caught even during the winter months.

Esteban Bird uses 50-pound- and 80-pound-class tackle and has hooked and lost blue marlin that he claims would have gone over 1,000 pounds. The waters off Puerto Rico are deep, and blue marlin often sound, so it is difficult to bring them to the surface again with light tackle. He uses a 9/0 or 7½/0 Fin-Nor reel with a Tycoon rod and monofilament line on the reels. For bait he uses bonefish, mackerel, and small barracuda rigged with a 12/0 Mustad hook. He also uses big mullet, which last longer in the choppy waters usually fished off Puerto Rico. The backbone of the mullet is broken and the hook emerges between the two pectoral fins.

Sport fishing for big black marlin has become very popular in recent years in Pacific waters. Raymundo D. Castro Maya, a Brazilian, has caught many of them off Peru. He finds that the marlin are usually seen moving north. He looks for a fin above the surface and then presents the bait, which is either a mackerel or a bonito. When the marlin swipes at the bait, he drops back and lets the fish think he has crippled it by letting it sink where the marlin can mouth it. The reel is in free spool and he lets the marlin swim away with the bait while he counts to ten. Then he throws the reel into gear and sets the hook.

Zane Grey went to New Zealand with Captain L. D. Mitchell back

This huge, 1,142-pound blue marlin was caught by Jack Herrington off North Carolina in 1974. He was fishing from Captain Harry Baum's charter boat *Jo Boy* when the big fish hit. (*Aycock Brown photo*)

in 1926, and they caught black marlin weighing 685, 704, and 976 pounds. Then, about 1951, Kip Farrington, Alfred C. Glassell, Jr., and other members of the Cabo Blanco Fishing Club, in Peru, started catching big black marlin in the Cabo Blanco area. Glassell caught the first fish over 1,000 pounds when he boated a black marlin weighing 1,025 pounds, on April 7, 1952. A year later, he caught a black marlin weighing 1,560 pounds. Other anglers started fishing there, and many black marlin, from 500 to 1,352 pounds, were caught.

Bart Miller runs the charter boat *Christel* and fishes off Kona, Hawaii, for Pacific blue marlin, black marlin, and striped marlin. In recent years he has achieved a reputation as one of the top skippers fishing those waters. (He has caught over one hundred of them in one year.) Bart finds that the marlin are present in Hawaiian waters the year round, with the late-summer months best.

Bart claims that the big marlin follow the 100-fathom line between the islands of Hawaii and Maui. He uses live and dead bait, preferably big, up to 20 or even 30 pounds. These are rigged and trolled at various depths. He also trolls the big Lucite or other plastic lures with rubber or plastic tails. These skitter, bounce, and weave on top of the water when trolled fast. He has hooked and lost marlin that he saw clearly, and estimated their weight at 2,000 pounds!

In the 1960's the black-marlin fishing scene shifted to Cairns, in Queensland, Australia. George Bransford has done more to pioneer black-marlin fishing off Cairns than any other man. He first saw this coast and these waters during World War II, then returned in 1963 and started to explore it for its fishing possibilities. He moved there soon after and had a 32-foot boat called the *Sea Baby* built.

Then he discovered reefs and shoals such as Jenny Louise, close to the continental drop-off, and started fishing along it. On September 25, 1966, his mate, Richard Oback, caught a 1,064-pound black marlin. Later on he acquired a larger, 39-foot boat, the *Sea Baby II*, and several black marlin over 1,000 pounds were caught on this boat. Other boats began fishing the area, and during 1973 there were thirty-three black marlin weighing over 1,000 pounds caught by various anglers. Two of the biggest marlin taken so far include the 1,417-pounder by Garrick Agnew and the 1,442-pounder by Michael Magrath. George Bransford and other anglers have had black marlin hooked and lost which they claim would have gone over 2,000 pounds. Most of the black marlin run between 500 and 1,000 pounds.

George Bransford uses mullet, bonito, little tuna, mackerel, and barracuda for bait; most of these run up to 10 pounds or so. Other anglers, however, use baits up to 20 pounds. They can be rigged Catalina style, and stainless-steel wire leaders have been found to be more effective than cable leaders in the clear water found there. When trolling, which is usually done blind, George Bransford looks for color changes, currents, rips, and birds. The peak months are from September through December, although marlin can be caught at other times of the year.

"Jo Jo" Del Guercio, Jr., also fished for black marlin at Cairns, with Captain Peter Bristow on his boat the *Avalon*. They would usually spend a few hours in the morning (since the best black-marlin fishing takes place in the afternoon) catching scad, bonito or small tuna for bait, plenty of which was needed. They tried to get at least two to three dozen baits, because they knew that many would be lost to wahoo, kingfish, and barracuda. On occasion, Jo Jo would use yellowfin tuna as big as 30 pounds for bait. He trolled these baits from outriggers, using 130-pound-test lines.

Del Guercio averaged three big marlin a day on his trips to Cairns. One of his best years was 1973, when he caught eighty-eight marlin in eighteen days of fishing. On one of those days, he caught twenty marlin, including one that went 1,127 pounds. On other occasions, he caught marlin going 1,211 and 1,271 pounds. Most of the marlin Jo Jo brought up to the boat, however, were tagged and released.

21

SAILFISH

Both the Atlantic and the Pacific sailfish are very popular with offshore anglers, because they are both more plentiful and easier to catch than the other billfish, such as the marlins. Sailfish are also caught closer to shore and are often taken from small boats. And you can use much lighter tackle than for the big marlin or swordfish. So it is no wonder that each year thousands of sailfish are caught in many waters all over the world. In recent years more and more fishing tournaments and private anglers and charter-boat captains have been releasing sailfish, unless they are trophies that will be mounted.

No one knows exactly when the first sailfish was caught on rod and reel. There are accounts of sailfish being caught on handlines and rod and reel just before and around the turn of the century. These were usually hooked on live baitfish, or small fish being fished or drifted for other fish. Then Captain Bill Hatch and Captain Charlie Thompson began experimenting with strip baits and the "drop-back" method of fishing, between 1910 and 1916. The strip bait they used was allowed to settle or drop back on a slack line when a sailfish hit it. This made it act like a crippled baitfish, and the sailfish would mouth and swallow the bait. During 1919 and 1920 Captain Bill Hatch caught 189 sailfish with this method. Then many other charter-boat captains and private fishermen joined in the fun, and sailfishing zoomed in popularity off Miami and the Palm beaches.

Captain Bill Hatch liked to use a small, 6-inch strip of mullet or bonito or dolphin for sailfish. Then small whole mullet and mullet strips became popular. Hatch discovered that if a sailfish hit a bait but failed to pick it up, you should reel in fast. This usually excites the sailfish and it will follow the bait and often hit it.

Harlan Major was one of the earliest anglers to use a kite to present a bait to a sailfish. He fished with Captain Tommy Gifford off Florida and caught sailfish on strip baits and small mullet. He was also an early advocate of light tackle for the sails and often used light rods and 6-thread line to make his catches. He used small, No. 5/0 hooks and sharpened them to a needle point to make them penetrate the jaws of a sailfish without straining or breaking the light line or limber rod tip.

When Captain Tommy Gifford and other Florida boatmen perfected the outrigger, sailfishing became much easier. You no longer had to hold the rod and reel when a sailfish hit. The line in the clothespin on the outrigger would be released automatically when a sailfish hit the bait and slack line would fall into the water, giving the sail more time to grab and mouth the bait.

Since those early days, however, it has been found that not every sailfish acts the same way and you cannot predict how a sailfish will take a bait. Some sailfish merely look over the baits and do not go for any of them. Another sail may hit the bait, pick it up, and then drop it, and repeat this several times. Captain Lew Parkinson, who was a charter-boat captain in the Palm beaches for many years, studied with binoculars the way a sailfish strikes a bait. He found that some sails will hit the bait with their bills but that others do not. He felt that many times when the sails looked as if they were trying to hit the bait with their bills they were actually trying to grab it with their mouths. He felt that the waving of the bill back and forth was done to get a better look at the bait at such a close distance. He and other captains have found that sailfish hit the bait with their bills more often when the water is choppy or the ocean is rough, than when the water is calm.

So experienced sailfish anglers usually wait to see how the sail acts or strikes before they decide when to set the hook. Many times, a sail will "crash" the bait and you can set the hook immediately or the fish will hook itself. Most anglers give the sail some line by thumbing the reel, and when they feel the spool speed up they set the hook. If the fish is not hooked, the best procedure is to reel the bait back to the surface; a sail will often return and hit it again. Then another drop-back or more line should be given before trying to set the hook

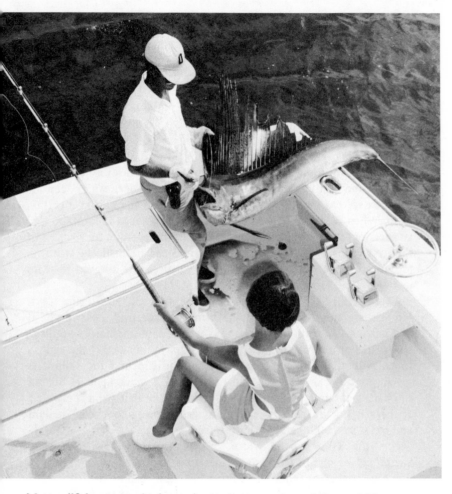

Most sailfish are caught from charter boats, such as this one fishing out of Miami, Florida. The charter-boat captain and mate supply the skill and know-how needed to make the catch. (*Miami-Metro Department of Publicity and Tourism photo*)

a second time. But, for most beginners, a long count of ten is still the best way to give the sailfish time to mouth or swallow the bait and avoid setting the hook too soon.

One trick anglers use for a hesitant sail that looks at the bait without taking it is to release it from the outrigger and let it drop back. Or you can reel in the line to release it and then keep reeling so that the bait acts like a frightened baitfish trying to get away. This often excites or angers the sail and he charges the bait and takes it.

Captain Bob Lewis, of Miami, helped to perfect kite fishing for sailfish. This is a very effective method for these fish and brings them up when straight trolling doesn't. He likes to use live blue runners for bait and hooks them through the back, near the head, with the hook on the fishing line. This line is then clipped to the kite line and both are let out with the wind while the boat drifts. He ties tiny bits of ribbon on the fishing line at the end of the leader, which can be watched so that the line can be adjusted to hold the bait at a certain level. When fishing with a kite, Captain Lewis keeps a constant vigil and lets out line or reels it in according to the position and action of the live bait. It should swim naturally and can be made to swim on top to create a commotion or splashing, or it can be allowed to swim just below the surface.

Captain Bill Self also uses a kite for sailfish, off the Florida Keys. He hooks a blue runner or a pinfish through the back near the head and lets out line from the fishing reel and the kite-line holder until the bait swims on top of the water in an attractive manner. If the sailfish hits the bait, the line is released from the clip and the sailfish is given some slack line to mouth the bait. If a shark appears behind the bait, Captain Self merely reels in to lift the bait from the water. If there is no breeze or wind, he inflates a big balloon with helium and ties it to the kite and flies it this way.

Jim Bob Tinsley, who wrote the excellent book *The Sailfish—Swashbuckler of the Open Seas,* mentions another way of rigging a live blue runner or other small fish when slow trolling or drifting for the sails: A short length of line is tied to the bend of the hook and is then run through the eye sockets, just in front of the eyeballs, and then run around the hook bend and into the eyes again so that the hook ends up about two inches from the nose of the bait. This gives the baitfish more freedom and it also swims head first in the water, rather than being dragged sideways, as often happens when the bait is hooked through the back.

Captain Earl Smith, skipper of the *Quail,* was fishing in the West Palm Beach Sailfish Tournament a few years ago. His angler was Mrs. Helen Grant and they weren't doing too well trolling with ballyhoo. Then Captain Smith found out that the sailfish were "balling" and feeding on sardines. He caught some of these for bait and then he searched for a school of the sailfish herding the small baitfish. The angler would then flip out a hooked sardine to a sail. Fishing this way, Mrs. Grant caught over fifty sailfish in three days!

Ted Chryst, who started fishing in the Gulf of Mexico for sailfish along Florida's West Coast back in the 1950s, used flying fish for bait. He would shoot them with a shotgun while they were flying, to obtain some for bait. Then he would rig them and troll them for the sails together with mullet strips. Chryst found that you had to go out to at least the 15-fathom curve, about twenty-four miles offshore, to get the sailfish in the Gulf of Mexico.

Bill Barnes recommends fishing a live bait under a float, or bobber, such as a small balloon or block of styrofoam as the easiest way to catch a sailfish. You can use a small blue runner or a pinfish, snapper, grunt, or pilchard for bait. One of these baits is hooked with a 5/0 or 6/0 hook and the balloon or float is attached about 4 to 5 feet above the hook. Then the baitfish is hooked through the back and is let out anywhere from 50 to 80 feet behind the drifting boat.

Dr. Roy B. Dean was using light tackle for Pacific sailfish way back in the 1940s, before spinning tackle and salt-water fly fishing became popular. He caught many sailfish on 3-thread line that had a breaking test of 9 pounds! In fact, he held the world record for sailfish on 3-thread line for many years. Dr. Dean fished mostly out of Acapulco and other Mexican ports.

Dr. Dean used a flexible 4-ounce rod tip with a 4/0 reel on it. Such an outfit wasn't balanced, but the big reel enabled him to retrieve line fast and held plenty of reserve line for any long runs. To raise sailfish Dr. Dean found out that if you dragged soft-drink bottles bottom first they made a lot of commotion and were good teasers for the sailfish.

He used mullet for bait and rigged them on big, 9/0 or 10/0 Sobey hooks. He trolled the baits on a flat line a short distance behind the boat. The rod was held with the thumb on the reel spool until a sailfish hit, then it was released and the boat was slowed down and stopped. He gave the sailfish plenty of time to swallow the bait, then set the hook.

After he either boated or lost a sailfish, Dr. Dean would immediately put another bait in the water, even before the boat started mov-

Mark Sosin, expert all-around angler, is shown with a sailfish he caught on a fly rod. These fish can be caught on long, streamer flies if they are first teased with fish or strip baits and brought close to the boat, where you can cast the fly to them. (*Mark Sosin photo*)

ing again, because he found that sailfish often travel in small schools or follow a hooked fish up to the boat.

Dr. Webster Robinson pioneered fly fishing for sailfish and caught one of the first sails on such tackle in 1961. He liked to use a 9-foot, 6½-ounce fly rod with a strong butt section that could handle a No. 10 salt-water taper fly line. He used a 12-pound-test tippet and a heavier shock leader up front.

Dr. Robinson did a lot of his sailfishing in Pacific waters in Panama and off Mexico. He worked out the system of trolling small whole fish such as ballyhoo, or mullet or other fish strips in the wake of a boat as teasers. These had no hooks in them but were used to raise the sailfish and bring them up to the boat. Then, when Robinson had the sail near the boat and excited, he would stop and cast the fly toward the waiting fish. He used a special plastic-foam popping bug with a 6/0 or 7/0 hook riding up. It had long, white saddle hackles or feathers tied around the hook. He could make it pop to throw a splash or make it travel underwater.

Stu Apte catches sailfish on light tackle such as spinning outfits with 8-, 6-, and 4-pound-test lines and also on fly rods. When using a fly rod it is considered unethical to troll the lure. You have to cast it to the fish and retrieve it. So Stu also uses decoy baits or teasers to bring the sailfish up and get them interested and excited. When a sailfish slashes at the decoy, which has no hook in it, it is quickly pulled away from the fish. Then it is dropped back again. If the sail rushes it again, it is pulled away once more. This is repeated until the sail becomes so agitated that it is ready to hit a lure. Then the fly is cast to the fish.

Fly designed by Lee Wulff for sailfish

Lee Wulff also catches Pacific sailfish on a fly rod, and he designed a special fly for this fishing. He tied a big streamer on two 4/0 hooks, using long white-and-yellow wings and red-and-yellow hackles up at the head. He felt that just a single hook resulted in too many short strikes.

Another angler who catches sailfish on lures is Pat Woodall, who fishes along Florida's East Coast. He was trolling a plug one day from his outboard boat, had a strike and was surprised to see a sailfish leap into the air. He fought it carefully on his 12-pound-test line and finally boated a 6-foot sail. This happened several years ago, and since that time he has caught other sailfish on plugs. His favorite plugs are the Pfeffer Shiner and the Banana. When trolling or casting plugs, no drop-back is necessary. The fish are hooked almost immediately after hitting the lure.

Larry Furman has also found that plugs can be highly effective for sailfish. He uses silver-and-gold minnow-type plugs similar to the Rapala and the Rebel and trolls them only 20 to 30 feet behind his boat. He has not only hooked and caught sailfish on the plugs but has discovered that they make good teasers, too. The sailfish often rise behind the plugs, and if you have a ballyhoo or mullet bait in the water they will often grab it.

Captain Skip Bradeen, who runs the boat *Blue Chip* out of Islamorada, in the Florida Keys, finds that live ballyhoo will often catch sailfish when they refuse other baits. He buys his live ballyhoo from commercial fishermen or catches his own on a hook with a tiny piece of shrimp on it. He keeps the ballyhoo alive in a bait well until he starts fishing.

Captain Bradeen hooks the ballyhoo with a short-shank 5/0 Eagle Claw hook by running it through the bottom jaw and out the mouth, with the hook facing up. Then he trolls the live ballyhoo from outriggers or a kite. If spinning tackle is being used, you can troll the bait on a flat line direct from the rod. The ballyhoo should be trolled very slowly so that it swims naturally. When a sailfish goes for the bait, there is a drop-back permitting some slack line so that it can mouth and swallow the ballyhoo.

Elmar Baxter fishes for Pacific sailfish off Mexico with spinning tackle. He started out originally with 15-pound-test line and worked down to 10-, 8-, 6-, and even 4-pound-test lines to catch the sailfish. He likes to use a spinning rod in the 7- to 10-foot length with a light tip but plenty of power in the butt section and a big salt-water spinning reel with mono line. He doubles his line for 15 feet and adds a 15-foot leader of 50- to 100-pound-test on the end. A new line is used for every fish, because the old line may have nicks and kinks.

Elmar uses flying fish and mullet for bait and makes sure that the hooks are needle-sharp. When trolling the baits directly from the reel, he lets them out from the stern into the wake. With outriggers the baits may be 100 to 150 feet out. But if there are a lot of fish around, he likes to hold the rod with the bail open or the line off the roller and use his finger to keep the line on the reel spool. When a sailfish hits the bait or grabs it, he releases the line from the spool and the boat is put into neutral. Then he keeps on letting the sailfish take more line while it is swallowing the bait. He may let it take up to a third of the line off his reel spool. With the boat (driven by another angler) moving ahead, he raises his rod high and sets the hook with a series of short jerks. Baxter likes to fight his sailfish standing up with the rod butt in a belt socket. He contends that he can feel a fish much better this way than when sitting in a chair.

Flying fish rigged for Pacific sailfish

22

TUNA

Tuna fishing for food in the Mediterranean Sea dates back to ancient Greek and Roman times. People have been using traps and nets to catch giant tuna off Sicily for centuries. And even in this country, commercial fishermen were catching big tuna in traps and nets and with harpoons and hand lines for a long time. They also trolled for the smaller, school tuna with metal squids, and cedar-and-bone jigs, long before sports fishermen started doing the same thing.

One of the first attempts to take giant tuna in a sporting manner is attributed to Thomas Patillo, a schoolmaster who went after them in a dory in Liverpool Harbor, Nova Scotia, back in 1871. According to one account, he used "32 fathoms of ordinary codline, wound it upon a swivel reel of some sort, fashioned a hook of steel ⅜ inch thick, 8 inches long with a 3-inch shank and a long, heavy beard." With this crude fishing gear, he caught a "horse mackerel," as giant tuna were called there, weighing 600 pounds.

Early attempts to catch tuna on rod and reel began in Pacific waters around Catalina Island during the 1890s. There one of the first rod-and-reel tuna was caught by W. Greer Campbell in 1896; it weighed 104 pounds. Colonel C. P. Morehouse was supposed to have caught a tuna during the same year too. But the tuna that got the most recognition was the one caught by Charles Frederick Holder, who caught a 183-pound fish in 1898. Soon after, he and a few other anglers formed the Catalina Tuna Club. Then, in 1899, Colonel C. P. Morehouse caught a 251-pound tuna. But tuna in Pacific waters do not reach the sizes of those found in the Atlantic, and the quest for the real giants began in earnest off Nova Scotia and New Jersey.

In Nova Scotia, Commander J. K. L. Ross started fishing for giant tuna in 1908. He hooked twenty-one big fish that year and lost them all. The following year, he hooked and lost thirteen more, including one that fought him for nineteen hours and towed the boat 120 miles. He fished from a dory, with another man at the oars. Finally, on August 28, 1911, he succeeded in catching a 680-pound tuna in St. Ann Bay, Cape Breton, after a five-hour fight.

Commander Ross, of course, was handicapped by the fishing tackle used for tuna in those days, which was really meant for tarpon and striped bass: 7-foot wood rods, small reels with no internal drag, linen lines, and no fighting chair. He used a herring or mackerel for bait and trolled it in harbors and in coves along the rocky coast of Nova Scotia. When he hooked a big tuna, he had to let it tow the boat for miles to tire itself out. He later discovered that he could shorten the fight with a big tuna when it sounded by rowing away from the fish and trying to get it back to the surface, where it could be fought to a finish.

In the meantime, a few anglers started fishing for tuna with rod and reel off New Jersey, and during the summer of 1910 a Mr. Townsend caught school tuna by trolling metal squids. One Colonel Shepley started fishing for school tuna off Block Island, Rhode Island; he and his daughter caught the first ones on August 10, 1911. In December 1914 the Atlantic Tuna Club was founded, in Providence, Rhode Island. Then, in 1915, Jacob Wertheim caught a 286-pound tuna off New Jersey, which was the American record for several years.

In the meantime the British angler L. Mitchell-Henry went to Port Medway, Nova Scotia, in 1914 and caught 520- and 480-pound tuna. Captain Laurie Mitchell caught a 710-pound tuna in the same waters that year. Captain Mitchell later met Zane Grey in New York, and the two men went up to Nova Scotia in 1924, where the Western writer caught a 758-pound tuna, which held the world record until 1933.

L. Mitchell-Henry worked on new rods, reels, and harnesses and with them caught big tuna first in Nova Scotia and then in British waters. He caught his first tuna, weighing 560 pounds, in 1930. Then, on September 11, 1933, he caught an 851-pound tuna in British waters, which set the world record for a time.

About the same time, Henry Strater and George Weare started fishing for tuna in Maine waters off Ogunquit and Bailey Island. In

1933 they caught their first tuna, and by 1935 more than fifty tuna had been caught. Most of these were small fish, weighing up to 271 pounds, but later on, bigger ones were caught. Tuna anglers fishing in Maine waters usually look for the fish on top chasing and feeding on herring, mackerel, or menhaden. Tuna have also been caught there trolling with big feather lures. Trolling with a whole mackerel has been a common practice there for years. But most of the tuna are caught by the mooring method, with the boat tied to a buoy while chumming with cut fish or whole fish and drifting out a whiting, hake, or mackerel bait in the tide. The best tuna fishing in Maine takes place during July and August.

Many of the early rod-and-reel tuna caught in Maine were taken by commercial fishermen or lobster fishermen who started to take out sportsmen in their boats. One such man, Elmore Wallace, harpooned tuna in Maine waters for years, then started to take out rod-and-reel anglers. He found out early in the game that the best place to fish for the giant tuna was where draggers and trawlers were hauling in their nets. There the tuna would gather and feed on trash fish being tossed overboard. Wallace would locate a dragger and drop an anchor attached to a buoy about 150 feet astern of the commercial boat. Then he would start tossing whiting and hake into the water as chum. For bait he would run a big, 14/0 hook through a whiting and add a cork about 30 feet above the bait. Then he would let the float and bait out in the current. When a tuna grabbed the whiting and the cork went down, he would start the engine of the boat, cast off the anchor line, and fight the big tuna in open water.

Things quieted down in Nova Scotia waters until 1935, when Michael Lerner went to Wedgeport with Captain Tommy Gifford and caught two tuna, one going 311 pounds and the other weighing 378 pounds. Kip Farrington arrived shortly with his wife and they each caught a tuna. From then on, the rush began to Wedgeport, and many other big-game anglers caught big tuna in those waters until the fish left the area and the action slowed down for many years.

In the meantime, anglers had been trying to catch big tuna in the Bahamas, especially those migrating past Bimini and Cat Cay. During the 1920s and 1930s, they hooked and lost many big fish. Then they started using heavier tackle successfully, but the tuna that were brought in were invariably mutilated by sharks. Finally, in 1935,

Ernest Hemingway succeeded in boating the first unmutilated tuna in those waters. After that, more and more anglers began boating big tuna before sharks could get to them. But many big tuna were still being lost when they headed for the drop-off, sounded in deep water and couldn't be raised with light tackle.

Captain Tommy Gifford was one of the first men to figure out how to boat a big tuna at Bimini on light tackle. He would look for a school of tuna and then present his "lollydo," which was a big white lure of pork-rind strips, in front of the fish. When a tuna grabbed it and was hooked, Tommy let it run for a while, then he maneuvered the boat and ran between the fish and the drop-off to herd it back toward the shallow flats. He would keep herding the tuna to keep it from reaching deep water. This soon tired the tuna and it could be brought up to the boat and gaffed.

The man who has caught more giant tuna on rod and reel than any other angler is William K. Carpenter, of Fort Lauderdale, Florida, former president of the International Game Fish Association. During a lifetime of fishing, he has caught more than six hundred of the giants. Bill Carpenter has fished for giant tuna in many waters, but one of his favorite spots is Bimini and Cat Cay, in the Bahamas. He has won the Cat Cay Tuna Tournament several times. In 1963 he caught fifteen tuna from 400 to 600 pounds in one day!

Bill Carpenter fishes with a Tycoon rod and a 12/0 Fin-Nor reel and 130-pound-test line. For bait he uses a mullet or a Spanish mackerel on a 12/0 Sea Mate Mustad hook. Much of his fishing has been done from his fast 37-foot boat the *Caliban,* which can get ahead of a school of speedy tuna and present the bait in front of them. The fast boat is also a big help in fighting a big tuna and keeping it from reaching deep water. Bill fights all his tuna hard, never giving them a chance to rest, and is always working to bring them close to the boat as quickly as possible for tagging. Most of the tuna he has hooked have been tagged and released.

Another great tuna angler who has caught many giant tuna—well over five hundred at last count—is Elwood K. Harry, currently the president of the International Game Fish Association. He has won many tuna tournaments in the years he has been fishing. Elwood has a great admiration and respect for a giant tuna's power, fast runs, and strength. He says, "There is no game fish anywhere that can pull like they can—peeling line off a reel against a drag set as high as 60

Bill Carpenter is shown with five tuna he caught in one day during the Cat Cay International Tuna Tournament. Carpenter has caught over six hundred big tuna during his lifetime. (*Bahamas News Bureau photo*)

or 70 pounds. For my money, they are the greatest fish of all."

He also likes to fish for big tuna at Cat Cay, and he makes sure he has a good captain, mate, and boat for this fishing. Elwood finds that for the best fishing there, you need some wind to ruffle the water. His captain searches for the schools of big tuna in fairly shallow water over a sandy bottom. The mate will have the mullet or other bait rigged usually with a sinker under its mouth. Then, when the captain feels the time is ripe, he slows down the boat and the bait is dropped into the water as the angler free-spools his reel and lets the bait drop back toward the approaching fish. The striking drag on the reel is set at 40 pounds as Elwood Harry waits for the fish to hit. A tuna may strike immediately, but other times Elwood may work his rod up and down to give the bait some added action and make it look alive. If a tuna hits and gets hooked, he loosens his drag to let the fish run. The boat is maneuvered between the tuna and the deep water so that it stays in shallow water. There is a big belly in the line now, and Elwood has to take up the slack as quickly as possible. Then he tightens his drag and gets to work pumping and gaining line. Elwood Harry uses a 12/0 Fin-Nor reel with 130-pound Dacron line, and has boated many big tuna in a matter of minutes. He also tags and releases most of his fish.

When Russ MacGrotty fishes for giant tuna off Rhode Island, he looks for schools of the big fish feeding on top on mackerel. Then he nets or catches some of the mackerel, hooks one through the back and lets it move ahead of the feeding tuna and swim toward them.

Other anglers, such as Harry Peters, who also fished in Rhode Island waters, would try to catch a live whiting on a spinning outfit or bottom rod and use it for bait. The live whiting was hooked through the back and fished 20 to 40 feet below a cork or plastic float. Or Peters would let the whiting settle, on a free line, into deeper water.

One of the most successful tuna-fishing guides in Massachusetts is Charley Mayo, who operates the charter boat *Chantey III* out of Provincetown. In 1971 he had forty-five big tuna taken on rod and reel from his boat, for a total weight of 28,081 pounds, averaging 624 pounds! Four of the tuna went over 800 pounds. Mayo got more than half of these fish during September on the northwestern corner of the Stellwagon Bank, halfway between Provincetown and Gloucester.

Mayo caught his first giant tuna in Cape Cod Bay back in 1937, and since then he has established a reputation for consistently catching the big fish. Charley Mayo, of course, knows his waters around Cape Cod and the best spots, rips, and tides at various locations. He looks for birds such as shearwaters and terns or for sharks cruising on top. He worked out a multiple-bait rig consisting of three herring or mackerel without hooks as teasers and a squid on the end with a hook in it. He usually trolls three such rigs, which are similar to the "daisy chain" rigs used in Canadian waters. Other captains use from eight to fourteen teasers and bait on such rigs. Still others are using spreader rigs, which have crossarms of heavy stainless steel with the baits suspended from the spreader.

But probably the main reason why Captain Mayo is so successful is his determination to get some fish for his customers. He fishes long and hard, going out early and staying out late.

In recent years, the activity for giant tuna has shifted to Canadian waters, especially at Conception Bay and Notre Dame Bay, in Newfoundland. Lee Wulff caught tuna on rod and reel in Bonne Bay and Conception Bay way back in 1938. But this was when Wedgeport, Nova Scotia, was in the spotlight and the "in" place for giant tuna, so anglers payed little attention to other spots in Canada. When the fishing dropped off at Wedgeport, anglers started looking for tuna in other Canadian waters. Conception Bay came into the limelight during the 1960s, when Bill Carpenter and a few other anglers started to fish there in earnest. In 1966 Bill Carpenter brought thirty-six tuna up to the boat in two weeks of fishing. They often saw several schools of tuna feeding on squid, herring, and mackerel during August and September. But this abundance of natural food also makes the tuna picky, so they do not hit the trolled baits too readily.

Mike Dunphy, owner of several charter boats at Conception Bay, also helped to develop the sport fishing for giant tuna in those waters. He would look for tuna schools "pushing" on the surface and then troll the daisy-chain rigs and baits on top, to attract the tuna. These were usually squid or mullet teasers and baits. Most of the fishing is done around Portugal Cove, Ore Head, and the Harbour Grace Islands.

Then the giant-tuna-fishing scene shifted to Prince Edward Island, which is a Canadian province just north of Nova Scotia and east of New Brunswick, in the Gulf of St. Lawrence. The first attempts to

One tuna caught and he's trying for another one. The scene is Conception Bay, in Newfoundland, where many big tuna have been taken in recent years from July to October. (*Canadian Government Travel Bureau photo*)

catch tuna there were made in 1966, but all the fish that were hooked were lost. The following year, Bruce Oland caught one weighing 855 pounds, and in 1968 a few lobster boats were fitted out and they caught fourteen giant tuna, including one going 960 pounds. In 1970 Mel Immergut caught a 1,040-pounder and the rush was on.

In 1973 there were 659 tuna caught at Prince Edward Island, and fifty-eight of these fish ran between 900 and 1,000 pounds, with six of them weighing over 1,000 pounds. The biggest one went 1,120 pounds. Very few "small" tuna, under 500 pounds, are caught in these waters; the big ones can be caught from July through October. It is claimed that the waters around Prince Edward Island are the spawning grounds of the mackerel, for they are present in great numbers there. In addition there are herring, capelin, hake, and cod, all of which attract the giant tuna.

Don Merten fishes for giant tuna around Prince Edward Island from his 52-foot boat *Valiant Lady*. He finds that the fishing is best there in the late afternoon and toward evening. He rigs up two or three daisy chains of mackerel or herring and trolls these to bring up the tuna. The last bait is usually a big mackerel rigged with a 12/0 hook, which is buried inside the bait. Heavy tackle, in the 130-pound class, with big, 12/0 to 14/0 reels, are used. Dacron line is preferred by Don to fight the big tuna on a tight drag.

Al Ristori decided to catch a big tuna the hard way—from a small, 19-foot outboard boat. And he caught one weighing 745 pounds from such a boat in Massachusetts waters. Al recommends a fighting chair in the bow of the boat if you want to go after the giants in a small boat. A rod with a 9/0 reel and an 80-pound-test Dacron line can be used for this fishing. You also need plenty of herring for chum and bait; Al cuts the herring into large chunks and dribbles these out in a steady but controlled stream. With small herring you can throw the whole ones into the water. He baits the 10/0 tuna hook with one big herring by inserting the hook in at the tail and then pushing it out through the back so it hangs head down. But he has also put two or three small herring on one hook if that was the only size available and was being used for chum.

Ristori will let out two lines from the drifting boat, one about 30 feet below a float and the other one down deeper, without any float. Once he sees a tuna in the chum line, he tries to hold its interest by

Al Ristori is shown gaffing a big tuna he caught the hard way—from a small boat. The tuna is allowed to tow the boat until it tires and can be boated. (*Lawrence J. Gronin, Jr., photo*)

throwing the herring into the water at regular intervals so that the fish gulps them and begins to look for more handouts. Then he drifts the herring with the hook in it as one of the offerings.

When a tuna grabs the bait, Al picks up his rod, puts the lever into the STRIKE position and sets the hook hard several times. Then he backs off the drag a bit so that he can get into the chair and put on the harness. When that is done, he tightens the drag so that the tuna can tow the boat without taking any line. Al finds that a tuna towing the boat tires fast and tends to stay on the surface.

Frank T. Moss fished for school tuna when he ran his charter boat out of Montauk, Long Island, and like most anglers he found that on some days they were easy to catch but on other days you couldn't get a strike. He looked for tuna leaping or feeding on top. And he also looked for birds such as shearwaters and fulmars wheeling and diving. Or he searched for oily slicks that indicated tuna feeding on baitfish below the surface.

Frank used Japanese feather lures in all white, all yellow, red-and-white, black-and-white, and green-and-yellow. Or he used nylon jigs, cedar jigs, metal lures, and spoons. These were trolled from five to nine knots anywhere from 20 to 80 feet behind the boat. At first, he would try various lengths, but when he started hitting tuna at a certain line length he would change all his lines to this particular length. This created a school-of-bait effect and he would often hook two, three, or more tuna at the same time.

Once he had one or two fish on, he would have his anglers reel them up to the boat, then have the other fishermen grab some rods rigged with metal squid or butterfish or bone jigs and drop these into the water and start jigging them as the boat slowed down. If he had any chum or blood in the boat he would also dump this from the stern to attract and hold the tuna near the boat and excite them to hit the jigged lures.

Captain Walter Drobecker, who also fished out of Montauk in his charter boat, would often come in with school tuna when other captains caught few if any fish. One of his favorite tricks was first to locate a school of tuna in front of his boat. Then, after trolling around the fringes of the school with no luck, he would deliberately speed up the boat and run it right through the school. This usually excited the fish and made them hit the lures.

When school tuna refused to hit lures trolled near the surface, Ray Jarry used a "planer," which took them down 30 to 40 feet, and then he would start to get fish. He found that such lures as feather jigs, nylon jigs, and cedar jigs worked best when they were trolled deep 200 feet behind the boat at about six to seven knots.

For years, school tuna were caught mostly from charter boats or private boats that spent many hours trolling all over the ocean for these scrappy fighters. Then Captain Fred Moore, who owns and runs the party boat *Teal* out of Great Kills, Staten Island, New York, started experimenting off New Jersey at 17 Fathoms, the Farms, and the Mud Hole, and found that you could catch school tuna there by chumming and using small live mackerel for bait. Other boats followed suit and soon a whole fleet was out there catching tuna.

Captain Moore recommends using a conventional salt-water rod

Pete Perinchief with a 56-pound yellowfin tuna he caught all alone in a 14-foot boat on the Challenger Bank, fourteen miles off the Bermuda coast. (*Bermuda News Bureau photo*)

and reel filled with 30- to 40-pound-test monofilament line. On the end of the line you tie a small, No. 2/0 or 3/0 albacore- or tuna-style hook. When hooking a small, 5- to 8-inch mackerel, you should bury the hook inside the fish's back as much as possible. If mackerel are not obtainable you can try other small fish, such as live whiting. Dead small mackerel and various baitfish can also be used but they are not as good as the live ones. Let these baits out in the chum slick usually without a sinker, but if the current is strong you can add a clamp-on or rubber-core sinker a few feet above the bait.

All kinds of tuna are tough fighters, but one of the toughest is the Allison, or yellowfin, tuna, and Pete Perinchief fishes for them in

Bermuda waters. There the best fishing is found at the Challenger Bank or the Argus Bank. These lie offshore, and boats drift or anchor and chum along the drop-off found there. Pete uses either mashed-up fish, small anchovies or hog-mouthed fry. These are often mixed with sand to obtain the best results. This chum will bring the yellowtail right up to the boat.

Pete likes to use 20- to 30-pound-test lines for most of this fishing but will go as light as 15- or 12-pound when casting lures to the fish. However, most of the time, he uses anchovies or pilchards or several hog-mouthed fry on a 4/0 to 7/0 hook. Because of the clarity of the water, you'll get more pick-ups, or bites, with the smaller hooks and lighter lines or leaders. Pete finds that the best fishing for the yellowfin tuna is from May to October in Bermuda waters.

Hook baited with tiny fry for yellowfin tuna

But in Mexican waters, where some of the biggest yellowfin tuna are caught, the fishing can be good in January. John Lighty, of Torrance, California, found this out when he fished off the Soccoro Islands and caught a 298-pound yellowfin, in January 1974. A year later, he went back and caught a 302-pound specimen. He claims that some of the yellowfins he lost would have gone from 400 to 500 pounds.

23

SHARKS

Sharks have been feared, hated, and respected by man since earliest times. They have also been caught—in nets, seines, traps, and on strong lines, or speared, harpooned, or shot with bow and arrow—through the ages. Sharks were caught on rod and reel by anglers seeking other species. A few anglers fished deliberately for sharks, but most fishermen considered them a menace and a pest and avoided them. For a long time, salt-water anglers looked down their noses at sharks and insisted that they weren't really game fish and provided poor sport on rod and reel.

But a few anglers, knowing better, sought sharks deliberately with rod and reel and found that most of them provide a lot of fun and sport. In recent years there has been a big spurt in shark fishing for sport in many parts of the world. There are now many shark-fishing clubs in this country and abroad.

One of the early anglers to discover that sharks were great sport and deserved to be considered game fish was Zane Grey. He fished for them in New Zealand, and on his first trip there, in 1926, he caught sixteen mako sharks. In one of his accounts he wrote, "The mako is the aristocrat of all sharks. It is really unfitting to call him a shark at all. I seldom use the word with regard to him. After he attains some weight—say over 400 pounds—he is indeed a magnificent sporting fish. His leaps are prodigious, inconceivably high above the water. The ease and grace of this leap is indescribable. It must be seen. He comes out slick, glides up, turns a somersault, and goes down head first, like a diving gull, almost without a splash. Then instantly he is out again."

Zane Grey also caught some white sharks, or man-eaters, up to 1,100 pounds and lost and saw some bigger ones. This was in

Australian waters, and he had a big reel built that could hold 2,000 yards of 54-thread line, weighed 37 pounds, and cost three thousand dollars; with this he hoped to catch one of the giant white sharks. On one of his later trips to New Zealand, Zane Grey hooked a big mako, which charged the boat and almost leaped inside the craft before it got away. He estimated that it was at least 17 feet long and would have weighed a ton.

In later years, other anglers caught makos up to 1,000 pounds, with one of the largest being the 1,061-pound mako caught by James Penwarden in New Zealand in 1970. Makos are not too plentiful anywhere and make a fine prize when captured. Many of them are mounted, and their streamlined bodies and blue color make them a handsome trophy. They also make excellent eating, and can be compared to swordfish in taste and texture.

But the man who has done the most to promote and popularize sport fishing for sharks is Captain Frank Mundus, of Montauk Point, New York. He started fishing for them soon after World War II and began calling it "monster" fishing. He exhibited at sports shows during the winter and signed up charters for the summer and early-fall months, when shark fishing is best. Since that time, thousands of sharks have been caught from his boats the *Cricket I* and the *Cricket II.*

Frank Mundus wrote a book, with Bill Wisner, called *Sportfishing for Sharks,* in which he gives some of his ideas on fishing for these marauders. Frank approaches shark fishing with the same care and attention to details as he would give to swordfishing. He makes sure his tackle, rigs, baits, and hooks are in good shape and ready to go. He doesn't like shiny hooks, feeling they make sharks shy away from a bait, so he uses dull, rusty, or painted hooks.

Frank finds that a chum made from ground-up pilot whale is best, but this isn't always available, and if you're going for an I.G.F.A. record it can't be used. However, the bloody meat of the whale will attract sharks quicker than anything else. Frank also uses menhaden (bunker), whiting, ling, or other fish as chum.

Mundus prefers a live bait to a dead one and uses frozen bait as a last resort. So he always tries to have his bait wells filled with plenty of live whiting or mackerel or other small fish. He hooks the live bait through the back with a hook big enough to hold the bait and the shark he expects to catch.

Captain Frank Mundus holds the fin of a 261-pound mako shark taken from his boat. Charles Meyer, on the right, who caught the fish, was one of the first anglers to use light spinning tackle for these fish. (*Charles Meyer photo*)

Mundus makes sure that the chum is dispensed at regular intervals, with no prolonged breaks. Once the rhythm and slick are established, they are maintained unless the boat is moved to a different area. If the boat is drifting slowly, he chums infrequently; if it is moving fast he chums more often.

Frank, of course, knows many spots around Montauk where

sharks gather and feed. But he will also look for schools of baitfish
or small fish such as mackerel or menhaden and fish under them.
Sharks often lurk beneath such schools of fish.

One trick Mundus will often try when fishing for sharks is to tie a
tuna to his boat and let it out in the water. When a shark grabs the
tuna, Mundus teases it by pulling on the line. This tug-of-war and
the commotion it creates attracts other sharks and makes them excited and more likely to take a bait with a hook in it.

Bill Wisner has fished often with Captain Frank Mundus and other
anglers for sharks. He has also made a lifetime study of these fish
and sport fishing for them through the years. Bill says that sharks
can be anywhere in the ocean, from just off the beach to many miles
offshore. They are great wanderers and will be plentiful in one area
one day and disappear the next. If Bill drifts and chums in one spot
for an hour or so with no action he will try a different spot.

Bill recommends hooks from 6/0 to 16/0, depending on the size
of the sharks in the area, and they should be attached to a wire
leader from 15 to 18 feet long. Rods and reels holding lines from 50
to 130 pounds are used, again depending on the size of the sharks
you expect to catch. The hook can be baited with either a live or a
dead fish: perhaps a bonito, mackerel, tuna, bunker, butterfish, or
whiting.

Wisner suggests drifting with three rigs. Two of them will have
cork or Styrofoam floats. One of these will be down about 20 to 30
feet, another will be down about 40 to 60 feet, and the third one,
without any float, will be down between 100 and 150 feet.

Frank T. Moss has caught sharks when trolling in areas where
school tuna are plentiful. These have usually been makos, porbea-
gles, and thresher sharks. They will sometimes rise to a trolled mackerel, mullet, squid, or eel. If he sees such a shark on top he will ma-
neuver his boat so that the bait passes close in front of the shark. He
finds that even the slower species, such as the blue, hammerhead,
and white shark will also rise to a slow-moving fish bait. He finds it
also helps to dribble blood from fresh fish such as tuna, albacore, or
bonito in the wake of the boat to attract and excite the sharks while
you are trolling the bait slowly.

Marshall Helfand and Bobby Killey also fish for sharks out of
Montauk. They look for them in tidal rips, waters where there are
thermal changes, where chumming is being done, where trash fish are

This big white shark, or man-eater, was harpooned by Captain Frank Mundus from the *Cricket II* off Montauk, New York. But sharks as big as this one have been caught on rod and reel, too. (*Captain Frank Mundus photo*)

being tossed overboard by draggers or trawlers, and under big schools of mackerel, school tuna, bonito, or false albacore. They also fish at night for the bigger sharks and have lost some monsters.

Captain Hal Scharp has been a charter-boat captain for many years in the Florida Keys, and many sharks have been caught from his boat by his customers. Most of them were caught for sport, but he has also caught sharks for research purposes and has worked with scientists to learn more about the fascinating creatures. To locate a good shark-fishing area, Hal advises anglers to locate local commercial fishermen. These men hate sharks because of the damage they do to their nets and lines, so they usually know where sharks are plentiful.

Hal recommends the regular menhaden or other fish chum, but also adds blood, which can be obtained from a slaughterhouse. For bait Hal Scharp will use a live fish such as a jack, bonito, mackerel, ladyfish, snapper, or grunt if he can get it. If not, he uses a dead fish. When a whole fish is used he cuts off the tail and slashes the sides of the bait with a knife in several places. He likes big hooks on a heavy, cable-wire leader 15 feet long when fishing for sharks. He sharpens the hooks to a triangular point to make them penetrate more readily. Captain Hal Scharp has also written a book, called *Shark Safari,* in which he tells all about sharks and also how to catch them.

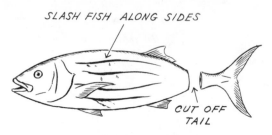

Whole-fish bait prepared for sharks

Thomas Helm has fished for sharks for many years in many waters. He disputes the belief that if you see porpoises there will be few sharks in the vicinity. Instead he finds that sharks will actually follow a school of porpoises to pick up the crippled fish or pieces of fish the porpoises miss or leave behind. He has caught some of his biggest sharks behind schools of porpoises. When fishing for sharks, Helm likes to chum near the mouth of a pass or inlet when the tide is running. He feels that this spreads a scent or slick over a wider area in a shorter space of time.

Eddie Barr and Tom Cunningham fish for sharks in Delaware Bay, and they find that the sharks come in and bite best when there are plenty of weakfish around. They will use a weakfish for bait on a 14/0 hook, but find that the best bait of all for big sharks is a live dogfish up to 2 feet in length.

Captain Jay Schick fishes for sharks off Long Island, New York, and he claims that the best bait he has ever used is a bunker and a squid on the same hook. He finds that they rarely refuse this combination.

Morton Newman also fishes Long Island waters for sharks, and he has a little gimmick that helps attract them. He mixes the regular mossbunker chum and adds some blood to it. Then he cuts up old newspapers into strips and adds these to the chum. The white strips drifting and twisting in the current seem to draw sharks to the area.

The man who has caught some of the biggest sharks ever taken on rod and reel is Alfred Dean, of Australia. He concentrated mostly on the big white shark, or man-eater. Three of his biggest went 2,344 pounds, 2,536 pounds, and finally one that went 2,664 pounds! He hooked and lost bigger ones and some that he did catch didn't qualify as records due to some infraction of the I.G.F.A. rules. He also hooked and lost one monster that towed his 30-foot launch twelve miles, for five and a half hours. He figured that this shark would have gone 4,000 pounds.

Captain Hal Scharp cleans the jaws of a big tiger shark. Many sharks have been caught, both for sport and research, from his charter boat *Que Pasa* in the Florida Keys. (*Captain Hal Scharp photo*)

Naturally Alf Dean used strong tackle for such brutes, with heavy rods, big reels, and 130- and 180-pound-test lines. Dean did a lot of his fishing in Denial Bay and at Ceduna, Australia, and he brought along plenty of chum and bait when he went after the big sharks. He liked to use whale oil and bullock's blood, which dripped from punctured cans into the water. He knew sharks are fond of whale meat and the scent of the whale oil drew them from great distances. When sharks appeared near the boat, he poured the bullock's blood into the water to excite them and make them take a bait more readily. Dean also shot seals and suspended these from the stern of the boat. He used seal livers and blubber for bait on a big hook.

Another angler who caught big sharks is Bob Dyer, of Sydney, Australia. He and his wife, Dolly, caught many sharks over 1,000 pounds. He held the former all-tackle record with a white shark that weighed 2,342 pounds. He also caught a 1,125-pound tiger shark on 24-thread line for another world record. Dyer also uses whale oil and whale blood for chum. He will also hang big pieces of whale meat over the side of the boat to bring a shark in close so he can judge its size. If it is less than 10 feet, he'll pass it up for a bigger one!

Frank Posluszny fishes for sharks in southern Florida waters and has won many of the prizes in the Annual Metropolitan Miami Fishing Tournament year after year for the biggest or most sharks caught. He catches many of them from party boats or drift boats, but he also fishes from charter boats and private boats. Frank likes to use a heavy rod; big, 12/0 reel; and 130-pound-test line, because he wants to be ready when a big shark takes the bait. He likes to use a whole bonito weighing about 5 to 6 pounds for bait, impaling it on a big, 14/0 or 16/0 hook.

Frank particularly favors fishing off the Florida Keys in a spot called "The Hump," about sixteen miles off Islamorada. There the bottom rises closer to the surface and all kinds of fish hang around, attracting big sharks.

Don Woodruff has been fishing for sharks for twenty-five years and figures he's caught three thousand of them during that time. He's caught them from Montauk, New York, to Florida, but in recent years he has been doing most of his fishing in Florida's Intracoastal Waterway or the Florida Keys. He fishes from a small, 17-foot dory-type boat and uses heavy rods and a 9/0 reel filled with 130-pound-test line. He anchors and fishes at night with a big chunk of moray eel, which he says makes the best bait. He lets out a lot of slack line so that the bait lies quietly on the bottom. Once he hooks a shark, he lifts the anchor and lets a big shark tow his boat while he fights it.

Walter Maxwell, of Charlotte, North Carolina, likes to fish for tiger sharks, and he caught one, going 1,780 pounds, from a pier at Cherry Grove, North Carolina. He finds that tiger sharks are most plentiful from May to September along the Carolinas. They come into shallow water then to feed and give birth. He found by examining their stomach contents that they eat mostly lemon sharks, stingrays, and skates. So he uses 3- to 4-foot lemon sharks for bait when going after the big tiger sharks and his equipment consists of a heavy rod, 16/0 reel, and 130-pound-test line for most of his fishing.

Maxwell lost some big sharks while fishing from piers, so in recent years he has been doing most of his fishing from boats.

Ben Pinsley used to fish for sharks in the surf from Long Island, New York, beaches. He used a heavy surf rod, a 4/0 reel, and 50- or 60-pound-test lines. Most of the sharks he caught were ground sharks or brown sharks, weighing up to 150 or 200 pounds. He used a 6-foot wire leader with a 10/0 hook and a piece of weakfish, half of a bunker, or a live eel for bait. Ben fished at the mouths of inlets or near them in the deeper holes, channels, and sloughs along beaches. He found that night fishing was best but also caught sharks in the daytime if the tide was favorable. This was usually during the period from half flood to half ebb. The best months for surf fishing for sharks in New York waters are July, August, and September.

But the most enthusiastic surf fisherman for sharks in this country is Herb Goodman, who fishes from the beaches along Florida's East Coast. He has caught many of them over 6 or 7 feet long, and one of his biggest was an 850-pound tiger shark. Herb uses 7- to 9-foot rods and 9/0 to 12/0 reels filled with 130-pound-test lines. He attaches a 15-foot wire leader with two 12/0 hooks on the end. He baits this with a large bonito or a 15-pound chunk of bloody fish.

To get this big bait and line out to deep water where sharks roam, he may let it out from a jetty in an inlet and let the tide take it out. He attaches two toy balloons 10 to 15 feet above the bait so he can watch it going out and keep it suspended above the bottom while it is moving out. In recent years, however, he has used a small boat run by a boy or a 3-foot radio-controlled boat to take the bait out up to 1,500 feet from shore. Then it is dropped into the water and allowed to sink to the bottom.

The biggest sharks caught from shore or piers are the giants hauled in by the sharkers of Durban, South Africa. Many sharks over 1,000 pounds have been taken from South Pier at Durban and along the rocks at Hermanus by anglers using 11-foot rods, big wooden reels, and lines testing 100 pounds or more. They use a piece of whale meat for bait and either heave this out from the pier or let it out with a big float from shore. Fishing this way, Wyn Moxley caught a 1,480-pound shark, Reg Harrison caught a 1,660-pounder, and W. R. Selkirk caught one going 2,176 pounds! Most of the sharks caught are white sharks, or "blue pointers," as they are called in South Africa.

Gil Drake usually fishes the flats in the Florida Keys or the Bahamas for bonefish or permit, but he also enjoys catching sharks in this shallow water. He finds that such species as the spinner shark, lemon shark, blacktip shark, dusky shark, and hammerhead shark will feed in shallow water and will often take a lure. He likes to use a fly rod or bait-casting tackle for the sharks and finds that with the casting tackle a surface plug will attract sharks. With a fly rod he uses big streamers and bucktails in white, yellow, orange, or red.

Gil finds that it is important when fishing for sharks to cast the lure in the right spot to obtain strikes. This means placing your lure on the side of the head nearest you opposite the shark's eye. Casting in front of the shark is not as effective, because this is a blind spot. Gil retrieves the lure fairly slowly but with plenty of action.

Norman Duncan, of Miami, also fishes for sharks with flies, but he teases and excites the fish before presenting the fly. He usually anchors the boat in a spot where sharks are likely to be cruising and chums with pieces of fish. Then he puts a piece of the fish on a casting rod, and when a shark appears he casts this in front of it. He teases the shark with the bait, even letting it grab it and take off a piece of the meat. When the shark is excited, Norm casts a fly toward it. This chumming and teasing usually makes the shark hit the lure.

Although most of the sharks caught while wading or from a boat in the flats in the Florida Keys and the Bahamas are on the small side, you never know when a good-sized shark will appear. Bart Foth caught a 272-pound lemon shark on a fly rod fishing this way.

The smaller sharks, like this one being hauled in, can provide a lot of fun and sport on light tackle. In recent years, more and more anglers have been fishing for them in the Florida Keys and the Bahamas. (*Florida Publicity Division photo*)

24

PACIFIC SALMON,
YELLOWTAIL, AND ALBACORE

Pacific salmon are caught from California to Alaska and provide top sport and fine eating for thousands of anglers, who catch them from shore and boats. Most of the fishing is done in the ocean, bays, river mouths, and the rivers themselves in salt or brackish waters. But some salmon are also caught upstream, in fresh water. All kinds of fishing tackle is used, from salt-water trolling rods and reels in the ocean, surf-fishing tackle from the beaches, and mooching outfits in the bays, to light spinning tackle, bait-casting outfits, and fly rods in fresh water.

There are many charter boats available for salmon fishing in such spots as Westport, in Washington, where you can go out for a day's fishing. One such charter-boat captain is Al Weathers, who fishes the Westport area and has caught thousands of salmon for his customers. He gets both Chinook and coho salmon by trolling and mooching. Captain Weathers finds some of his best fishing along a ragged line of floating seaweed and debris where two ocean currents meet and create a rip. There herring, needlefish, and other baitfish are found, and these in turn attract the salmon.

Bob Behme also fishes for Pacific salmon, and he favors the two-hook mooching rig to hold the herring bait: A big single hook is run through the herring's head and another single hook or treble hook on a short nylon dropper is run through the tail. The bait can be given a slight curve, which produces a slow looping movement and makes it look crippled. Bob also likes to paint a few stripes along the sides of the herring with red Merthiolate.

When mooching for salmon, he adds a crescent weight ahead of the bait, lowers it to the depth he wants to fish, and drifts with the current or wind. If there is no current or wind to move the boat he'll use the engine to move the boat 20 to 30 feet, cut it off, run it again, cut it off, and so on, to give the bait movement. This also makes the bait rise and then sink, which gives it that disabled look salmon go for. Bob finds he catches his biggest salmon during September and the first week of October.

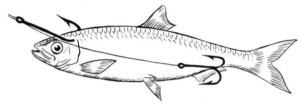

Two-hook mooching rig used for salmon

Chester Chatfield looks for coho or silver salmon in the most turbulent water he can find. He looks for two currents meeting, swirls, whirlpools, and tidal rips, where baitfish get trapped and tossed around, and there he usually finds the cohos feeding. Most of the better spots are two to three miles from shore.

Chet uses a 2- to 4-ounce crescent sinker about 6 feet above his two-hook rig. He likes No. 2/0 Eagle Claw hooks tied about 3 inches apart on the end of his leader. He cuts a long, tapered fillet from the side of a herring, puts this on the front hook and lets it out from the boat anywhere from 30 to 120 feet. When trolled, the bait should flash and spin and look like a live herring in the water. When straight trolling doesn't produce, Chet tries a zigzag course. He also reels in his bait, then lets it out again, repeating this at regular intervals.

Francis H. Ames fishes for "jack salmon," which are the immature Chinook and silver salmon that often run up rivers from California to Oregon during the summer months. He uses a sliding cork float on the end of his line baited with salmon eggs and he adds a quarter-ounce sinker to the leader. This is cast out, and the lead weight on the leader pulls the hook and bait down while the cork float rests against a knot in the line. He casts this rig out, and when the cork is pulled under by a fish, he waits a few seconds and sets the hook. He also catches jack salmon on plugs, spoons, and flies. He finds these lures work best when the salmon are trapped in pools.

Leonard Miracle likes to troll for coho salmon out of Newport, Oregon, using a long, limber rod, a 20-pound-test line, and a herring bait in front of a crescent sinker. He finds that you have to try various weights and trolling speeds to get down to the level where salmon are feeding. At times, they will take a herring moving just below the surface. But, other times, they want a herring trolled 10 to 20 feet down. He lets out about 100 feet of line, but often the coho hit closer to the boat if the bait reaches the right depth.

Don Holm fishes for Pacific salmon from Oregon to Alaska, and he feels that too many anglers mooching or trolling for salmon with herring bait strike these fish too soon and too fast. When he feels a fish taking the bait, he feeds some slack line so that a salmon can swallow the herring. Then he sets the hook.

Don Holm fishes for coho salmon in the surf, from the beaches in Oregon. He looks for terns and gulls feeding close to shore where cohos are chasing candlefish or other baitfish. Then he casts coho flies with a weight and a plastic bubble on the line to reach the feeding fish. He has caught coho salmon up to 12 and 15 pounds by fishing in this manner.

Dick Knowles has been taking out fishing parties for coho salmon on the Campbell River, in British Columbia, Canada, for many years. His favorite and most effective method is to troll big, polar-bear bucktails in shallow water during the summer and fall months. He looks for the coho over reefs and bars and along kelp beds, where he does most of his trolling. At times, he also sees coho chasing and feeding on herring and needlefish. If he sees a school of bait, he trolls past it and then runs the boat out so that the flies travel through the eddies and undisturbed water and drift sideways across the current.

Bob Olsen fishes the San Pedro Bay area of California for Pacific salmon, and he has a reputation for coming in with big salmon when everyone else is getting small ones. Like most expert salmon fishermen, Bob Olsen looks for the "black water"—clean, clear water free of weeds, kelp, or heavy plankton growth—and that is where he fishes. It is so named because it appears dark to the eye if you look down into the depths. Bob will also try to find a school of feeding salmon, and then he tries to determine the direction in which it is moving and feeding. If he locates such a school, he will drop his boat back toward the tail end of the body of fish and let out more line. He believes that the smaller salmon feed closer to the surface, while the larger ones lie in deeper water. He catches most of his big salmon on a whole anchovy rigged so that it has a curve in its body, which makes it wobble from side to side.

Dave Stewart fishes for Pacific salmon in the more remote spots, where fishermen are scarce, like the West Coast of Vancouver Island, British Columbia. There are numerous coves, reefs, inlets, islands, rocky shores, and beaches that can be fished here. Dave catches his Chinook salmon by mooching with a whole herring in 50 to 100 feet of water with gravel bottoms. He lets out the 1- or 2-ounce crescent sinker and bait until he feels it hit bottom. Then he reels in a few feet and drifts at that level. Other times, he will use a 2-ounce all-silver jig with a 3/0 treble hook and a yellow or orange skirt. He lets this down to the bottom and then jigs it up and down.

Enos Bradner has spent a lifetime fishing for Pacific salmon in the Northwest. When he went up to Alaska, he found that anglers believed that the sockeye, or red salmon, wouldn't take artificial lures. But he tried the same bucktail flies he used for steelhead and found that the sockeyes loved them. The fishing for these salmon is best when they run up the rivers, in July. He looked for the salmon in shallow riffles, where they were thick, and cast the fly out and retrieved it fast to get strikes.

Gene Round believes in changing lure sizes, colors, and types every fifteen to twenty minutes when he is trolling for coho salmon. He holds the rod in his hand in order to feel the steady beat, or action, of the lure. If this stops or changes, he reels in to see if the lure is fouled or has picked up weeds, kelp, or other debris.

When Wesley Blair wants big Chinook salmon, he heads for Rivers Inlet, in British Columbia, where the average fish caught runs about 40 pounds! They have been caught going 70, 77, and even over 80 pounds from late July to late August, which is the peak period for the big ones. Blair trolls with a conventional rod and reel with 3- to 5-ounce weights and a herring bait. The big salmon lie near the bottom, so you let out line until you feel the sinker bounce on the bottom and then reel in a couple of turns. The best fishing usually occurs at dawn and dusk.

Allen Bonenko fishes for Pacific salmon in many waters in the Northwest. He catches salmon by trolling and mooching, and he finds that the angle of the line into the water while mooching should

This is a day's catch of big Chinook, or tyee, salmon caught at Rivers Inlet, British Columbia. The smallest was 40 pounds and the biggest went 54½ pounds. (*Allen Bonenko photo*)

be 45 to 60 degrees for Chinook salmon and about 20 to 45 degrees for coho salmon. And the depth you fish is very important. It should be varied, and the motor can be used every so often to raise and lower the bait. He finds that for coho you usually don't have to go much deeper than 30 feet. But Chinook should be fished deeper, from 60 to 90 feet, just off the bottom. However, early in the morning and toward evening, Chinook may come closer to the surface and can be caught at the same depths as the coho.

When searching for salmon, Bonenko looks for the tide rips where two bodies of water with different densities come together. These rips hold small baitfish and other food, and salmon are often found there. He also watches for birds wheeling and diving for bait. Or he looks for schools of baitfish, or "bait balls"—clusters of bait on or just below the surface. He finds that tides vary from place to place, but as a general rule an hour before to an hour after a tide change is a good time to fish. If these occur at dawn or dusk your chances of catching salmon are excellent.

Bonenko finds that coho will often take a fast-trolled bait or lure, but that Chinook like slow-moving baits and lures. A herring that has a slow, looping roll is best for Chinook.

David Smith fishes for big Chinook, or king, salmon in Pacific Coast streams with tackle suitable for fresh-water bass. He uses light spinning rods with reels loaded with 6-pound or 8-pound lines and has caught Chinook salmon up to 50 and 60 pounds on such tackle!

He finds that these big salmon will lie or hold in deep, slow-moving water. The best time to fish for them is early in the morning, when they will hit a plug, spoon, spinner, or cherry bobber.

Bob Nauheim also catches big Chinook, in such waters as the Smith River, in California, in September, October, and November. He uses a fly rod and has caught them in the 20-, 30-, and 40-pound classes, up to 49 pounds. They have also been caught up to 52, 53, and 56 pounds on a fly!

Bob prefers a heavy fly rod and a fly line with a shooting head. He finds that high-density and lead-core lines are best for this fishing. The monofilament running line he uses tests 20 pounds. The flies are tied on No. 2 to 6 hooks and are mostly hair, with silver or gold tinsel bodies. Some of the flies also have Mylar piping.

Fly used for Chinook salmon

Bob uses a small boat to reach the best spots where salmon lie. Sometimes the fish show themselves or can be seen in the clear water. He tries to cast the fly anywhere from 10 to 20 feet upcurrent of where the fish are lying and then let it sink and drift in front of the fish so that they can see it. He finds that the salmon hit best early in the morning and late in the evening when the water is low and clear. When rains raise the water and discolor it slightly, the fishing usually improves.

Some of the pools Bob Nauheim fishes are studded with boulders and logs, which cause him to lose a lot of flies and even fly lines, so he brings plenty of flies and spare fly lines when he fishes the Smith River.

The California yellowtail is a scrappy fish related to the amberjack and is usually caught from the "live bait," or party, boats in Pacific waters. One angler who has fished for them for many years is Harry Bonner. He recommends a spinning or conventional rod from 8 to 10 feet long with a light, limber tip but a stiff butt section. Big spinning reels or conventional reels filled with 20- to 25-pound-test monofilament line are required. He ties a small, No. 4 tuna-style hook directly to the line, baits this with a live anchovy and casts it without any weight if the yellowtail are on top. If they are deeper he may add a light weight above the hook.

When the yellowtail are really deep, near the bottom, Bonner uses an 8-ounce cigar sinker on the end of his line and then attaches a 6-foot bronze-wire leader to the weight. Then he ties on an 8/0 tuna hook and baits it with a strip of mackerel 6 to 7 inches long. He lowers the bait to the bottom, then starts reeling it back slowly.

Bill Beebe also fishes for yellowtail, and when they refuse a live anchovy or sardine, he uses a live mackerel for bait. He chums with ground or crushed anchovies, catches live mackerel on small feather lures and keeps them alive in his specially built bait tank. When he reaches the kelp beds where yellowtail are found, he starts chumming with live anchovies to bring them up to the boat. When he sees yellowtail near the boat, he baits a mackerel through the lips and lets it swim around freely. When a yellowtail grabs the bait, Bill gives it plenty of line so that it can swallow the bait. Then he sets the hook. For this fishing, he prefers conventional rods and reels with lines testing from 15 to 40 pounds.

Captain George Wyer, who runs the boat *H & M 80* out of San Diego, California, makes long trips to Guadalupe Island, off Baja

Action can be fast and furious when yellowtail or albacore show up near a boat. You often get several anglers hooked up at the same time. (*Phil Clock photo*)

California, for the fast yellowtail fishing often found there. He also likes to use live mackerel for bait and catches them at night using a series of ten or twelve hooks with colored yarn tied around them to catch the mackerel. The best-sized mackerel to use for bait will run from 8 to 12 inches.

When anglers are fishing with live mackerel on his boat, Captain Wyer tells them to give the yellowtail plenty of time to run and swallow the bait. If an angler does set the hook and misses the fish, he advises throwing the reel into free spool and letting some line out. The yellowtail will often come back and take the bait again.

Chuck Garrison fishes for yellowtail from a small boat on the inshore beds. He looks for floating "clumps" or "paddies" of kelp, because he finds that yellowtail will lie and feed under patches of floating kelp. Chuck may toss a few live anchovies near the kelp and if he sees boils or yellowtail after the bait, he casts toward the spot.

Chuck will often use fresh or frozen squid for bait, and he casts one of these on a hook with a ½-ounce rubber-core sinker on the leader to take it down. The yellowtail will often grab the squid as it is sinking. If not, he retrieves the bait with an up-and-down action of the rod to make the squid look alive. Other times, Chuck uses metal jigs and casts these toward the kelp or any fish he sees boiling. The jig is retrieved fast to give it plenty of action.

Dick Underwood fishes for yellowtail from party boats in waters off Baja California. He usually starts off fishing with big, 7-inch, 6½-ounce casting jigs which he prefers with a chrome, purple, or red nose, and clear reflective finish on the body. He rigs up three outfits, each with a different-color jig, so that he doesn't lose time changing lures.

Dick will let the jig down to the bottom and then reel in a couple of turns. Then he holds the rod with his left hand on the foregrip and starts jigging the lure up and down with his right hand on the rod butt, raising and lowering it in a steady action.

When jigs don't work, Dick uses his bottom-fishing outfit with an 80-pound mono line on a 6/0 reel. He uses a rig with several sliding sinkers up to a total of 8 or 9 ounces in weight about 4 feet above the 9/0 hook. A barrel swivel acts as a stop to keep the sinkers from sliding down to the hook. Then he baits a live mackerel through the nose with the hook and lets it down to the bottom, reeling in a couple of turns to keep the rig clear of the rocks.

Many anglers who fish for yellowtail from the party boats also catch the Pacific long-finned albacore from them too. Claude Kreider, who spent a lifetime fishing for these speedy fish, discovered early in the game that they are shy, wary, and sensitive fish with keen eyesight. He found that they would refuse a feather jig that was even slightly stained with rust. Or they would pass up one color in favor of another. He also found you couldn't use too small a hook or too fine a leader for these fish. Claude liked a No. 2 tuna-style short-shank hook when he used live anchovies for the fish.

Like most albacore fishermen, Claude looked for boils, or fish showing on top, and then cast his live anchovy toward them. But other times, when the albacore were down deeper, he added a small clincher sinker on the leader above the live bait.

Clint Hull also fishes for albacore from the live-bait boats off California. He keeps a close watch on the lines and lures being trolled behind the boat when they get to the fishing grounds. This is the way the fish are located. If albacore hit the lures and are being brought in, Clint waits until the crew starts tossing live bait as chum into the water to hold the albacore near the boat. Then he quickly hooks an anchovy through the nose and drops him into the water as the boat slows to a stop. He usually gets a quick hook-up this way from a school of albacore, which tend to follow a hooked fish right up to the boat and begin feeding on the live bait thrown out as chum.

When Robert S. Mikkelson fishes for albacore from the live-bait boats, he brings plenty of extra spools of line for the spinning reels he uses. He finds you lose a lot of line in break-offs or tangles during this fishing. And you also have to cut off the bad sections of line during the fishing day.

Mikkelson uses a No. 1 or No. 2 hook on the end of his 25-pound-test line and baits a live anchovy through the gill collar. He finds that when albacore become shy or selective, a fresh, lively bait on the hook every minute or two will bring more strikes. It also helps to turn the reel handle slightly to make the bait move a bit and look alive.

Don Holm fishes for albacore off Oregon and Washington by running far offshore for these fish. Don looks for "tunny birds," or gulls that follow the albacore schools. He also looks for porpoises, which often signal the presence of tuna under them. He finds that trolling, with feathers, jigs, bone or plastic lures, and spoons, is a good way to catch and locate the fish. Trolling at eight to nine knots with long lines out is most effective. Once you hook an albacore or two, its a good idea to double back and cover the same water again. You can also try trolling in a square pattern.

Jim Martin fishes for Pacific albacore, and he says that you should use fairly heavy tackle and lines when trolling and trying to locate a school of albacore. He advises using 50- or 60-pound-test lines and

Claude Kreider is shown with a good-sized long-finned albacore he caught from a "live-bait" boat in the Pacific. (*Claude Kreider photo*)

trolling the lures fast when searching for albacore. The reason for the heavy tackle is that you can't afford to lose the first fish you hook. Albacore are school fish, so they tend to follow a hooked fish. If you lose the hooked fish, the rest of the school will follow him away from the boat. Once the hooked fish is close to the boat and other albacore are around, Jim hooks an anchovy through the nose and flips it out into the water even before the boat stops moving. He finds that he has to work fast, because the first baits in the water get hits and fish on while anglers who wait too long fail to get hook-ups.

25

BOTTOM FISHES

The term "bottom fishes" covers a wide variety of salt-water species, from tiny panfish, running a few ounces in weight, to big grouper and jewfish running several hundred pounds. These are the fish usually caught by the average angler from piers, bridges, shore, private boats, rental boats, and party boats in the Atlantic, Pacific, and Gulf of Mexico waters.

Scott Simons fishes for the big "humpback" porgies at Montauk, New York, and he finds that fresh skimmer clams make the best bait. He also uses clams as chum; he fills a chum pot with them and lowers it to the bottom under the boat.

Scott likes to use a two-hook rig with No. 1 Eagle Claw baitholder hooks. He ties one hook about 6 inches above the sinker and the second hook about 12 inches above the first one. He uses short, 2- to 3-inch snells to hold the hooks to the line or leader because he feels that they tangle less than longer ones. Scott baits the hooks with small pieces of clam and lets his rig down with a one-handed spinning outfit with 10- or 12-pound-test line. This light line enables him to feel the porgies bite better. He sets the hook right after the second rap.

Matt Ahern fishes for sea bass in New York and New Jersey waters, and he finds that the squid makes one of the best baits for these fish. He cuts the squid into strips 3 to 4 inches long and runs the 4/0 or 5/0 hook through the strip two or three times. He may also pound the squid bait with a mallet to make it give off juices or a scent, which attracts sea bass. Matt will also use a diamond jig for sea bass, also adding a small strip of squid to the hook.

Staff Carroll enjoys fishing for the big blackfish, or tautog, found off the rocky shores and on the reefs of Rhode Island. He catches some of his biggest ones, going from 5 to 15 pounds, at Brenton Reef, near the Texas tower. Record blackfish, weighing over 20 pounds, have been caught there.

Staff uses a small whole green crab or half of a bigger one on a hook for bait. One of his tricks is to chum with crushed green crabs so that the big blackfish leave the holes and crevices and start feeding actively. Once they are out in the open, it is easier to hook and boat them on lighter tackle. He finds September and October two good months for catching blackfish off Rhode Island.

Many skilled anglers such as Max Payne also believe that chumming is a must for catching flounders. Max takes mussels or clams, crushes them and puts them in a sack or a mesh bag. Then he adds a brick or a stone for weight and lowers the chum bag to the bottom. Every so often, he pulls on the line attached to the chum bag to release some of the chum and scent.

Max looks for flounders over mud bottoms and where the mud meets and mixes with sand and gravel bottoms. He also looks for the edges of channels, and oyster and clam beds. He believes in using small baits for flounders because of their small mouths. A bit of clam or worm no bigger than a small elbow macaroni is the size he likes to use.

When Max feels a nibble, he lowers his rod to give the flounder a chance to swallow the bait. Then he lifts the rod slowly, and if he feels the weight of the fish, he sets the hook.

Captain George F. Glas, who runs a party boat and fishes off Block Island, Rhode Island, for big, snowshoe flounders, recommends a No. 4 Chestertown hook for these fish. This is baited with a skimmer-clam lip impaled several times along the bend and shank of the hook. Or you can cut the clam into long, narrow strips and use these. Once anchored over a good spot, Captain Glas chums with broken skimmer shells or smashed mussels to bring the snowshoes under the boat.

Milt Rosko is an avid fluke fisherman, and he seeks these tasty flatfish wherever they are found along the Atlantic coast. Milt uses the standard fluke outfits, with conventional reels, and lines testing from 15 to 30 pounds. The heavier lines are used for big fluke in deep water over broken or rocky bottoms. The lighter lines are fine for the smaller fluke in shallow water and clean bottoms. Milt will use a regular fluke rig with 30-inch leader and a single hook for live

Fluke, or summer flounders, provide sport and good eating for many anglers. This one was caught in South Carolina, but they run along most of the Atlantic Coast. (*Ted Borg photo*)

killies if these are being used for bait. For dead baits and long strips, he prefers the two-hook rig on the end of the leader. These are baited with long strips of squid, strips cut from a fluke or sea robin, or big baitfish such as smelt.

While Milt does a lot of drifting for fluke, he has also found that power trolling is even more productive in most waters. It is especially useful when there is no wind or tide to move the boat. He finds that such trolling can be effective in both shallow and moderate depths. And when a fluke grabs the bait while you're trolling, you don't have to hesitate or give line as you do when drifting, because the fluke usually hooks itself almost immediately.

Judd York and Frank Lovello fish for big, "doormat" fluke at the end of Long Island, New York. During the summer months, they catch fluke up to 14 and 15 pounds! They use a small, whole squid or a whole smelt for these big fish. The baits are hooked on a two-hook rig, with the first one a 5/0 single hook about 5 or 6 inches above a small, strong treble hook. The single hook is run through the tail of the squid, while the treble hook impales the head. The leader, with bait, is tied about 2 feet above the sinker to keep from hanging up in the rocks or the bottom too often.

Small squid on two-hook rig for big fluke

At one time, cod were caught mostly during the winter months, but now many party boats and private boats go after these fish the year round. You just have to fish in colder and deeper waters during the summer months than you do during the winter. One angler who fishes for cod in many of the top spots is Pete Byrnes. He feels most anglers use too much bait on their hooks, and he recommends using only half of a clam on the hook, leaving the point of the hook exposed. He also feels that too many anglers lose fish because they are too eager to set the hook and yank the bait out of the cod's mouth. He advises the angler to raise the rod slowly, lifting the bait from the bottom about 3 feet, and then lowering it again. Cod will usually grab the bait as it is being raised.

Pete Byrnes has also caught cod on lures such as the spoons and tube lures trolled with wire lines or weights along the bottom. He recommends letting the sinker or weight hit bottom, then reeling it back up a few feet. You can also reel the line all the way in from the bottom and then let it drop back again. Keep repeating this until you get a hit.

Captain Carl Forsberg was a party-boat skipper out of Montauk for many years and was one of the first to discover and fish the famed "Cox's Ledge" from that port. Carl always felt that anglers use too much hardware such as swivels, snaps, spreaders, and beads on their rigs. He advocated a simple cod rig, without any hardware. He would tie one big loop on the end of the line to hold the sinker, then another, smaller loop about 2 feet above the sinker to take the snelled hook on an 18-inch leader, and another loop 3½ feet above the first one to take the second hook. That way, the snells on both hooks would never meet and get tangled.

Captain Forsberg advised the anglers on his boat to let the bait down to the bottom and let it lie still, with no lifting or jerking of the rod. He felt you could catch more cod that way. He also told anglers to use small baits rather than two or three big clams on a hook.

Captain Ralph Selva, who runs the *Spook III* out of Lindenhurst, Long Island, has a trick he uses in cod fishing that he feels gets him more fish. Like many skippers, he will chum with empty clam shells under his boat. But he also gets a quart of cod liver oil and dumps this over the clams to be used as chum and also in the bucket where the clams have been shucked for bait.

Max Payne likes to jig for his cod in Rhode Island waters, and he uses light tackle and chrome-plated diamond jigs from 4 to 8 ounces. He lets these go down to the bottom and then starts jigging with quick, sharp lifts of the rod tip at the rate of a lift every 5 to 6 seconds. He finds the cod usually take the jig as it flutters down, but he hesitates a second or two after a hit to give the cod time to mouth the lure.

Jigging is also used to catch big cod in Maine on such boats as the *Magnum,* run by Captain Ransom Kelley out of Boothbay Harbor. Many cod in the 40-, 50- and 60-pound classes are caught there each season, and one going 86 pounds was taken in those waters. Heavy jigs are used over the codfish grounds, located about twelve miles from shore. The best season runs from June to September.

Up in New England and Canada they catch cod like this one on big metal jigs during the summer months. (*Canadian Government Travel Bureau photo*)

Pollock are also caught on diamond jigs on many party boats, and if you want big ones you should sail with Captain Howard Bogan, skipper of the *Jamaica,* out of Brielle, New Jersey. He fishes a spot he calls "Bogan's Mountain," making the long run to those grounds in the spring and fall, when the fishing is best. Pollock running from 30 to 40 pounds are often taken on these trips. You need a sturdy rod and a good-sized reel holding 50-pound-test monofilament or Dacron line for this deep fishing. Big diamond jigs, up to 14 ounces, are used, and these are lowered to the bottom and then reeled back immediately.

Also caught in deep water from party boats sailing out of New

York and New Jersey ports is the little-known tilefish. A. R. Wickers likes to fish for them, and he uses a fairly stiff boat rod 6 to 7 feet long and a 4/0 reel filled with 40- or 50-pound-test mono line. Sinkers up to 2 pounds may be needed to get down to the 300- to 500-foot depths usually fished. His rig consists of a single 9/0 hook tied on a snell about 2 feet above the sinker. For bait he uses a small whole squid. This should be hooked securely in two or three places.

Although tilefish can be caught most of the year, Wickers finds that the warmer months, June to September, provide the weather and calm seas that make for good tilefishing.

Most anglers who fish for red snappers, in our warmer waters, use heavy rods, strong lines, and heavy weights to get down to the depths where these fish are usually sought. But Frank Komitsky has found that you can take these fish on light tackle when they come closer to the surface to feed. He has caught red snappers up to 20 pounds within 70 feet of the surface of the water.

Fish strip on jig used for red snappers

Frank likes to use a spinning rod and big salt-water spinning reel filled with 20- to 30-pound-test line. He ties a 2-ounce jig on the end of his line and baits it with a strip of fish, which can be cut from a bluefish, bonito, blue runner, or almost any other fish. This strip should be shaped like a pennant and be 4 to 8 inches long and 2 to 3 inches wide. He runs the hook of the jig through the widest part of the fish strip.

Frank Komitsky finds that the best way to use this jig and bait is to cast it out from a boat and let it drift with the current to various depths. If the lure and bait reaches a spot where it is suspended by the tide, he reels in and casts it out again. Frank will cast uptide, downtide, and across the tide all around the boat so that he covers various spots and depths.

Max Hunn and his wife, Kit, enjoy fishing for mangrove snappers in Florida's Everglades country and other spots where these cagey and smart fish are found. Max uses a light spinning rod with 6- to 8-pound-test line and a heavier, 10- to 12-pound-test shock leader at least 8 to 10 feet long.

Max catches the snappers on live and dead shrimp but prefers to get them on small white jigs. A ¼-ounce jig is a good size to use and cast with the light outfit he likes. He usually adds a piece of shrimp to the hook of the jig to obtain more strikes. He looks for snappers under mangrove trees or in the deeper holes and channels. Such spots are located at low tide and fished when the tide is up.

When Louis Mowbray wants to catch mangrove snappers in Bermuda waters, he first gets some hog-mouthed fry (tiny salt-water minnows) and then heads for a reef, anchors, and starts chumming with the fry to bring the snappers up to the boat.

Phil Francis finds fishing for sheepshead a challenge, because these fish are so adept at stealing a bait off the hook. He finds that a sliding-sinker rig is best for these fish. He adds a barrel swivel about a foot above a No. 1/0 O'Shaughnessy hook, and an egg sinker with a hole is threaded on the line above the swivel. He baits the hook with a fiddler crab. Phil finds that with this rig he can feel the sheepshead bite and can give a bit of slack and hook more fish. At the slightest tug, he lowers his rod a second, then sets the hook. If you fail to hook the fish, you might as well reel in, because the bait will be gone. Francis looks for sheepshead around rocks, piles, mangrove roots, and other spots where there are barnacles. Oyster beds are also good spots to try for them.

Jack Stark fishes for grouper in Florida, and one of his favorite spots for these fish is Turtle Rock, off Key Largo. He either trolls or drifts with ballyhoo or mullet strips. He uses large egg sinkers to get the baits down to the right depth. He also fishes the edge of the Gulf Stream, and there he looks for drop-offs in 90 and 100 feet of water.

Max and Kit Hunn have a lot of fun and sport catching grouper in shallow water along Florida's Gulf Coast on lures. They use light spinning rods and reels filled with 8- to 10-pound-test lines. While surface plugs will often raise grouper, they find that underwater or sinking models work best. These plugs are cast out and retrieved near the holes, or hide-outs in the rocks. Then, when you hook a grouper, you have to keep it from returning to its hole. Most of the grouper caught in these shallow waters run small, from 2 or 3

Max Hunn holds a mangrove snapper he caught on light spinning tackle and 4-pound-test line. These fish are especially numerous in the Florida mangrove country and make fine eating. (*Photo by Kit and Max Hunn*)

pounds up to 10 or 15 pounds, but they put up a great fight on the light tackle Max and Kit use.

Emmett Gowen liked to fish for jewfish in the Gulf of Mexico from a small boat. He found that the best bait was a big, live blue crab hooked through the outer tip of the shell. He fished the crab when the tide was slack by lowering it into holes around wrecks and rock jetties, and under bridges and piers. When a jewfish took the bait and got hooked, Emmett immediately applied pressure to keep the fish from getting back into a hole, where it could cut or foul the line.

One angler who has taken big jewfish on extremely light lines is Ralph Delph, of Miami. He has caught them going 307, 319, 343, and 349 pounds on lines testing from 10 to 20 pounds on plug-casting tackle. One of his tricks in luring a big jewfish out into the open and away from its hole is to lower a small live fish on another line, and when the jewfish comes up from the bottom for it, he offers it a bait or lure on his light tackle.

Harry Bonner fishes for big black sea bass from party boats off California and Mexico. He uses a sturdy trolling rod with roller guides and tip top and a big, 9/0 reel filled with 80-pound-test line. He attaches an 8-ounce cigar-shaped sinker to the end of this line with a husky ball-bearing swivel and snap. To the other eye on the sinker he ties a 6-foot wire leader. At the other end of the leader, he puts an 8/0 or 9/0 hook. The hook is baited with a live mackerel, barracuda, bonito, squid, queenfish, or white croaker and is lowered to the bottom.

Or he may remove the sinker from his line and push it into the stomach of a whole-fish bait which is then hooked through the nose and lowered to the bottom. Then he will retrieve it slowly, while raising and lowering it to make it look alive.

Bonner also finds that black sea bass will often hit a 3- or 4-ounce metal jig worked near the bottom, especially if you add a small live squid to the hook of the jig.

J. Charles Davis II fished for black sea bass off California for many years, at Anacapa, Catalina, San Clemente, and the Coronados. He found the best fishing for them around islands, near shore, around rock piles and sunken wrecks, and near kelp beds.

Davis used live baits such as whitefish and mackerel on a big, 9/0 to 12/0 hook with heavy tackle. He added a sinker above the bait

This huge, 465-pound black sea bass was caught off California, around the Channel Islands, with husky tackle and big fish baits. (*Pierpoint Landing photo*)

and kept it about 10 feet off the bottom. For baits he punctured the air bladder of a whitefish to keep it from coming up to the surface and hooked it on the underside just back of the vent, to keep it swimming in a natural position. He hooked a live mackerel the same way through the nose or back. When a black sea bass grabbed the bait, Davis didn't wait very long to set the hook. Then he applied pressure to keep the big fish from heading for a hole, a rock, or the kelp, where it could foul the line.

Surf perches provide a lot of fun and sport along the Pacific coast, and anglers such as Larry Green fish for them often. Larry catches them with such baits as prawns or mussel worms, but he has also found that they will take artificial lures. He casts tiny spoons or spinners with light spinning tackle, and finds his best fishing in inter-tidal pools and around old pilings, wharfs, piers, and rocks. He also uses a fly rod and a shrimp-type fly, which he casts in the intertidal pools at low water and around kelp beds.

Another angler who fishes the Pacific beaches for surf perch is William Hunter. He finds that along open beaches surf perch do most of their feeding just beyond the white breakers. The best fishing takes place during the incoming tide anywhere from three to five hours after it starts coming in. Hunter finds his best fishing along beaches where razor clams are dug, since the perch move in with the tide to feed on the broken or discarded clams. He uses the razor clams for bait if he can get them. He also uses sand shrimp, which can be dug on the mud and sand flats at the mouths of bays or rivers. He ties the shrimp around a hook with pink thread so that it stays on.

William Hunter also fishes for rockfish along the rocky shores of Washington and Oregon. He fishes from rocks and casts into the deeper holes or pools and over kelp beds. During the daytime, he finds herring the best bait for these fish, either whole if small or a chunk if large. The herring can be fished on a 4/0 hook and with a weight to get it out to the best spots.

Hunter has also found that toward dusk the rockfish will hit lures such as the weighted spinners used for bass and trout in fresh water. He likes those with red-and-yellow bodies and casts and retrieves them just above the rocks and kelp.

Most anglers catch the ling cod found in Pacific waters on bait, but Guy Porter Fones uses metal jigs for them and gets some big fish. He fishes along the California coast and finds May, June, and July the best months for this fishing. He uses various colored jigs, with the chrome, white, yellow, and copper finishes the most effective. He uses the lighter colors on bright, sunny days and the darker colors on overcast, cloudy days. These jigs are let down to the bottom and then are worked up and down to catch ling cod up to 30 pounds or more.

Jig used for ling cod

26

OTHER SALT-WATER FISHES

This chapter will cover some of the salt-water fishes not dealt with in previous chapters. Most of these are great game fish and provide sport and fun for thousands of anglers who fish in the ocean, bays, tidal rivers, and surf, and from boats, jetties, bridges, piers, and shorelines.

One of the fastest of these is the wahoo, which is found in warm waters. It makes long, sizzling runs that peel the line off the reel at an unbelievable speed; many anglers rate the wahoo as one of the fastest fish in the ocean. Captain Russell Young, skipper of the *Sea Wolfe,* fishes for big wahoo in Bermuda waters. He often tries for them on the Challenger Bank mentioned earlier in this book as a good spot for yellowfin tuna.

Captain Young is very careful about how he rigs his baits for wahoo and will choose the best flying fish, ballyhoo, and pilchards he can obtain. He sharpens his hooks to a needle point, because wahoo have big, tough, bony mouths, which the hook must penetrate. He tells the anglers on his boat to set the hook hard when a wahoo hits. Captain Young also avoids shiny swivels and hardware and either uses black ones or tapes them, so that the wahoo won't hit them and cut the line.

Captain Young trolls the baits at about seven knots but varies the speed from time to time. He looks for birds working and small fish leaping, but finds that wahoo will often appear suddenly and hit the baits blind. And at times, you'll get two or three hook-ups at the same time, when a small school of wahoo show up. Once it's hooked, there's nothing an angler can do but let the wahoo make its first, long run. Trying to stop the fish or even slow it down at this time will lead to a break-off and a lost fish.

Feather lure with strip bait for wahoo

Jerry Klink fishes for wahoo off Baja California, Mexico, and he catches a lot of them. Here he finds that fast trolling with such lures as plugs, spoons, feathers, and jigs is best. But they will also take strip baits cut from the belly of a bonito or mackerel. At times they will also take a slowly trolled live fish. But Jerry finds that blind trolling done fast over a wide area is most effective for the wahoo, which are usually scattered and not too thick in any one spot.

This beautiful, streamlined wahoo was caught from a charter boat off the Bahamas. These waters have produced record wahoo, up to 149 pounds. (*Bahamas News Bureau photo*)

George Bernstein also likes to catch wahoo, and he uses light tackle for them in Bermuda, the Bahamas, and off Panama. He finds them most plentiful off Coiba Island, in the Pacific off Panama, during the summer months. There they can be caught very close to shore because of the deep drop-offs near land.

Bernstein uses lines as light as 12- and 6-pound-test, and he caught a record, 74-pound wahoo on 12-pound-test line. He used a 3-ounce white-and-red Jap feather lure with a 4/0 hook to make this catch. But he also uses spoons and underwater plugs for wahoo.

Another fish, which looks somewhat like a wahoo and also runs fast and fights hard, is the king mackerel. A. C. Becker fishes for them off Texas and Louisiana around offshore oil rigs. The oil rigs in deep water, beyond eight miles, are better than those close to shore, according to him. He also looks for shrimp boats anchored offshore during the day. The shrimpers clean their nets and often dump trash fish overboard, which attracts king mackerel to the spot. He also looks for the "blue-water line," where the blue offshore waters meet the green inshore waters, and trolls or drifts there. And to bring king mackerel up to the boat, Becker will often chum with fish or suspend a chum pot or bag in the water.

John H. Wootters, Jr., also fishes for king mackerel in the Gulf of Mexico, and he finds trolling the most dependable method for taking the kings, day in and day out. He likes a feather jig weighing about 3 ounces for this. He also uses underwater plugs, spoons, and other metal lures. These should be trolled at various depths and speeds until the right combination is found. At times, he finds that the kings will be right in the wake of the boat, and then lures on short lines will get hits. John carries a flag buoy with a weighted anchor line when trolling for king mackerel. If he gets hits or fish, he throws this buoy overboard to mark the spot so he can troll in the same area.

Wootters also looks for gulls and terns wheeling and diving over baitfish and will then troll or cast lures in that spot. Or he will just drift in a good spot and cast spoons, jigs, or underwater plugs. Or he lets out a baitfish such as a cigar minnow, mud minnow, sand trout, or ribbonfish. He finds such drifting is most effective if you also chum with ground-up or chopped-up fish.

Another fish that is popular with many salt-water anglers is the colorful dolphin, caught offshore from Cape Cod to Florida and in the Gulf of Mexico. In fact, Mark Sosin feels that the dolphin is one of the greatest light-tackle fish that swims in the ocean. He finds that they can be fussy at times, so he likes to rig up two fly rods, two spinning rods, and two bait-casting rods, all with different lures. Then he can switch outfits and try various lures to find out what the fish want.

Mark uses surface and underwater plugs, jigs, spoons, and flies with the various outfits, and rather than troll, he likes to cast these near floating seaweed, logs, boxes, or other debris. But he will often troll until he hooks a fish and will then hold that fish near the boat to keep other dolphin near, where he can cast to them. Chum also helps to hold their interest and keep them near the boat.

Bill Barnes found that dolphin can lurk under almost any floating or swimming object. He was fishing with a friend when they saw a big turtle on the surface. As they came close, they saw that there was a school of dolphin under it; his friend cast and hooked a 45-pound bull dolphin near the turtle.

Peter J. Frederikson fishes for false albacore off New York and New Jersey and catches most of them by trolling. He uses six lines, putting two short lines with the lure in the first wake, two lines near the second wake, and two lines on the outriggers, 80 to 100 feet out. He finds that spoons, bone jigs, cedar jigs, and feathers are the most effective for these fast, streamlined members of the tuna family. When using spoons or bone jigs, he adds a 4- to 8-ounce trolling weight ahead of the lures, depending on water conditions and seas encountered.

Jerome B. Robinson finds that one of the few places where false albacore can be caught from the surf is along the Outer Banks of North Carolina. They run from May to November, with the spring and fall months best. Robinson finds that the fishing is best when the water is fairly calm and clear and the wind is light from the south. He fishes the deeper holes and sloughs at Cape Hatteras Point and the mouth of Ocracoke Inlet. False albacore can also be caught from some of the piers along Hatteras Island.

Robinson often sees schools of false albacore slashing at bait and churning the water. Then he casts ahead of the school, so that the fish come up to his lure. Fast reeling produces the most strikes, while metal squids, Hopkins lures, and heavy spoons are the most effective lures.

Herbert F. Meyer catches bonito on a fly rod in the Pacific Ocean from a live-bait boat fishing around the kelp beds. The trick is to bring the bonito up to the boat within casting distance by chumming with live anchovies. When the school is boiling, he casts a fly toward them. Meyer likes a 3-inch white marabou streamer with a Mylar skirt wrapped around it. He finds this fishing is best during the summer and early-fall months off California.

When it comes to amberjack, Al Pflueger, Jr., catches these tough battlers on a fly rod. He uses several tricks to make the big fish hit his fly. First, he looks for gulls, pelicans, or frigate birds wheeling and diving. Then he races to the spot and starts chumming with ground fish to attract bait to the boat. Then, if he sees amberjack in the chum slick, he starts tossing out live pilchards toward them. When the "feeding line" on the amberjack's head and body starts to turn dark, Al knows the fish are excited and ready to hit a lure, and then he casts his fly to them.

Another trick he uses to excite the amberjack is to tie a live blue runner or some other small fish without any hook in it to the end of a long pole and let it struggle on top of the water. When an amberjack goes for it and tries to grab it, Al lifts it clear of the water. This drives the amberjack mad, and they hit almost any lure or bait cast toward them.

Mark Sosin catches amberjack by deep jigging with heavy, 2- to 4-ounce jigs in white, yellow, or green. A strip of Mylar on the jig usually increases its effectiveness. The best spots for jigging, he finds, are underwater wrecks, drop-offs, rocky bottoms, and coral reefs, in water from 50 to 200 feet deep. This is where the big amberjack like to hang out. Mark uses a popping rod or spinning rod and sends the jig down to the bottom, then he retrieves it with long, fast sweeps of the rod.

Karl Osborne fishes for cobia in many spots along the Atlantic coast from Virginia to Florida. He finds that baits and methods vary according to the locality being fished. In Virginia he often trolls for the cobia in Chesapeake Bay with spoons, underwater plugs, and plastic eels. Around Ocracoke Island and Morehead City, in North Carolina, he uses a bottom rig with a sliding sinker and an 8/0 or 9/0 hook baited with squid or a small fish such as spot, mullet, pigfish, or herring. Off Beaufort, South Carolina, he finds that live eels free-lined in the current without any float or weight work best. And when fishing near Savannah, Georgia, he uses a live catfish hooked just behind the head and drifts it out to a waiting cobia. There he often uses a float to keep the bait at a certain level.

Lefty Kreh looks for cobia around wrecks, offshore oil towers, lights, oil rigs, and channel markers and buoys. To get them excited, he uses a "popping"- or "chugger"-type plug with no hooks on it and casts this into spots where cobia are hanging out. Then he works this teaser back to the boat with plenty of commotion and splash, and when a cobia appears under it, he yanks it away and casts a lure or bait toward the fish, which usually takes it.

Roy Martin has caught many cobia from the pier at Panama City, Florida, and from small boats cruising just off the beaches. They run in April and can be caught by casting plugs, metal lures, or jigs to fish that can be seen. The cobia will also take live fish such as blue runners, cigar minnows, or pinfish. When using a lure, Roy Martin tries to cast about 8 to 10 feet in front of a cobia and then retrieves it in short jerks. If a cobia shows interest, he lets the lure sink and hesitate. Once a cobia clamps its jaws down on the lure, he sets the hook hard.

Mark Sosin fishes for barracuda around Walker's Cay, in the Bahamas, especially during the winter months, when they are most plentiful. Then they come into the shallows or flats or cruise along the edges of sand patches. Mark finds that one of the most effective lures he has used for the barracuda there is a lure made from surgical tubing. He makes these himself and uses chartreuse, fluorescent red, or green tubing, cutting it into 11-inch lengths. After which, he attaches a treble hook to stainless-steel wire and pulls it through the tube. The treble hook rests inside the tube, with just the bends and points emerging. Then he threads a slip sinker on the wire and pushes it into the other end of the tube. He forms an eye next to the weight, and the lure is ready to troll or cast.

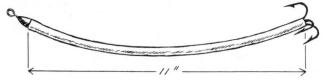

Surgical-tube lure used for barracuda

Gordon Young fishes for pompano at Cape Florida, not far from Miami, and he finds that this fishing can be red hot during April and

Mark Sosin with a barracuda he caught on a tube lure. These fish often come into shallow water in Florida and the Bahamas and can be caught on light tackle. (*Mark Sosin photo*)

May. He casts small jigs for the pompano in the finger channels in that area and prefers a small yellow nylon jig, either plain or with a tiny piece of shrimp added to the hook. The best way to work the jig is to let it settle to the bottom and then bounce it along slowly so that it raises puffs of sand.

Paul Kalman also fishes for pompano; only, he does it around the oil rigs found off Louisiana. There the pompano run from October to March, with January one of the top months for this fishing. He finds that a small nylon jig with a piece of shrimp on the hook is the best combination for pompano. But it should be retrieved with the current or tide so that it moves naturally. This means you have to cast it into the current or tide. Paul finds that stormy weather will ruin the fishing for a while, but when it gets calm right after the blow, the fishing often gets hot.

Another relative of the common pompano is the palometa, or longfin pompano, which is caught in Bermuda waters. Pete Perinchief often fishes for them there when a school comes close to the beaches or surf. Pete finds that they provide great sport on a light, one-handed spinning outfit. They will hit tiny jigs, spoons, or salt-water flies. To hold a school of the palometa in an area, he will often chum with pieces of bread.

Alain Wood-Prince also fishes for palometa, in the Bahamas, and he finds that the fishing is best where there is some surf breaking. Then he wades out into the water and casts parallel to the shore and retrieves the lure so that it comes in along the bottom right in back of the breaking waves. But he has also found that the bigger fish often hang out in deeper water, and then he casts out as far as he can and retrieves the small jig he uses from the deep to shallow water.

Anglers fishing in Mexican waters often run into the tough, fighting roosterfish and have great sport with these colorful fish. Norman Phillips fishes for them along Baja California—off Mulegé, Loreto, La Paz, Buena Vista, and Cabo de San Lucas. To locate the roosters, he cruises close to shore looking for gulls, petrels, and pelicans diving and feeding on baitfish. He then approaches the school, cuts his motor, and drifts through the fish, using a live grunt on a hook for bait.

Norm will also try trolling along the edges of the school, using various lures such as spoons, feathers, jigs, or plastic lures. He finds these should be trolled at high speeds—six to ten knots—to make

They're admiring a fine specimen of palometa caught from a Bermuda beach. Also called the gaff-topsail pompano, this fish is a tough little scrapper on light tackle. (*Bermuda News Bureau photo*)

the lures skip and obtain strikes. Norm uses spinning tackle with 15-pound-test lines for ultimate sport and has caught roosterfish up to 60 pounds on this gear.

Chris Blough fishes for the smaller roosterfish, up to 15 or 20 pounds, with a fly rod and bucktail fly. He finds that when they are chasing baitfish on top, they will hit the fly.

Roosterfish are also caught from party boats such as the *Red Rooster II*, run by Captain Danny Palm out of San Diego, California. He makes long trips to the Gulf of California, and the anglers on his boat catch a lot of roosterfish. He recommends either a spinning or conventional outfit with 20- to 40-pound-test line. The bait used is a scad (a small fish), which is hooked through the nose with a 6/0 or 7/0 hook. The roosters will also take a heavy spoon, jig, or metal lure cast from the boat. Captain Palm runs the boat close to the beach, and anglers cast their bait or lure toward the surf. Chumming with live anchovies is done to bring some of the roosterfish close to the boat and also to excite them into taking a bait or lure.